Some INI

The reader may find puzzling as t(printed in 1987. The point lies i. Imperfections' to 'EX PARTE AND GIPPERGATE'. If you fast-forward to pages 10 and 11 you will find two pages wherein counsel for Mr. and Mrs. Danny Kaye, two of the principles in the book, authored two letters and filed them with the Federal Communications Commission Administrative Law Judge Thomas B. Fitzpatrick who was presiding over the renewal of the Broadcast License held by the Kayes and their business associate Mr. Lester M. Smith.

That license was for KISW-FM, Seattle, Washington. It was due for renewal as were all licenses on the West Coast.

At renewal time any citizen or entity could file a competing application since the Courts had ruled that a new licensee may well operate in the public interest better than the incumbent.

A Licensee does not own the channel they are operating on but are only stewards of public property and that privilege can be lost if the incumbent licensee does not operate in the public interest, convenience, and necessity. That, of course includes being law abiding. A Challenger does not have to prove that an incumbent has violated the law by any higher degree than the preponderance of evidence. That is established by the courts and the Commission in the WSIB, Sea Island Broadcasting, FCC 78 – 841 M.O. & O., released December 11, 1978. SEA Island lost their license based upon making deliberate misrepresentations and misleading and deceptive statements in order to conceal violations of rules. KAYES violations were infinitely worse.

While this author, Hoffart, was dismissed for reporting payola to the CEO, Mr. Lester M. Smith, KISW-FM Seattle and also holders of seven other licenses, denied the payola and a large number of acts of perjury and forgery surfaced at a hearing before Judge Fitzpatrick held in December of 1982. The judge granted the KISW renewal. Even though KISW-FM personnel engaged in at least sixteen acts of perjury and six acts of phony-signed exhibits, the judge agreed with KISW counsel that the law violations were 'innocent error', unfortunate and should not have happened, Hoffart's exceptions and appeals to federal judges fell on deaf ears and each of the many efforts to get a ruling that the FCC judge engaged in preferential treatment to the Kayes and Mr. SMITH WERE DENIED. It was obvious that the judge had been subject to ex parte, no other judge would overturn the re-licensing of KISW and dismissing Hoffart's filing which had zero demerits and preference due to not holding any other licenses and would be in control 100 percent of the time.

Hoffart's filing charged listed the phony notarized exhibits and perjury as warranting non-renewal but the judge and all subsequent FCC and court personnel upheld the judge. Obviously someone helped the Kayes prevail.

That 'someone' surfaced when RONALD REAGAN released some of his documents and Hoffart had an FOIA on file for any document that would show that FCC CHAIRMAN MARK FOWLER MET WITH REAGAN.

As the reader no doubt knows, the GOP has some of his documents. Congress passed a law that permits a president to withhold his documents for twelve years after leaving office. This law was the result of President Nixon's records being released and proved that he was a liar.

It was Reagan who signed the new law. Hoffart had obtained some information, the source of which will not be revealed due to possible retaliation even at this late date, that FCC Chairman Mark S. Fowler had visited Reagan in the oval office.

Since Hoffart was aware that Mr. Fowler was giving special treatment to some broadcast licensee, he may have done so in the Danny Kaye renewal of the KISW Seattle license. Hoffart then filed an FOIA with the FCC, not knowing about the twelve year freeze on Reagan documents. A letter from the library advised Hoffart that the earliest date that documents could be released is after Reagan is out of office for 12 years.

That set the earliest date that documents could be released was January 20, 2001.

However, while cataloging some of the documents, FCC personnel advised me that they had located 71 pages and some pictures and they would check with Reagan personnel to see if they could be released. I then received a letter telling me that the 71 pages and some positive prints of photos could be released.

Hoffart then ordered the 71 pages plus two black and white photos. Four pages were withheld and are still being withheld even though they should have been released on January 20, 2001.

They have been classified as an invasion into Reagan's personal privacy. I have sought them under court subpoena with the court reviewing them 'in camera' and releasing them only if they were being validly withheld. The courts refuse to do that.

This withholding of documents leaves Hoffart with no avenue to obtain the truth, and the truth is that Reagan sold out to his Hollywood friends, the Kayes and as such also to their business associate, Mr. Lester M. Smith, Bellevue, WA.

The reason for reprinting the book titled 'A Case of Notarial Imperfections' with a new title is to try to get some persons interested in obtaining the documents withheld, first by Reagan and now, apparently, by President BUSH since he has extended the time that the REAGAN documents can be released. Hoffart is hopeful that this new book will force BUSH to release all of the REAGAN documents to historians and that the four pages being withheld will be released.

The picture on the cover allegedly shows FCC Judge Fitzpatrick. Former FCC Chairman Mark Fowler is easily identified as shaking hands with Reagan. Fowler, however, denies that the man standing behind him is FCC JUDGE FITZPATRICK. Some of the 71 pages released support that the 'unidentified staffer' is the judge who sat in judgment of the KAYES radio station renewal. Those documents will be released in a sequel. I am looking for an author since I am 89 years old and not able to write the story. I am hoping that Mike Moore will be interested. There can be no greater story than coercing a president to intervene in a case at bar before the FCC or any other tribunal. Did REAGAN sell out to the KAYES? THE PUBLIC HAS A RIGHT TO KNOW.

EVIDENCE, STANDARD OF PROOF

QUOTING FROM SEA ISLAND BROADCASTING DOCKET No. 19886
DATED DECEMBER 11, 1978

The standard of proof for administrative agencies should be the PREPONDERANCE OF EVIDENCE rather than the more stringent evidence standards due to the unique element of public trust that Commission licensees hold.

THE SPOKESMAN-REVIEW
Spokane Chronicle

REVIEW TOWER
999 WEST RIVERSIDE AVENUE
P O BOX 2160
SPOKANE, WASHINGTON 99210-1615
(509) 459-5000

January 8, 1985

ANNOTATION BY AUTHOR HOFFART.
PRESIDENT HARRY TRUMAN, WHEN HE
WAS AT THE SPOKANE ARMORY ON HIS
BID FOR REELETION STATED: THE
SPOKESMAN REVIEW IS THE WORST
NEWSPAPER IN THE UNITED STATES.
TRUMAN WAS RIGHT AT THAT TIME AND
IS STILL RIGHT TODAY. V.L.HOFFART

Vincent Hoffart
N1748 Lacey St.
Spokane, WA 99207

Dear Mr. Hoffart:

The code of ethics of a newspaper editor and reporter calls
for their fairly assessing the newsworthiness of a story or
potential story. And that's exactly what happened with you and
your allegations.

Mr. Morlin and his editors gave a good deal of their time
and expended a good deal of their energy looking at the material
you provided them. They concluded, after this time and energy,
that there weren't sufficient grounds to proceed with their research, and told you so. Mr. Morlin then returned the 550 pages
worth of documents to you.

You got a fair shake, Mr. Hoffart, from this newspaper and
from one of the finest reporters in this business. You got an
honest answer and you got your material back.

I think we acted ethically all the way along. Thus, I resent
your implication that it was any other way.

Sincerely,

E. Curtiss Pierson
Editor

ECP:dh

cc: Bill Morlin

Gippergate

Before the
FEDERAL COMMUNICATIONS COMMISSION
Washington, D.C. 20554

In re Applications of

DENA PICTURES, INCORPORATED AND
ALEXANDER BROADCASTING COMPANY,
a joint venture, d/b/a
KAYE-SMITH ENTERPRISES

For Renewal of License of Station
KISW(FM), Seattle, Washington

VINCENT L. HOFFART,
d/b/a HOFFART BROADCASTING
Seattle, Washington

For Construction Permit

       BC Docket No. 82-265
       File No. BRH-801001UZ

       BC Docket No. 82-266
       File No. BPH 801229AE

A TRUE STORY

by
VINCENT L. HOFFART

*Printed in Victoria, BC, Canada. Printed on paper with minimum 30% recycled fibre. Trafford's print shop
runs on "green energy" from solar, wind and other environmentally-friendly power sources.*

TRAFFORD
PUBLISHING™

Offices in Canada, USA, Ireland and UK
This book was published *on-demand* in cooperation with Trafford Publishing. On-demand
publishing is a unique process and service of making a book available for retail sale to the
public taking advantage of on-demand manufacturing and Internet marketing. On-demand
publishing includes promotions, retail sales, manufacturing, order fulfilment, accounting and
collecting royalties on behalf of the author.

Book sales for North America and international:
Trafford Publishing, 6E–2333 Government St.,
Victoria, BC V8T 4P4 CANADA
phone 250 383 6864 (toll-free 1 888 232 4444)
fax 250 383 6804; email to orders@trafford.com
Book sales in Europe:
Trafford Publishing (UK) Limited, 9 Park End Street, 2nd Floor
Oxford, UK OXI IHH UNITED KINGDOM
phone 44 (0)1865 722 113 (local rate 0845 230 9601)
facsimile 44 (0)1865 722 868; info.uk@trafford.com
Order online at:
trafford.com/05-2716

10 9 8 7 6 5 4 3

CONTENTS

APPENDIX EXHIBITS

The author supports this story with seventy-eight Exhibits which are indexed separately at the back of this book. References to these documents will be made throughout this book as an offer of proof that this is a true story.

TABLE OF AUTHORITIES AND CITATIONS

Following the Appendixed Exhibits, the author lists case histories, rules and regulations, policies and statutes in support of his charges of preferential treatment to Kaye-Smith in this hearing before the Federal Communications Commission.

PREFACE

In a decision handed down by U.S. Court of Appeals, D.C. Circuit on September 28, 1978, the so-called WESH-TV case, Judge Malcolm Wilkey, a highly respected jurist, remanded the renewal of the Cowles Broadcasting Company's license to operate WESH-TV in Orlando, Florida back to the commission. While the court subsequently affirmed the commission's renewal, based on further argument, Judge Wilkey had said:

> Aside from the specific facts of this case, there is other evidence indicating the state of administrative practice in commission comparative renewal proceedings is unsatisfactory . . . Its paradoxial history reveals an ordinarily tactic presumption that the incumbent licensee is to be preferred over competing applicants. Because the Communications Act fairly precludes any preference based upon incumbency *per se*, the practical bias arises from the Commission's discretionary weighting of legally relevant factors.
>
> The Commission's rationale in this case is thoroughly unsatisfying. The Commission purported to be conducting a full hearing whose content is governed by the 1965 Policy Statement on Comparative Renewal Criteria. It found favorably to Central on each of diversification, integration, and minority participation, and adversely to Cowles on the studio move question. Then simply on the basis of wholly noncomparative assessment of Cowles' past performance as "substantial," the Commission confirms Cowles' renewal expectancy. Even if we were to agree, (and we do not agree) with the Commission's trivialization of each of Central's advantages, we still would be unable to sustain its action here. The Commission nowhere even vaguely describes how it aggregated its findings into the decisive balance: rather we are told that the conclusion is based upon "administrative feel." Such intuitional forms of decision making, completely opaque to judicial review, fall somewhere on the distant side of arbitrary.
>
> The development of commission policy on comparative renewal hearings has now departed sufficiently from the established law, statutory and judicial precedent, that the commission's handling of the facts in this case make it embarrassingly clear that the FCC has practically erected a presumption of renewal that is inconsistent with the full hearing requirements of Section 309 (e) (of the Communications Act.) We are especially troubled by the possibility that settled principles of administrative practice may be ignored because of the commission's insecurity or unhappiness with the substance of the regulatory regime it is charged to enforce. Nothing would be more demoralizing or unsettling of expectations than for drifting administrative adjudications to quietly erode the statutory mandate of the Commission and judicial precedent. (Central Florida Enterprises, Inc., v. Federal Communications Commission, Case 76-1742, (9-25-1978).)

Officers And Directors of Dena Pictures, Incorporated And
Alexander Broadcasting Company

1. The officers and directors of *Dena Pictures*, Incorporated are
   as follows:
   - *-Danny Kaye*   – President & Director
   - *-Sylvia Fine Kaye* – Secretary, Treasurer & Director
   - -Herbert Bonis   – Vice President & Director
   - -Julius Lefkowitz – Vice President

2. The officers and directors of *Alexander Broadcasting Compa-*
   ny are as follows:
   - *-Lester M. Smith*   – President, Treasurer & Director
   - -Bernice R. Smith   – Vice-President & Director
   - -William A. Palmer – Secretary & Director
   - -Irvin H. Karl   – Assistant Secretary & Director

On January 24, 1985, Alexander Broadcasting reported
that Mr. Palmer had resigned and Mr. Karl was elected that
corporation's secretary and vice president.

Lester M. Smith purchased the 80 percent holdings held by
Mr. and Mrs. Danny Kaye in April of 1985.

In late 1986 the media reported that Mr. Lester M. Smith
sold KISW (FM) to Nationwide Communications, a sub-
sidiary of Nationwide Insurance.

On March 3, 1987, Mr. Danny Kaye (born Daniel Kamin-
sky) died.

Mark S. Fowler declined to seek renomination as an FCC
commissioner and gave his farewell speech before the convention of the National Association of Broadcasters held in
Dallas, on March 31, 1987. Dennis R. Patrick, one of the
incumbent commissioners, is to assume the FCC chair-
manship.

1-12-85　　　　KAYE-SMITH ENTERPRISES—Bellevue, WA.

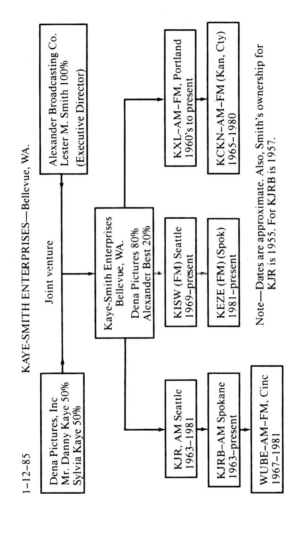

Dena Pictures, Inc
Mr. Danny Kaye 50%
Sylvia Kaye 50%

Joint venture

Alexander Broadcasting Co.
Lester M. Smith 100%
(Executive Director)

Kaye-Smith Enterprises
Bellevue, WA.
Dena Pictures 80%
Alexander Best 20%

KXL–AM–FM, Portland
1960's to present

KCKN–AM–FM (Kan, Cty)
1965–1980

KISW (FM) Seattle
1969–present

KEZE (FM) (Spok)
1981–present

KJR, AM Seattle
1963–1981

KJRB–AM Spokane
1963–present

WUBE–AM–FM, Cinc
1967–1981

Note—Dates are approximate. Also, Smith's ownership for
KJR is 1955. For KJRB is 1957.

THE ACTIVE CAST

KAYE-SMITH ENTERPRISES—appearances
    Lester M. Smith, Executive Director
    Stephen L. West, General Manager, KISW
    Eric S. Bogel, Program Director/air personality
    Margit E. Noren, Administrative Assistant/Notary Public
    Carrie Matthew, Traffic Director/Notary Public
    Craig Siegenthaler, Chief Engineer, KISW
WITNESSES—KAYE-SMITH ENTERPRISES, non-employees
    Julie McCullough, Trustee, Greenpeace, Seattle
    Shawn Taylor, Boy Scouts of America
    Judy Balint, Office Coordinator, Focus
    Charles E. Blacksmith, Roundup Music Dist.
    David Watkins, Assistant General Manager Supersonics, (ex)
    J. Daniel McConnell, President, McConnell Co
TESTIMONIAL LETTER AUTHORS, non-witnesses
    John R. Taylor, Promotion Director, Bumbershoot
    Bob L Curran, U.S. Army (retired) Seafair Coordinator, Mil.
    C. Clark Griffin, President, CC Griffin and Co., Inc.
HOFFART BROADCASTING, Spokane, Washington
    Vincent L Hoffart, *pro se.* Owner
FLY, SHUEBRUK, GAGUINE, BOROS, SCHULKIND AND
BRAUN, attorneys
    Jerome S. Boros, Esquire
    Stuart J. Young, Esquire
FEDERAL COMMUNICATIONS COMMISSION
    The Honorable Thomas B. Fitzpatrick, Assistant Chief,
        Administrative Law Judge, presiding.
    Daniel Sarno, Broadcast Bureau, Hearing Division
    Charles E. Dziedzic, Chief, Mass Media, Hearing Division
    Robert A. Zauner, Mass Media, Hearing Division
    Joseph A. Marino, Chairman, Review Board.
    Mr. Jerold L. Jacobs, Member, Review Board
    Mr. Norman B. Blumenthal, Member, Review Board
    Mark S. Fowler, Chairman, FCC.
    James H. Quello, Commissioner, FCC
    Mimi Weyforth Dawson, Commissioner, FCC
    Henry M. Rivera, Commissioner, FCC (resigned 9-13-1985)
    Dennis R. Patrick, Commissioner, FCC

THE KAYE-SMITH/KISW (FM) PHONY NOTARIZATIONS
TESTIMONIAL LETTERS.

Author	Exhibits	Date of Letter	Notarized by	Correction Date
C. Clark Griffin	17-p. 8/8(A)	October 21, 1982	*Christine Woolson	November 23, 1982
David Watkins	17-p. 5/5(A)	October 22	*Anthony Tucker	November 17
Julie McCullough	16-p. 6/6(A)	October 22	Carrie Matthew	November 16
C.E. Blacksmith	16-p. 24/24(A)	October 27	Carrie Matthew	November 17
Judy Balint	16-p. 14	October 29	Carrie Matthew	None filed
Dan McConnell	17-p. 6/6(A)	October 29	Carrie Matthew	November 16
Shawn Taylor	16-p. 7/7(A)	November 5	Carrie Matthew	November 23

OTHER QUESTIONED LETTERS

Author	Exhibits	Date of Letter	Notarized by	Correction Date
John R. Taylor	16-p. 13/13(A)	October 25, 1982	Margit Noren	November 22, 1982
"Bob" Curran	16-p. 28	no date	Margit Noren	none filed

Notes: *John R. Taylor* letter was re-executed due to failure of Ms. Noren to date her notarial act on his original letter.
Bob Curran original letter was notarized by Ms. Noren on October 26th.
Nina L. Evers—Her November 8th letter, Exhibit 16, page 5, was notarized November 10th. Eric Bogel averred she was an affiant on the 9th.

* The original C. Clark Griffin letter, notarized by Ms. Woolson and the original Watkins letter notarized by Anthony Tucker are not claimed to be other than legal notarizations. The *corrections* are questioned.

CALENDAR OF EVENTS October, 1982

Sun	Mon.	Tue	Wed	Thur	Fri	Sat
17	18	19	20	21 date of earliest K/S Exhibit	22 date of first Watkins letter	23
24	25	26 Bob Curran letter notariz-ed by Noran.	27	28 McCul-lough letter phony notariz-ation.	29	30
31						

November, 1982

	1	2	3	4	5 Original Exchange Date and S. Taylor phony N.	6
7	8 Date of Nina Evers letter.	9 Date of all Smith Affidavit also Bogel and West	10 Date of Nina Evers Notariz-ation.	11	12 Exchange Date of Kaye/Sm. Exhibits (Rcv'd)	13 7 letters written to letter authors
14	15 Judy Balint Receives Hoffart's letter.	16 Date of Judy Balint response	17 Date of Watkins phony notariz-ation by Noren.	18 Judge not-ified of phony verific-ations.	19	20
21	22	23 Correct-ions by KISW filed	24 Correct-ions by KISW filed.	25 Thanks-giving	26	27 Subpoena requests filed by Hoffart
28	29	30 Hearing Smith & West				

December, 1982

			1 Hearing West Bogel Matthew	2 Hearing Noren Watkins and others	3 Hearing Hoffart Graves Smith.	4

1.

INTRODUCTION

This is a true story. The names of the principals have not been changed. Truth is a valid defense in any court of law. This book is being written so that the public may know what is involved in a so-called "mutually exclusive" application for a broadcast station construction permit. In this case the author filed an application with the Federal Communications Commission for a construction permit to install an FM station in Seattle, Washington. The application was for Channel 260, which is occupied by KISW (FM). Such applications are called mutually exclusive since only one licensee can operate on a specific channel in a specific location.

Challenging applications can be filed at a period of time when an incumbent files for renewal. This filing window is between 120 days and 30 days before the station's license is to expire. In the case of KISW, the author filed an application challenging the KISW renewal on December 29, 1980. The KISW license was due for expiration on February 1, 1981, and a renewal application had been filed in October of 1980, as required by the Rules and Regulations. Once a renewal application is filed, the Federal Communications Commission is mandated, by law, to accept challenging applications that are substantially complete and meet the commission's other criteria as outlined in the Rules and Regulations and the Communications Act of 1934, as amended.

Both the courts and the commission have repeatedly held that this "competitive spur" of filing challenging applications at renewal time is in the "public interest." The courts have held that the public may benefit if one station licensee is replaced by another who would continue to provide the best practical service. Competing applications are among "friendly weapons" in the public's arsenal provided by the Communications Act and FCC rules. The Communications Act recognizes the unique concept of a private attorney general who, because of an economic interest, is permitted to participate in FCC proceedings to litigate public interest questions. A challenger has to raise important public interest questions and issues in order to win. The commission recognizes that they cannot be aware of operations of every broadcast licensee and as such must rely upon the public to bring to their attention a licensee's conduct through the filing of complaints, petitions to deny renewal, or challenging applications at renewal time.

A licensee does not own a station's license. They have no vested right to renewal. Broadcast licensees have been designated, by the courts, as public trustees of the air waves, and as public trustees, they must exercise a high degree of stewardship in their stations' operations. The Communications Act contains the statutory mandate that a broadcast permit or license cannot be granted unless the "public interest, convenience or necessity is served thereby." The commission relies primarily upon a licensee's past record as being indicative of whether a renewal will serve the public interest. The reasoning behind this thinking is that if an incumbent has served the public interest in the past, he or she is likely to continue such service.

This book is appendixed with fifty-four exhibits and a Table of Authorities and Citations in support of the author's charges that the case you are about to read was decided on the basis of who was involved and not the record evidence. Relevant factors were simply left out of the Findings of Facts or swept under the rug. For example, perjury by the station manager at the hearing was not even mentioned by the judge in the Initial Decision.

The author charges that the commission exercised preferential treatment in this case and afforded such treatment to Kaye-Smith Enterprises, licensees of KISW (FM), Seattle, in order to renew their license. The judge's conclusion that the unlawful conduct and abuse of the commission's processes, that the author will prove, beyond any doubt, should not have happened, sets a new precedent in administrative hearings. To rule that the statutory violations are mitigated because they should not have happened defies analysis and supports the author's charges of preferential treatment to an influential broadcaster.

The author will prove, beyond any doubt, that Kaye-Smith Enterprises, through their counsel, initially filed five testimonial letters solicited from Seattle area community leaders upon which the notarial verifications were phony, that is to say, the notarizations were performed outside the presence of the affiants and without the knowledge of the affiants. These five documents, patently forgeries due to the addition of the notarial attestations, were filed with a federal agency, the FCC, and represented as true and correct in all respects. Such acts are prohibited by statute, both federal and state.

The author will prove, beyond any doubt, that Kaye-Smith Enterprises, through their counsel, filed two more documents as "corrections" where again the notarial attestations were affixed outside the presence of the affiants. The "corrections" came after the author detected the phony verifications. In one of the corrections, the signature was not that of the author of the letter even though it was represented that the author had appeared before a notary. This will be proven untrue.

The author will prove, beyond any doubt, that the illegal notarizations were orchestrated by the KISW general manager and were carried out by two of the KISW employees, both of whom were commissioned Washington State notaries.

The author will prove, beyond any doubt, that this station manager perjured himself on the witness stand when he stated, without equivocation, that one of the affiants had appeared in his office, and his solicited testimonial letter was then notarized in his presence by his administra-

2

tive assistant. In actual fact, the letter author had not appeared before the notary, and the signature on the letter was not affixed by the so-called affiant but by his secretary.

The author will prove, beyond any doubt, that the corrections, which also were affixed with phony verifications, were performed after all of the difficulties came to the attention of the station manager and his administrative assistant. Counsel for Kaye-Smith had advised the station manager that "you can't do that," with reference to affixing notarial attestations outside the presence of the authors of the letters. This warning came after the author had detected the initial five phony verifications.

In other matters, the author will prove, beyond any doubt, that Kaye-Smith/KISW installed and operated unauthorized and unlicensed radio apparatus in connection with a translator installation. In this matter the author will charge the commission with misrepresentations and untruths with regard to their statement, in their order upholding the ALJ and the review board, that the application for a directional antenna for use in rebroadcasting KISW programming had been granted. No documents exist that specifically granted KISW the authority to use a directional antenna.

These are just some examples of the charges in this book—termed a hodgepodge of accusations . . . much ado about nothing . . . by the review board.

Now let's look at the facts, as adduced from the record.

2.

THE HEARING DESIGNATION ORDER

The author's challenging application was found to be substantially complete and as such entitled the author to a hearing before an administrative law judge who would issue an Initial Decision on whether the incumbent or the challenger should be the next licensee for Channel 260, Seattle, Washington. The hearing designation order was released on June 1, 1982, some one and one-half years after the filing of the challenging application.

The hearing designation order specified the following issues that were to be resolved at the hearing:

1. To determine whether the author (Hoffart) is financially qualified to construct and operate the proposed station;
2. To determine which of the proposals would, on a comparative basis, better serve the public interest;
3. To determine, in light of the evidence adduced pursuant to the foregoing issues, which of the applications should be granted.

The latter two issues are basic to all applications. The administrative law judge found, in his Initial Decision, that Hoffart was financially qualified. That left only issues two and three which also had to be resolved on the basis of the evidence adduced at the hearing. Both of these issues were resolved in favor of KISW.

The reader should know that, even though not specified, truth and candor are always at issue since the commission expects applicants to be truthful, as a matter of law. Misrepresentations are untruths in matters before the commission. A misrepresentation finding requires that there be falsity, materiality, and an intent to deceive. If any of the three criteria for a misrepresentation issue are absent, the commission will not make any adverse findings against the party charged with untruths. In this case the conclusion reached by the ALJ was that there was no intent to deceive anyone, a ruling not supported by the record.

The cryptic title of this book should alert the reader that the author charged KISW personnel with misrepresentations before a federal agency. The fact that KISW prevailed shows that the commission did not find all three elements that involve misrepresentations present. The administrative law judge found that there was no intent to mislead anyone in this case. He ruled that the myriad of unlawful conduct was due to ignorance and as such, involved innocent error. He assessed a slight demerit upon Kaye-Smith. The review board upheld the ALJ and called the author's charges a hodgepodge of accusations, typical adversarial puff and much ado about nothing.[1] The five commissioners subsequently upheld the ALJ and the review board, ruling that the alleged transgressions amount to nothing more than innocent errors on the part of the licensee, apparently unfamiliar with these particular intricacies of the commission's rules.[2]

Kaye-Smith, however, was represented by counsel. The Commission's ruling appears to state that counsel was also ignorant of the commission's rules.

Nearly all cases before the commission involve some charges of misrepresentations and/or lack of candor. In a case decided by the U.S. Supreme Court, that Court stated:

> The Commission's ability to fulfill its statutory responsibility rests in a considerable measure upon being able to rely upon the representations of those whom it licenses. Therefore the Commission must demand candor and refuse to tolerate deliberate misrepresentations made in or out of hearing, made in writing or orally . . . one who is not candid and trustworthy in all circumstances cannot be accorded the privilege of a Commission license.[3]

This is just one precedent cited by the author in his filings with the commission. It appears that the wisdom of our Supreme Court judges has to yield to the sagacity of those sitting in judgment in this case.

---

[1] 98 FCC 2d at pages 680, 681.
[2] Order 85-192, released April 19, 1985.
[3] *WOKO, Inc.*, cited as 329, U.S. 223 (1946).

3.

THE PRE-HEARING

It is customary for the presiding administrative law judge to call a pre-hearing conference to lay down the guidelines to be followed by the parties. Such a hearing was held in Washington, D.C. on August 6, 1982.

For the purposes of this book the author will take verbatim excerpts from the pre-hearing, the hearing, and the oral argument. This method of conveying to the reader the story which is about to unfold should leave no doubt as to the authenticity of issues being brought to the attention of the public by the author. (TR: refers to transcript.) Washington, D.C., August 6, 1982:

TR:104   *Judge Fitzpatrick*: I guess I can assume, Mr. Boros, that you are going to want to come in with the sworn testimony of community leaders attesting to how the station during the renewal period was sensitive to, conversant with, and met the needs and problems of the community. Am I correct on that?
Mr. Boros: That is correct, your Honor.

Well, there is nothing like starting out a case and having the presiding judge tell counsel for the incumbent licensee what he wants brought into the case so that he can support the grant of a renewal.

The judge was then Assistant Chief Administrative Law Judge Thomas B. Fitzpatrick of Washington, D.C. Mr. Boros, senior member of Fly, Shuebruk, *et al*, Attorneys at Law, represented Kaye-Smith Enterprises, licensees of KISW (FM) Seattle. Also in attendance was Mr. Stuart Young, assistant to Mr. Boros. The commission was represented by Mr. Daniel Sarno, Esquire. The author, Hoffart, appeared on his own behalf, that is, appeared *pro se*. Hoffart is a radio engineer, and has no legal background.

TR:106   *Judge Fitzpatrick*: Do you intend, Mr. Hoffart, to be adducing any evidence through any members of the public that Kaye-Smith is not meeting the needs of the community in its operations of the station in the last renewal period?
Mr. Hoffart: You mean bring in affidavits by other people in the Seattle area?
Judge Fitzpatrick: Well, it is in the form of an affidavit, but it is sworn testimony and in the affidavit, that is one thing that I should say, Mr. Boros, that in the affidavit as

submitted, it should show in its face that these people know it is being given to the commission, and that it is sworn testimony, you know, and that it is testimony in a docketed proceeding, and also they should be aware that they are going to be subject to being called for cross-examination . . .

Mr. Hoffart: At this time I do not know of anybody I would be bringing in to say that they are not programming, well, that their programming is not meritorious.

TR:108   *Mr. Boros*: Your Honor, as your pre-trial order directs, this will be a written case insofar as our presentation is concerned. You have expressly so instructed us, that is why . . .

TR:110   *Judge Fitzpatrick*: I did that, did I? What I said, Mr. Boros, is that the presiding judge is of the view that the submission of the parties of their affirmative case in writing will add significantly to the disposition of this proceeding . . . Mr. Hoffart, do you know what we are talking about? We are talking about, a direct written case is that instead of just the witness getting on the witness stand and giving his name and then testifying, that there is prepared in advance his written testimony, for which he signs and has it notarized, you know, sworn to before me, and it is accurate and complete, and it is exchanged well in advance of the hearing so that the other lawyers, parties to the proceeding, can study it, and then they are required to give notification, as to what witnesses they want to call for cross-examination, and to what areas of cross-examination are going to be.

Prior to the above exchanges, and earlier in the prehearing, the judge admonished Hoffart for filing some of his documents which were not notarized. Hoffart had argued, "counsel (for Kaye-Smith) does not have to verify their . . . "

TR:17   *Judge Fitzpatrick*: That's correct, because they are counsel, because the rule specifies, they can be disbarred if they make a statement that is improper. They can lose their right to practice law if they file a pleading that isn't correct.

Mr. Hoffart: Now, I may be getting out of line, your Honor, . . if I file an affidavit and I depose falsely, what happens?

Judge Fitzpatrick: You can go to jail.

Mr. Hoffart: Does that apply to Kaye-Smith?

Judge Fitzpatrick: Does that apply to Kaye-Smith? If they file any affidavits that are false, they can go to jail, too, if the prosecutors decide. The commission doesn't send people to jail. U.S. Code Title 18, section 1001 provides that any statement knowingly made to the United States Government or its officials or agents, can be prosecuted as a felony.

TR:18   *Mr. Hoffart*: My case rests on that, pretty much.

Hoffart's questions to the judge were rooted to the fact that he has several notarized statements in his files relating to previous encounters with Kaye-Smith in which the author alleges false statements were made. Hoffart had filed his challenging application based upon the existence of these documents. As it turned out, the judge limited the hearing to matters relating only to KISW (FM) and only to the renewal period between February 1978 and February 1981. This is the same ruling in most cases. A challenger may not probe into an incumbent's operations at other stations, or probe matters not connected with broadcast station's operations. A challenger may not bring known violations of rules by an incumbent licensee to the attention of the judge unless a nexus can be established between the violation and the operation of the station challenged.

The pre-hearing established a timetable. Each party was to take oral depositions from the other in early September. Discovery orders were issued wherein there would be an exchange of documents requested by the other party. In addition, Hoffart advised the judge that he intended to research the public file at KISW (FM) at this same time. The files are open, however, to the public during business hours and no notice is required for an inspection. The date for the exchange of the parties' Direct Written Case was set for November 5, 1982; rebuttals by the 19th; and the hearing was to start on a Tuesday, November 30, 1982, in the federal court house, Seattle, Washington.

4.

ORAL DEPOSITIONS AND DISCOVERY

Author Hoffart reviewed the KISW public file and copied some hundred or more pages of documents for later scrutiny. One set of documents was a copy of the KISW equipment performance measurements that are to be made annually, with one such proof made within four months of the filing of a renewal application. The application engineering section requires a "check-mark" to indicate that the measurements had been made. The proof documents gave the date of the proof as being made on September 29th, 1980. The renewal application, however, was dated on the 26th. In the renewal application Mr. Smith, executive director of Kaye-Smith Enterprises, represented to the commission, by virtue of dating and signing the renewal application on the 26th, that the measurements had been made. This was proven untrue by the station's engineer who testified, under oath, that the measurements had not been made prior to the 29th. He did not know who placed the "checkmark" on the page of the application that he signed.

The renewal application also stated that Kaye-Smith Enterprises operated Concerts West. In actual fact this concert booking business had been sold in 1977. This was another misrepresentation in the renewal application. Smith had certified the application as being true and correct to the best of his knowledge and belief, under penalty of Title 18, U.S.C. section 1001, the stricture against knowlingly filing false information with an agency. No demerits were issued against Kaye-Smith for these acts. Smith's excuse was that the events were "oversights."

It is well-known that a person who signs a document is responsible for the accuracy of its content.

The file review also revealed that KISW had received a construction permit to install a translator to rebroadcast their programming on channel 283.[4] The permit authorized the installation of a GIBSON, 3 Colinear vertical dipole antenna. Kaye-Smith, without authorization, installed a directional antenna, a TACO model Y51, five element Yagi. This antenna was orientated 204 degrees from their Queen Anne location in order to cover Alki Point. Alki Point is in a dead spot, being shadowed to all stations transmitting from Cougar Mountain. This unauthorized and illegal installation will be covered in a later chapter in this book when it will be alleged that the commission's Order Granting Renewal contained misrepresentations regarding the grant of a license to permit the use of a TACO directional antenna. The author charged

---

[4]File BLFT-780822IA.

KISW with a statutory violation in the installation and use, for over four years, of unauthorized and unlicensed radio apparatus.[5]

Discovery also revealed that KISW had changed their microwave transmitter, linking their studios with Cougar Mountain, to a higher powered transmitter of a different manufacture without application to the commission and without authorization. This also violates the Communications Act of 1934, which prohibits the installation and use of unauthorized radio apparatus.

The author obtained copies of a six-month period of KISW operational logs. These logs were analyzed by Hoffart and a tabulation of their Emergency Broadcast System (EBS) programming showed that KISW did not log EBS actions approximately 50 percent of the time. Airing and logging tests are a vital public interest programming requirement. More on this rules and regulations violation in a later chapter.

The public file review uncovered a "memo" addressed to the public relating to the airing of a non-fact event by KISW on March 26, 1982.[6] This memo, authored by program director "Beau Phillips," was notarized by Ms. Margit Noren, senior notary at the station. More about this notarization later. The document was placed in the public file to "clear up" an erroneous announcement, aired over a period of approximately thirty hours in March of 1982, which declared that advanced time (daylight saving time) would begin one month early. Mr. Phillips stated, in explanation to the event, that "it was an honest mistake." Author Hoffart will devote a chapter in this book to this "honest mistake" and the reader can draw his or her conclusions as to whether or not the airing was an honest mistake or a preplanned publicity stunt.

The oral depositions did not amount to much. The author brought to Mr. Smith's attention the fact that he had made two misrepresentations to the commission in his renewal application. First, he had certified the application on September 26th and by so doing represented to the commission that the performance measurements had been made. Second, Smith was made aware that he had certified that Kaye-Smith Enterprises operates Concerts West when in actual fact Smith had sold this business in 1977.

In previous applications Mr. Smith had represented to the commission that Mr. and Mrs. Danny Kaye, 80 percent owners of Kaye-Smith Enterprises, jointly owned Belmont Television. The author asked Smith about this representation. Smith said he never heard of a Belmont Television, but had heard of a Belmont racetrack. Author Hoffart subsequently checked this out. At one time Mr. and Mrs. Danny Kaye had each owned 50 percent of a Belmont Television, but had dissolved the

---

[5]Title 47, U.S.C. Section 301, The Communications Act.
[6]Appendix page 33. Copy of the "memo."

corporation. Hoffart's records show that Smith continued to represent, in renewal applications for nine stations over a period of six years, that one of the business interests of the Kaye's was Belmont Television. These representations came after the dissolution. The point is that Smith stated, under oath before the notary at depositions, that he had never heard of such a Belmont Television. Smith had his renewal prepared by his administrative assistant, Mr. Melvin Mandren Bailey, who apparently was no more concerned about the accuracy of the representations made to the commission than Mr. Smith or the Kaye's. These prior misrepresentations, repeated some eighteen or more times, could not be entered into the case since the 1980 renewal did not mention the ownership of Belmont Television by the Kaye's. As stated earlier, Hoffart was limited to keeping licensee's conduct to the period between 1978 and 1981. This limitation severely limited the author's arguments before the judge.

One other matter that surfaced at the depositions bears mentioning. Author Hoffart had filed his application specifying the same site Kaye-Smith was leasing on Cougar Mountain. In his application Hoffart allocated one thousand dollars per month as lease costs for this site. Kaye-Smith, in an effort to prove that the author was not financially qualified, represented to the commission, on two occasions, that leasing the site for this amount was "wishful thinking." As a matter of discovery, then, the author requested a copy of the lease held by KISW. After some arguing, counsel for KISW released a copy of the lease. The documents showed that, in actual fact, the KISW lease had expired prior to Hoffart's application, and while in force, Smith was paying three hundred dollars per month for the Cougar Mountain site of the KISW transmitter. Smith negotiated a new lease shortly after the challenging application was filed. This new lease was for five hundred dollars per month, with escalation clauses. The expired lease and the new lease both supported the authors representation that he had allocated sufficient funds for a site. Without this proof Hoffart would have been declared financially short since he could not prove that Smith was paying less than he had allocated. As the review board stated later—Hoffart just squeaked by on that issue.

In sum, then, the trip to Seattle produced the following results. Smith made two misrepresentations in his 1980 renewal application. KISW had installed and was operating a microwave transmitter without prior authorization from the commission. KISW had installed an unauthorized and unlicensed antenna on its translator so that they could cover the dead spot at Alki Point. KISW had aired a non-fact event by broadcasting to their listeners that advanced time would begin in March of 1982 instead of April. KISW had repeatedly violated the rules governing Emergency Broadcast matters. KISW had no valid lease on their Cougar

Mountain site at the time the challenging application was filed. Smith did not, at any time, reveal this to the commission but instead told the FCC that Hoffart's representation of one thousand dollars per month a valid figure was "wishful thinking." The author submits to the reader that Smith lacked candor in this matter. Lack of candor has been defined by the commission as being evasive, lack of forthrightness, and beating about the bush in matters by failing to bring to light information that might illuminate a decisional matter. Smith lacked candor, but candor is apparently only required of challengers and not incumbents.

The licensee's actions and conduct were all related to the renewal period, with the exception of the airing of the untrue broadcasts about advanced time. Thus a nexus between the KISW operations and conduct was established. It would appear that the matters raised were not in the "public interest, convenience or necessity"; the statutory basis that must be met before a permit or license can be issued. Author Hoffart submits that he should have prevailed on these revelations, all proven beyond any doubt. Just what the commission ruled has already been revealed—the conduct and events were due to ignorance and as such warranted only a "slight demerit."

This is just a preview, however, of what is yet to come. Feigned ignorance is now a valid defense, at least before administrative bodies. The question arises, however, whether ignorance was involved or negligence and indifference on the part of Mr. Smith and Mr. and Mrs. Danny Kaye, 20 percent and 80 percent owners of Kaye-Smith Enterprises. As will be seen, Kaye-Smith counsel proved, to the satisfaction of the judge, the review board and the commissioners that the upper echelon KISW employees were ignorant, and this ignorance mitigates their unlawful acts.

These employees owe this characterization to Kaye-Smith and their counsel. They were branded as being ignorant of the very fundamental acts in veracity, that is to say, they did not know right from wrong. In actual fact, their acts in this case came about due to orders given them, and the ignorance and stupidity is self-serving and feigned. The author does not believe that ignorance was involved in this case. It was a case of supporting one's employer or look for work elsewhere. There is no doubt in the mind of the author that the witnesses were briefed to show ignorance so that their conduct would mitigate the wrongful and unlawful acts they engaged in on behalf of their employer, Kaye-Smith.

5.

THE DIRECT WRITTEN CASE EXCHANGE

The author met the November 5th, 1982 exchange date for his Direct Written Case. Kaye-Smith did not. About one week prior to the exchange date set by the judge, Hoffart received a phone call from Mr. Stuart Young, co-counsel for Kaye-Smith. Mr. Young requested that Hoffart agree to a one-week extension for the filing of their Direct Written Case. Mr. Young stated that there were "steno" problems. The author reluctantly agreed to the extension and so notified the judge immediately by letter. Later that same day Hoffart received a letter from the Washington, D.C. office of these same lawyers in which it was stated, to the judge, that the reason for the requested delay was that documents had to be obtained from the Seattle area and from the Federal Communications Commission. The reasons given the author for the needed extension did not check out. Hoffart immediately filed an objection to any extensions. He was advised, however, that the judge had already granted the extension. Counsel for Kaye-Smith, therefore, had the author's Direct Written Case before them before they completed their mandated Direct Written Case. In actual fact Kaye-Smith used the one-week extension to obtain additional testimonial letters for filing in support of their renewal application. One such solicited letter of commendation was allegedly notarized on the original due date of November 5th and another was notarized on November 10th, 1982. Since there were no stenos involved, the excuse given Hoffart for the need of extra time was clearly not true. The author is relating this matter since it has a bearing on what is to come and also because the judge mentioned it at the opening of the hearing.

The one-week extension granted Kaye-Smith by the judge set the new exchange date as November 12, 1982. Hoffart received the Kaye-Smith Direct Case on the morning of the 12th.

A review of the exhibits showed that fourteen documents had been notarized by a Ms. Carrie Matthew and only two of these notarial attestations were dated as to the date Ms. Matthew notarized them. In addition, four of the exhibits were shown to have been notarized before a Ms. Margit Noren. Three were notarized on November 10th, in Seattle, and one was not dated.

The author knew Ms. Noren was employed by KISW. With fourteen documents notarized by Ms. Matthew, Hoffart suspected that she was also a Kaye-Smith employee. This was proven correct at the hearing.

With eighteen notarial verifications before him in which fifteen were not dated as to when the affiants had appeared before these two notaries, the author suspected that some of the affiants had not appeared before the notaries.

Seven of the suspect attestations were affixed to testimonial letters solicited by KISW from area community leaders and were filed in support of the renewal application. Five of these letters were notarized by Ms. Matthew and two by Ms. Noren.

The author immediately wrote letters to these authors of testimonial letters, asking if they had appeared before the notaries. Copies of their notarized letters were sent to them. The letters also included a self-addressed stamped envelope for a reply. They were all mailed on November 13th, a Saturday, one day after Hoffart received the Kaye-Smith Direct Written Case.

One of the verified letters in suspect had been solicited from a Ms. Judy Balint, of Focus, a non-profit organization.[7] This letter was purportedly notarized before Ms. Carrie Matthew on an unknown date. The author's letter to Ms. Balint read as follows:

Dear Ms. Balint:

Vincent L. Hoffart, d/b/as Hoffart Broadcasting, is in a hearing before Federal Communications Commission Administrative Law Judge, the Honorable Thomas B. Fitzpatrick, scheduled to start on November 30, 1982, room 514, Federal Building, Seattle, Washington. This hearing is to determine whether Hoffart Broadcasting or Kaye-Smith Enterprises is to receive a license or construction permit for the channel presently used by KISW. In connection with the Kaye-Smith Direct Written Case, filed with the Judge, the Broadcast Bureau and Hoffart, are several letters of commendation solicited from a number of firms and individuals by Kaye-Smith. These were filed in support of the KISW renewal application. Hoffart notes that a number of these letters, including yours, do not show that the author appeared personally before a notary public, and deposed to the content of the letter as being true, correct, etc—I am therefore enclosing a copy of your letter, dated 10-29-82, which shows it was notarized by a Carrie Matthew-no date given.

Please advise, by return letter, self-addressed stamped envelope enclosed, if you personally appeared before Ms. Carrie Matthew, and give the date and location where this was so notarized. A copy of this letter is being sent to the judge in rebuttal.

cc: rebuttal filing—FCC   Vincent L. Hoffart
    certified# P 25 5417057   Hoffart Broadcasting.
cc: Fly, Shubruk, *et al*
    Counsel for Kaye-Smith.

---

[7]This Kaye-Smith exhibit is appendixed as page 1. The Carrie Matthew notarization is a phony.

The certified letter return receipt showed delivery to Focus, 509 Tenth Avenue East, Seattle, 98102 on Monday, November 15th, 1982. A Carol Madigan had signed for it.

The author received a reply from Ms. Balint dated November 16th. The letter, reads as follows:

Dear Mr. Hoffart,
In response to your letter of November 13, 1982, I did not appear in front of a notary with regard to my letter of support for KISW. I was also not aware that the purpose of these testimonials was to bolster a legal case.

Sincerely,
(S) Judy Balint
Judy Balint[8]
Office Coordinator

The receipt of this letter verified the author's suspicions that fraudulently notarized documents had been filed with a federal agency. The letter, however, did more than just prove that phony verified testimonial letters had been filed by Kaye-Smith. Ms. Balint stated that she was not aware that the letter solicited by KISW would be used to bolster a legal case. The author takes leave to reprint, verbatim, the judge's pre-hearing instructions, a response to the authors query:

TR:106   *Judge Fitzpatrick*: Well, it is in the form of an affidavit, but it is sworn testimony and in the affidavit, that is one thing that I should say, Mr. Boros, that in the affidavit as submitted, it should show in its face that these people know it is being given to the commission, and that it is sworn testimony, you know, and that it is testimony in a docketed proceeding, and also that they should be aware that they are going to be subject to being called for cross-examination . . .

In an effort to comply with these explicit and unambiguous instructions, Kaye-Smith duly filed supporting affidavits with the testimonial letters to prove that all of the affiants had been so informed. The supporting affidavits, executed by KISW station manager Stephen West, and by Mr. Eric Bogel, KISW program director, also known as "Beau Phillips," filed in support of Kaye-Smith exhibits 16 and 17, the testimonial letters, read as follows:

State of Washington) ss   Kaye-Smith Exhibit 16
County of King)   (page 15)

Stephen L. West, being duly sworn, deposes and says:
1. Each of the affidavits described on the attachment was obtained by me

---

[8]Appendix page 2.

or those under my direction. It was explained to each affiant that his or her affidavit would be used as testimony in a proceeding before the Federal Communications Commission.

(S) Steve West

Subscribed and sworn to before me
this ___ day of November, 1982.
(S) Carrie Matthew
     Notary public (seal)
     My Commission expires June 1, 1986.[9]

West signed two such affidavits, the other one supporting Kaye-Smith exhibit 17. Mr. Bogel signed an identical affidavit, also supporting Kaye-Smith exhibit 16, the testimonial letter exhibits. In all three of these affidavits the date the document was notarized is blank. Subsequently, Kaye-Smith filed affidavits signed by Ms. Carrie Matthew that she had notarized the above three affidavits on the 9th of November, 1982. Similarly, she filed affidavits that six other affidavits, wherein she did not date the notarial act in the exhibits were notarized before her on this same date, November 9th. This date is significant, as it will later prove that one of the attachment lists mentioned in the affidavit above could not have been in existence on the 9th.

The author will prove, in this book, that Mr. and Mrs. Danny Kaye's and Mr. Lester M. Smith's employees willfully and repeatedly filed, or caused to be filed, testimonial letters solicited from Seattle area citizenry upon which the notarial attestations were affixed outside the presence of the signatories. These illegal acts were performed by KISW employees who are also Washington State commissioned notaries. They followed instructions and suggestions from the station manager, Mr. Stephen West.

The filing of false information with a federal agency is prohibited by statute. Title 18, U.S.C. Section 1001 states:

> Whoever, in any matter within the jurisdiction of any department or agency of the United States knowingly and willfully falsifies, conceals, or covers up by any trick, scheme, or device a material fact, or makes any false, fictitious or fraudulent statements or representations, or makes or uses any false writing or document knowing the same to contain any false, fictitious or fraudulent statement or entry, shall be fined not more than $10,000 or imprisoned not more than five years or both.[10]

It is axiomatic that the laws apply equally to everyone, or so this author thought, until this case proved to him this untrue. Employees of influential broadcasters can file documents with fictitious entries in the

---

[9]Appendix pages 3 through 8 are the three affidavits and attachments.
[10]Title 18, U.S.C., Section 1001, Crimes and Criminal Procedure.

16

form of notarial attestations with impunity. The author will prove, beyond any doubt, that there was intent to deceive involved and that the acts were repeated when the author discovered that phony verifications had been affixed to five solicited testimonial letters and that these letters were filed upon the FCC by counsel for Kaye-Smith, owners of KISW.

After reading this book, the reader can decide for him or herself if the facts presented warrant only a slight demerit and that Kaye-Smith should prevail due to meritorious service to the people of Seattle. Hoffart will devote chapters to a non-fact airing in 1982 and also print a series of letters alleging KISW aired pornography repeatedly.

6.

THE SUSPECT TESTIMONIAL LETTERS

The author has established that a testimonial letter solicited from Focus, a non-profit public service organization, and authored by a Judy Balint, had been affixed with a phony verification by a KISW employee. Exhibits 16 and 17 of the Kaye-Smith Direct Written Case consisted of twenty-four letters of commendation and this book will focus primarily on these two exhibits. The letters had been solicited by KISW employees to impress upon the judge that the Seattle area citizenry is solidly behind KISW and as such renewal should be granted. The reason why only twenty-four civic leaders supported KISW becomes evident when the reader is exposed to the actual programming and complaints thereto by concerned citizens.

Initially the author, Hoffart, suspected that seven out of the twenty-four letters submitted to the FCC were affixed with phony verifications. The suspicion was raised because some of the letters did not show the date of notarization and five had been notarized by the same notary. Two others had been notarized by Ms. Margit Noren and the author knew that she was employed by KISW.

The suspect letters, then, were authored by:

Ms. Judy Balint, Focus.
Shawn Taylor, Boy Scouts of America.
John Taylor, Bumbershoot
Charles E. Blacksmith, Roundup Music/Fred Meyers
Bob. L. Curran, Major, U.S. Army (retired) Seafair.
J. Daniel McConnell, President, McConnell Co.
Julie McCullough, Greenpeace.

The affidavits filed by KISW which were signed by Mr. Steve West, station manager, and Mr. Eric Bogel, program director, had attachment lists upon which the above names were listed as authors of the solicited letters. The content of the affidavits, which attested to the fact that all authors were advised that their letters would be used in an FCC proceeding will be proven untrue by some of the affiants who were required to appear as witnesses. These seven people were sent letters by Hoffart on November 13, the day after receiving the Kaye-Smith Direct Case.

The author also received a response to a letter written to Ms. Julie McCullough, Greenpeace. The letter sent her was similar to the one written to Ms. Balint.

Hoffart had asked Ms. McCullough if she had appeared before Ms. Carrie Matthew, the notary who attested to her signature. She did not respond to the question asked by the author but sent the author a copy of her letter, now notarized before a Ms. Diane Blane. The fact that she sent a letter notarized by someone else is sufficient proof that the original letter filed by Kaye-Smith,[11] was not notarized before Ms. Carrie Matthew.

Ms. McCullough is one of the witnesses who was ordered by the judge to testify. Others who were required to appear, and did appear, were Shawn (Sean) Taylor, Ms. Judy Balint, Mr. J. Daniel McConnell, Mr. Charles Blacksmith, Ms. Carrie Matthew and Ms. Margit Noren. The latter two are the KISW notaries involved in this case. The burden of producing these witnesses had been placed by the judge upon Kaye-Smith.

Two other authors of testimonial letters, Mr. John Taylor and Mr. Bob Curran, were also to appear. The judge, however, ruled that their testimony would be cumulative and thus they were excused. The author will charge that this ruling by the judge prejudiced his case. He was denied cross-examination of two authors of testimonial letters. The accuracy of the notarial attestations on their letters is only supported by one of the KISW notaries. Cross-examination may have revealed perjury by this notary, over and above that which will be proven, beyond any doubt. Repeated perjury would be of significance since there is no need for a showing of willfullness when acts are repeated.

Each of the affiants and the notaries will be featured in a chapter in this book, with their verbatim testimony taken from the transcript of the hearing.

The rules of procedure require all parties to keep all other parties, the judge and the commission, informed, and make service and full disclosures on all aspects of a case.

Hoffart filed information with the judge, the Broadcast Bureau and counsel for Kaye-Smith in which he stated he suspected that some of the testimonial letters had been notarized outside the presence of the authors of the letters. After Kaye-Smith counsel had been so advised, (allegedly they received Hoffart's filing on the 22nd of November, 1982, as rebuttal to their Direct Written Case) counsel filed two letters with attachments with the judge and all other parties. The letters were dated November 23rd and November 24th. The letter dated the 23rd reads, in part:

---

[11]Appendix page 9. This original McCullough letter was affixed with a phony verification by Ms. Matthew.

Dear Judge Fitzpatrick:

I am enclosing herewith corrections to Kaye-Smith Direct Exhibits 5-10, 13 and 16 and 17. These will remedy notarial imperfections in the foregoing exhibits . . . the pages enclosed under attachment II are to be substituted for the existing exhibit pages identically marked and paginated . . . I am supplying Mr. Hoffart and Mr. Sarno of the Broadcast Bureau with these corrected pages.

Very truly yours,
(s) Stuart J. Young.[12]

The November 24th letter was similar in nature but had reference to corrections submitted to what turned out to be some of the testimonial letters affixed with phony notarial verifications by Kaye-Smith notary/ employees.

The trickery counsel attempted to pull off here is self-evident. They wanted the illegally notarized letters to be withdrawn and substituted by properly notarized letters bearing the identical page numbers. This shystering failed. For one thing, Hoffart would not have agreed to a simple substitution. Falsely notarized documents had been filed by counsel and the phonies had been detected and reported by Hoffart days before Kaye-Smith counsel admitted, albeit by filing correctly notarized letters, that willfull misrepresentations had been filed with an agency of the federal government, clearly a violation of Title 18, U.S.C. section 1001.

Enclosed with the transmittal letters were nine affidavits executed by Ms. Carrie Matthew on the 16th of November, attesting to the fact that the nine undated affidavits which were not connected with the testimonial letters had all been correctly notarized on the 9th of November, and with all of the affiants, Mr. West and Mr. Bogel, appearing before her and attesting to the accuracy of their exhibits. These exhibits related to such things as programming, employment roster, bibliographies, and other topics that are immaterial to the issue at hand; that issue being that KISW had tried to deceive Hoffart and all others concerned, including the public, by illegally notarizing testimonial letters and filing them in support of their renewal application.

The enclosures also included "corrected" letters solicited from Shawn Taylor, Julie McCullough, John Taylor, Charles E. Blacksmith, J. Daniel McConnell, David Watkins and C. Clark Griffin. The author had questioned the notarial acts on seven letters, and seven corrections were received, *but not the same seven!* Author Hoffart had not question-

---

[12]The transmittal letters for the corrections are appendixed as pages 10 and 11. Kaye-Smith did not request leave to file these corrections and they were filed 11 days and 12 days after the second due date. The corrected testimonial letters were not the same as the originals since they now were notarized by different notaries, without permission from the judge. All of the corrected testimonial letters were dated after the November 12 due date and should have been rejected out-of-hand for failure to prosecute.

ed the notarization of the letters solicited from David Watkins of the Seattle Supersonics or that obtained from C. Clark Griffin, nor had Hoffart written letters to these two affiants. Their letters had appeared to be properly notarized although the Watkins letter lacked the date of notarization.

The author reproduces the original testimonial letters and the corrected versions in the appendix.[13] The author will refer the reader to these documents as this story unfolds.

No corrected letter was filed from Focus. The original letter, as the reader is already aware of, was affixed with a phony verification by KISW employee Carrie Matthew. The transcript supports the fact that a corrected letter was solicited from Ms. Balint, but she did not give them one. Instead a corrected letter may have been signed by a Ms. Ann Burnes, the head of Focus. Such a letter was purportedly picked up by Ms. Tamara Kern, secretary to Mr. Eric Bogel, the KISW program director. If so, it was not filed as a correction by counsel for Kaye-Smith.

The judge ordered all corrected exhibits affixed with the suffix (A) to distinguish them from the originals. This was necessary since counsel for Kaye-Smith used identical page numbers on the corrections in their attempt to have the illegally notarized documents substituted for correctly notarized letters. This identical numbering led to considerable confusion at the hearing and to some of the witnesses, who apparently were not aware of what was going on, giving contradictory testimony regarding their exhibits.

It is one thing, of course, to file corrections for typos and unintentional errors or honest mistakes. Here, however, counsel for Kaye-Smith attempted to withdraw documents that were proof of statutory violations. This shystering failed when Kaye-Smith was required to place both the original letters and the corrected versions where corrections were filed into the official record.

As has been said earlier, the author will prove, beyond any doubt, that the illegal acts were orchestrated by the KISW station manager and that two more illegally notarized documents were filed as corrections after the author detected the initial five felonious acts.

Hoffart received the Kaye-Smith corrected testimonial letters on Friday, November 26th, 1982. The hearing was to start on the 30th. The judge had ruled that all documents were to be exchanged well in advance of the hearing so that opposing counsel could study them and file witness notifications. The reader will readily see that Hoffart was shortchanged in this matter. Not only do we have the judge granting a one-week extension to Kaye-Smith for the filing of their Direct Case, we now

---

[13]Appendix pages 1, 9 and 12 through 27 are the original and corrected testimonial letters.

have Kaye-Smith filing documents four days before the start of a hearing and doing so without leave from the judge.

The author had a new mystery on his hands. Counsel for Kaye-Smith filed corrections of two testimonial letters that Hoffart had not questioned.[14] One was a corrected letter purportedly signed by David Watkins, an official with the Seattle Supersonics professional basketball team. The other was a correction of notarial imperfections in a letter solicited by KISW employees from a C. Clark Griffin. The author had not written letters to these two letter writers. The original Watkins letter was undated as to when a Mr. Anthony Tucker, another Supersonics official, had notarized it. The Clark letter had been notarized before a Christine Woolson purportedly eight days after it was authored.

Hoffart compared the original Watkins letter with the corrected version. He immediately recognized that the two David Watkins signatures were different. Obviously one of the letters was not signed by Mr. Watkins but both had been notarized before Washington State notaries, the original by Mr. Anthony Tucker on an unknown date and the corrected letter purportedly before Ms. Noren, the KISW senior notary, on November 17, 1982.

The author suspected that the original Watkins letter had not been signed before Mr. Tucker. When Ms. Noren's testimony is presented in this book, it will be established, beyond any doubt, that it was the corrected letter that had a forged Watkins signature and that no one had appeared before Noren on November 17th, 1982 in regards to the Watkins letter.

This was clearly an act of defiance. KISW personnel engaged in two more statutory violations by submitting two more testimonial letters, as corrections, wherein the affiants had not appeared before the notary. Ms. Margit Noren, administrative assistant to Mr. West, had notarized both of the corrected letters. She did this after all of the difficulties regarding the original five (or more) phony notarial attestations had come to her attention. She so admitted on the witness stand. This is proof beyond any doubt that there was intent to engage in further deception. She would have gotten away with these felonious acts except for the fact that Hoffart detected the two different styles of the David Watkins signature.

The hearing testimony also revealed that Ms. Noren had notarized the C. Clark Griffin corrected letter without benefit of Mr. Griffin being present. Just why his original letter had to be re-submitted and corrected will be dealt with later in this book.

Neither Kaye-Smith nor their counsel advised the judge or Hoffart that two of the corrected letters had again been notarized outside the

---

[14]Appendix pages 14 and 27 are the David Watkins and C. Clark Griffin corrected letters.

presence of the authors, nor did they advise anyone that the corrected David Watkins letter had not been signed by him. The reader may wish to compare the signatures on the original and the corrected David Watkins's testimonial letters, appendix pages 13 and 14.

The reader already knows what the judge ruled in this matter. He stated that the acts were unfortunate, should not have happened, and that there was no intent on the part of Kaye-Smith to mislead anyone. Just how such a finding can be reached on the basis of the record defies analysis. The judge clearly engaged in preferential treatment and failed to judge the case upon the record evidence.[15]

The time element was such as to foreclose the filing of the discovery of apparently additional felonious conduct by Kaye-Smith with the judge in Washington, D.C. Counsel for Kaye-Smith had sent their latest corrections to the judge in care of the FCC field office in Seattle. The author followed suit.

In his presentation to the judge, Hoffart attached subpoena forms requesting the appearance of Mr. David Watkins, Ms. Noren, Ms. Matthew and others. The forms used had been previously obtained from the FCC and needed only the signature of the judge to make them valid. Hoffart served this filing upon counsel for Kaye-Smith at the opening of the hearing on Tuesday, November 30th. This, then, was the first notice which Kaye-Smith received that Hoffart had detected additional statutory violations of Title 18, U.S.C. 1001, the statute against knowingly filing false information with a federal agency.

The judge received the mailing and reviewed the subpoena requests and supporting documents at the opening of the hearing.

With reference to the time element, Hoffart received Kaye-Smith's corrections to the phony verified testimonial letters on Friday, November 26th, the day after Thanksgiving. The next two days were non-working days. Monday would be the day the judge would be traveling to Seattle; the hearing was to start on Tuesday, November 30th. It should be clear that Kaye-Smith counsel waited until the last minute to advise both the judge and Hoffart that they had filed false information with the Kaye-Smith direct case. If Mr. Young's testimony, as co-counsel for KISW, is believed, he "perceived" on the 12th of November that illegally notarized documents had been filed in the case. The fact that he did not pick up the phone and call Hoffart on the 12th, or anytime before the corrections were filed proves that Kaye-Smith attempted to mislead and deceive Hoffart at the last minute.

---

[15]Preferential treatment, or an appearance of preferential treatment, is prohibited. FCC Rules and Regulations, Part 19, sections 19.735—101, *et seq*, and specifically section 19.735—201a.

7.

THE HEARING

The comparative renewal hearing convened as scheduled at 10:00AM in Seattle, Washington. It is now twenty-three months since the challenging application was filed. The judge requested the appearances for the parties. The author stated that he was appearing *pro se*, that is, representing himself. Mr. Jerome S. Boros and Mr. Stuart Young, both attorneys from New York stated that they were representing Kaye-Smith Enterprises. When the judge asked if anyone represented the Broadcast Bureau, no one responded. In the pre-hearing chapter it was shown that Mr. Daniel Sarno, Esquire, had appeared on behalf of the bureau. However, in October Mr. Sarno called Hoffart, and presumably all parties, to advise the author that he had been taken off the case, therefore no one would represent the bureau, and as such, the public, at the hearing. The judge mentioned that he had been told that the Broadcast Bureau would not be represented. This is highly unusual. The bureau has the responsibility of representing the commission and the public. It appears, at least in this case, that the bureau did not wish to appear since they had a responsibility to file the incumbent's record as it exists at the field offices and in Washington, D.C. The author, to this day, does not know if any complaints relating to the operations of KISW (FM) that are in these files relate to the renewal period of 1978 to 1981.

The judge read from the designation order which had set the issues that were to be the basis of the hearing. These have already been outlined in the chapter on the designation order. The ALJ (judge) further read from a previously released order to all parties: "Each affirmative of the Direct Case Exhibits must be accompanied by the affidavit of a sponsoring witness." Going further into the preliminaries, and his opening statements:

TR:140   *Judge Fitzpatrick*: On November 11th, 1982, Kaye-Smith counsel filed their Direct Case Exhibits with the judge. Subsequently, however, by letter dated November 23rd, 1982, Stuart J. Young, an associate of Mr. Boros, by letter to myself enclosed direction to Kaye-Smith exhibits 5 thru 10, 13 and 16 through 17 and it was stated quote, "these will remedy notarial imperfections in the forgoing exhibits." Subsequently ... in a subsequent letter dated November 24, 1982, filed another letter with additional corrections of notarial imperfections ... filed by Mr. Young.

24

I have studied the so-called corrective pages of the Kaye-Smith exhibits and the purported notarial remedying of the purported notarial imperfections and there arises, as a result of my study, a serious question with respect to this matter, and then on my own motion I am going to enlarge the issue in this proceeding to include an issue to determine all of the facts and circumstances surrounding the so-called notarial imperfections relative to the Direct Written Case of Kaye-Smith and what impact, if any, whatever evidence is adduced will have on the basic and/or comparative qualifications of Kaye-Smith to continue to be a broadcast licensee. The burden to proceed with the introduction of evidence and the burden of proof will be upon Kaye-Smith. There arises a serious question as to whether or not the Direct Written Case of this applicant was prepared properly or whether there were any misrepresentations to this Commission with respect to the actual notarization of the sworn testimony of these witnesses. I expect that in each case I want to have as it relates to Exhibit 16, I want all of those public witnesses to appear and I want the notaries to appear and I want also the people in Exhibit 16 who say that they arranged for the notarization . . . arrange for the testimony to be developed . . . to appear and be prepared to testify as to what instructions, if any, they gave to these various public witnesses, what arrangements they made to assure themselves that the testimony was appropriately prepared and that there wasn't any misrepresentations to the Commission.

TR:144   The Commission takes very seriously the integrity of it's hearing process and when we arrange for the exchange of the Direct Written Case, it's with the clear understanding that all of the testimony prior to it's submission to the Commission will be appropriately prepared. So you're on notice as to what the problem is. All right?

In response to a logistical question from Mr. Boros, Judge Fitzpatrick stated:

TR:145   *Judge Fitzpatrick*: Mr. Boros, only you and your client know the facts. You are the people who have come in and asked leave to correct certain exhibits and you are the people who have told us there are notarial imperfections. Now, what is incumbent upon you people is to explain what these notarial imperfections have been . . .

Even though the author had filled out subpoena forms and they were before the judge, the judge ruled that Hoffart would not have the burden of producing the witnesses who had questionable notarizations on their letters, the notaries, or Mr. Bogel and Mr. West—the two Kaye-Smith employees who filed the affidavits attesting to the fact that all affiants had been told their letters would be used in a proceeding before the Federal Communications Commission. Witness testimony will prove that both Mr. Bogel and Mr. West stated untruths in those affidavits, already appendixed, as page 3 through 8.

It is significant that the judge's enlargement of issues was comparative or basic. Had he found that Kaye-Smith and counsel had abused the commission's processes and had willfully filed documents and affidavits that violated both federal and state laws, he could have disqualified Kaye-Smith. Once an applicant is basically disqualified, and it is upheld by the commission, that applicant has no further standing in a case before the FCC.

Similarly, had he found that KISW personnel willfully filed falsely certified testimonial letters and as such intented to mislead and deceive, Kaye-Smith could have been basically disqualified, or, at the very least, given a substantial demerit that would have disqualified Kaye-Smith on a comparative basis.

The fact that the judge ruled in favor of Kaye-Smith supports the author's charges that this case was decided on the basis of who was involved and not on the record evidence. Hoffart, therefore, states that he is fully justified in charging all concerned with giving an appearance of preferential treatment to an incumbent licensee; such conduct is prohibited. The author, for one, has lost all confidence in the integrity of the FCC to judge cases on the basis of the record evidence.

The witnesses in this case appeared at their convenience. The author will present their testimony in the order they appeared. Leave will be taken to paraphrase. Redundant and insignificant testimony will be deleted.

Now for the sworn testimony, as adduced at the hearing.

8.

LESTER M. SMITH

Lester M. Smith, executive director of Kaye-Smith Enterprises was the first hearing witness to be called. Smith was 20 percent owner of KISW. Mr. and Mrs. Danny Kaye owned the other 80 percent by virtue of 100 percent owners of Dena Pictures. Since the Kaye's owned most of the stock, they were controlling owners. The responsibility for the illegal acts in this case rests with the Kaye's as well as with Mr. Smith. This is the well-known *respondeat superior* concept of the law.

Mr. and Mrs. Kaye did not appear at the hearing in support of their renewal application.

Smith was duly sworn upon oath by the judge. Mr. Boros proceeded with his direct examination regarding the content and accuracy of the Kaye-Smith Direct Case exhibits which he had directly sponsored and had supported by affidavit. These notarizations are not in dispute. All of Smith's affidavits attached to exhibits purportedly prepared by him had been notarized by his secretary, Ms. Anne Curtis. All of the exhibits were shown to have been notarized on November 9th, 1982.

One of the exhibits, however, related to the Arbitron Company ratings of KISW. This exhibit, filed as No. 15, contained an internal document notarized by Mr. Anthony Kelsey attesting to the accuracy of the Arbitron rating book that was part of the exhibit.

Smith's affidavit, dated the 9th of November, attested to the fact that he had read all of exhibit 15.[16] The Anthony Kelsey affidavit, an internal page of exhibit 15, however, was not notarized until the 10th.[17] Hoffart had brought this to the attention of the judge in his rebuttal to the Kaye-Smith Written Case. Purportedly the judge received the rebuttal on the 22nd of November.

Smith's exhibit 15 affidavit content is not true.

Since this book relates mostly to "notarial imperfections," the author goes directly to the transcript testimony regarding this misrepresentation by Mr. Smith.

TR: 189   *Judge Fitzpatrick*: But you had a copy of Mr. Kelsey's . . .
            Mr. Smith: I had a copy of it, typed copy, but it was not signed.
            Judge Fitzpatrick: Were the attachments to Mr. Kelsey's affidavit there when you signed it?

---

[16]Appendix exhibit page 28. Smith's preexecuted affidavit.
[17]Appendix exhibit pages 29/30. Kelsey's affidavit.

Mr. Smith: The attachments I have had, are you talking about the book itself?

Judge Fitzpatrick: Well, it's been marked as Kaye-Smith exhibit 15, pages 18 thru 21 . . .

Mr. Smith: That I have had and read many, many times.

Judge Fitzpatrick: Well, did you have this, as the exhibit appears today, before you when you signed . . .

Mr. Smith: Yes, I did.

Judge Fitzpatrick: And it was all before you except the copy of the affidavit you had of Mr. Kelsey and was not executed . . . had you checked with him to find out whether he had . . .

Mr. Smith: Counsel did that. Counsel told me that it would be forthcoming.

Judge Fitzpatrick: Do you have any qualms about executing an affidavit saying that everything was true and correct when in fact there was an unsigned affidavit as part of the exhibit?

Mr. Smith: Your Honor, I would call your attention to what Mr. Kelsey says in his . . .

Judge Fitzpatrick: I read what Mr. Kelsey said, now please answer my question. Did you have any concern about signing this affidavit on the 9th of November saying everything was true and correct when in fact you didn't have a signed affidavit of Mr. Kelsey before you?

Mr. Smith: No, I didn't. Because I was assured he was going to sign it.

Judge Fitzpatrick: Did you inquire of anybody as to whether it was appropriate of you to . . .

Mr. Smith: I inquired of counsel.

Judge Fitzpatrick: What did he tell you?

Mr. Smith: He said it was fine.

Judge Fitzpatrick: He did? Let me tell you it isn't fine.

Mr. Smith: Yes, sir.

Judge Fitzpatrick: Did you receive Mr. Kelsey's affidavit that . . . was it forwarded to you, this affidavit that he purportedly subscribed and swore to at, on the 10th day of November, 1982?

Mr. Smith: It was read to me on the phone, sir.

Judge Fitzpatrick: Did you hear my question?

Mr. Smith: Yes, sir.

Judge Fitzpatrick: Will you, please?

Mr. Smith: The content of the affidavit, itself, was given to me on the phone.

Judge Fitzpatrick: So Mr. Kelsey never forwarded this affidavit to you, is that correct?

Mr. Smith: Yes, he did afterwards, sir, but it was after the time.

Judge Fitzpatrick: When did you receive it?

Mr. Smith: Sometime later. Counsel received it as of the date he signed it. I didn't receive a lot of this material until sometime later.

Judge Fitzpatrick: Mr. Kelsey executed this in New York. He gave it to counsel in New York?

Mr. Smith: Yes, sir.

Judge Fitzpatrick: So it was never sent out to you . . .

Mr. Smith: Later on.

Judge Fitzpatrick: When did you first see this as Mr. Kelsey's executed affidavit?

Mr. Smith: When all of the material was sent out to me a couple of weeks ago.

Judge Fitzpatrick: As a package?

Mr. Smith: Yes.

Judge Fitzpatrick: Do you have any questions?

Mr. Hoffart: Well, I would object to this entry because the affidavit says I read the foregoing Case Exhibit 15 and Exhibit 15 contains page 16 and page 16 is an affidavit that was signed one day after he said he read it.

Mr. Boros: Your Honor, the witness volunteered and made clear the methodology involved. If there is a fault on the part of his counsel in terms of logistics . . .

Judge Fitzpatrick: It wasn't much to volunteer when you execute an affidavit on the 9th saying that the exhibit is true and correct and part of the exhibit is an affidavit executed on the 10th, Mr. Boros. There isn't a heck of a lot that you have to make a true on it's face, it didn't appear to be proper.

Mr. Boros: Well, your Honor, I submit that we are dealing strictly with a technical matter as opposed to a substantive matter in that . . .

Judge Fitzpatrick: Well, Mr. Boros, we ought to get a little technical then.

Mr. Boros: We don't object to that, your Honor. But the affidavit, when you say offered in terms of what the Commission is concerned with for substance Mr. Kelsey's affidavit obviously was obtained for authenticity purposes only and the problem is not the fault of the client; it's the fault of counsel, your Honor, in not . . .

Judge Fitzpatrick: Many clients have gone down the drain because of the fault of his attorney, Mr. Boros; you know that as well as I do, don't you?
Mr. Boros: Yes, your Honor.
Judge Fitzpatrick: Right.

The testimony continued with the admissibility of the exhibit and the judge ruled that it was admissible after Mr. Boros explained it was being offered to show that KISW (FM) had a high listenership during the Saturday and Sunday early morning hours; a time when KISW (FM) airs blocks of non-entertainment programming. The judge referred to these early morning hours as the "ghetto hours." These hours, as a general rule, have a lower listenership than other hours and days of the week. The author, some twenty months later, located a series of complaint letters in the Washington, D.C. files of the FCC enforcement division wherein area citizens complained that KISW was airing obscene and indecent language, some on Saturday and Sunday mornings. These letters were outside the renewal period upon which the hearing was being held. The letters, some of which post-dated the hearing, will be highlighted and reproduced in a later chapter in this book under the heading of Pornography Complaints.

Smith's testimony regarding the pre-execution of an affidavit filed as true and correct in all respects needs to be analyzed. Did Mr. Smith file a misrepresentation with a federal agency? Are his self-serving statements in the testimony credible? Do you believe that Mr. Kelsey called Mr. Smith on the phone on the 10th of November and told him he had signed an affidavit and had read the context to him over the phone? Would it have been proper, assuming that it was counsel who read the context to Smith over the phone, to also read Mr. Kelsey's signature to him as proof that the affidavit was signed? Did Mr. Kelsey, on the 10th of November, know what Mr. Smith had before him in Seattle on the 9th or 10th? Should the exhibit been admitted by the judge over Hoffart's objection since it was established, beyond any doubt, that Smith had made misrepresentations in connection with the exhibit?

The author has already stated that truth and candor are always at issue, and the elements of misrepresentation are falsity, materiality and intent to deceive. Let's look at Mr. Smith's testimony in the light of these three elements.

First, was there falsity? Unquestionably yes. Smith had stated in his affidavit, under oath, that he had read all of exhibit 15. This has been proven untrue. Second, was materiality involved? Mr. Boros has proved that. He stated that the exhibit was being submitted to prove that KISW had a high listenership at times when their non-entertainment programming was being aired. This, then, would be material to a "meritorious programming" finding. Third, was there intent to deceive? The author says yes. Smith testified that counsel had told him it was OK to pre-execute his affidavit. Smith, by his own testimony, acknowledges that he was aware that counsel would insert a page into the exhibit that was not in existence, at least not in the form that it was submitted to the commission and to Hoffart. Author Hoffart submits that, by the commission's own standards, Kaye-Smith engaged in misrepresentations to a federal agency on advise of counsel, and counsel was directly involved and actually initiated the misrepresentation.

It is a well-established legal precept that a client is responsible for the actions and omissions of his or her attorney.[18] These listed in the footnotes are just some of the FCC cases on record where the commission has held a licensee responsible for the acts of counsel.

The Kaye-Smith Direct Case exhibits relating to the renewal period programming were supported by the affidavits of station manager Stephen West and program director Eric Bogel. Mr. Bogel used the professional name of "Beau Phillips." Mr. Smith, when asked by the judge regarding aspects of the programming outside the Arbitron rating exhibit, referred the judge to Mr. West and Mr. Bogel. The judge, however, had some more questions to ask Mr. Smith after Mr. Boros stated that he had completed his questioning of Lester M. Smith.

TR:200   *Judge Fitzpatrick*: Let me ask you a couple of questions. Did you have any knowledge as to whether there was any difficulty in getting direct testimony in meeting the schedule we have?
Mr. Smith: Well, Federal Express has been a life-saver. Getting stuff clear across the country by U.S. Mail is for the birds.
Judge Fitzpatrick: Did it come to your attention that some of the public witnesses whose testimony is to be submitted did not have their signatures notarized?
Mr. Smith: Yes. Earlier counsel said everything had to be notarized and had everybody scurrying around after these people and getting them notarized, and the two people that are notaries are employees, Carrie Matthew and . . .
Judge Fitzpatrick: Anne Curtis?
Mr. Smith: Anne is my secretary, but the other two that were mentioned . . .

---

18 *Wadeco Inc.*, 628 F 2d at 122, 128 (D.C. Cir., 1980)
California Broadcasting Corp., 98 FCC 2d at 1040, (1984)
Community Broadcasting Co., 18 FCC wd at 686, 688 (1969)
Midwest Broadcasting Co., 70 FCC 2d at 1489, (1979).

Judge Fitzpatrick: Carrie Matthew?

Mr. Smith: Right, and Meg Noren.

Judge Fitzpatrick: Were you aware that Carrie Matthew affixed her signature to documents . . .

Mr. Smith: I personally . . . I think that particular question you should address to Steve West.

Judge Fitzpatrick: I am asking you. Did you have any knowledge . . .

Mr. Smith: I know we had a problem.

Judge Fitzpatrick: What problem did you have?

Mr. Smith: We had a problem with dating and the manner in which they were done.

Judge Fitzpatrick: When did you learn about the problem?

Mr. Smith: I learned about it just about a day or so after these pieces of paper started to be assembled.

Judge Fitzpatrick: Well, prior to the letter of November 11th, transmitting what has been marked and is in booklet of Exhibits 1 thru 18, table of content for Kaye-Smith; prior to that being submitted to myself, were you aware that some of the notarizations were phonies?

Mr. Smith: No, sir.

Judge Fitzpatrick: When did you find out that there might be a problem?

Mr. Smith: Well, when it was called to my attention by counsel.

Judge Fitzpatrick: That was subsequent to the exchange?

Mr. Smith: Following that.

Judge Fitzpatrick: But prior to the submission, you had no knowledge that there was any problem at all?

Mr. Smith: No.

Judge Fitzpatrick: All right.

Mr. Smith: Your Honor has to understand that papers were coming from various sources. They were coming from the station, coming from my office, being funneled through Mr. Boros in New York.

Judge Fitzpatrick: I realize that. You were responsible for certain exhibits . . .

Mr. Smith: Right.

Judge Fitzpatrick: You have to stand here and be responsible for them. Isn't that right?

Mr. Smith: Right.

Judge Fitzpatrick: Others weren't responsible for the exhibits, were they?

Mr. Smith: Right.

Judge Fitzpatrick: But you are the number one man here in Seattle?

Mr. Smith: No question about it.

Judge Fitzpatrick: And at no time did Mr. West or Mr. Bogel or anybody tell you, "hey, we have a problem here. We have got some letters and we want to put them in as part of our Direct Case, but they're not notarized and so we are going to have somebody else notarize them?"

Mr. Smith: Counsel brought it to our attention.

Judge Fitzpatrick: Counsel brought it to your attention?

Mr. Smith: Yes.

Judge Fitzpatrick: Explain that to me?

Mr. Smith: He called on the phone and I said if you have a problem, call the radio station.

Judge Fitzpatrick: What did he tell you?

Mr. Smith: He said we are getting things taken care of. Some of the stuff we have had before, we can't use it. I also brought in a man who had worked with me and retired at the end of the year, Mr. Bailey, whose name was mentioned here, and I said, "Mel, go down there and straighten the young people out and get all of the information," but my age group, this is not important as far as I am concerned. We have got to get people who listen to the age group that we are talking about in connection with the operation of this radio station.

Judge Fitzpatrick: And that age group is?

Mr. Smith: In the 30 ... 25, 30 year old age group. We can't start ... I could bring in people who have worked with the station close, like the Mayor or whoever, but they have had personal experience working with this radio station. This is a rock and roll radio station.

Judge Fitzpatrick: Can I ask you, as the number one man, what role did you play when it became necessary to start proposing these exhibits. Did you give instructions?

Mr. Smith: Yes.

Judge Fitzpatrick: What did you tell them?

Mr. Smith: We had many meetings down at the radio station to say, "OK, this is a hurry up, we need them quickly, and even though we are in a very busy time of year, we are to drop everything we are doing and go after the next information that counsel wants." We didn't know until ... I don't know what date this was, but sometime in October, that we had to go ahead and get all this stuff. If we had plenty of time to do it, we would have been in great shape, but it was a rush job.

Judge Fitzpatrick: You didn't know until October?

Mr. Smith: Yes.

Judge Fitzpatrick: On August 10, 1982, I issued my order which established November 5 as the date for the exchange of the Direct Written Case of the applicants. You were not aware of that?

Mr. Smith: I was aware, sir, but the papers would have been required. What I was unaware of was the form which it was to be in, which I was leaving up to counsel.

Judge Fitzpatrick: Well, were you aware . . . ?

Mr. Smith: I was aware of the date in November.

TR:205   *Judge Fitzpatrick*: Were you aware that if you were going to submit statements by public officials or people in various organizations that said you're doing a great job, it was to be submitted before the FCC?

Mr. Smith: Yes.

Judge Fitzpatrick: But are you aware of any such statements that they had to affix their signatures . . . ?

Mr. Smith: Yes.

Judge Fitzpatrick: When were you aware of that?

Mr. Smith: All along.

Judge Fitzpatrick: Now, as the number one man, did you instruct the people who were going out to get these statements, the written testimony that they were to notify the people that it was to be submitted to the FCC, and it was considered testimony before government agencies and that they were to sign and get it notarized?

Mr. Smith: I think in a matter of translation, some people thought, well, I have got all these letters, all I have to do is put on a notary and say, I have received these letters and so on and so forth. To take each person and have them sworn, I think this came by counsel sometime in the latter part of October.

Judge Fitzpatrick: Were you aware of what was considered proper?

Mr. Smith: No, sir. Frankly, in all the years I have been in this broadcast business, I have never gone through a situation like this before. I have never gone through a comparative hearing before. I have had to rely on counsel to tell us precisely what documents are going to be required to make this case, and being 3000 miles away, he said well, we need this and that and I said fine, we will see that they're provided and we will provide the staff to do it.

Judge Fitzpatrick: Now, Exhibit 16 is the testimony concerning KISW and both Mr. Bogel and Mr. West have given affidavits, sworn testimony?

Mr. Smith: They are both here in the courtroom.

Judge Fitzpatrick: Now, both of them said in their testimony that they instructed the people as to what had to be done . . .

Mr. Smith: Yes.

Judge Fitzpatrick: Did you have talks telling them what they had to do?

Mr. Smith: We had a meeting in Mr. West's office with Mr. Bogel and Meg Noren, the notary, and Bailey, and we got this letter that we received from counsel, and I said, "I don't care what you have to do, but you have got to drop everything you're doing and get the particular chore done." I remember that very distinctly.

Judge Fitzpatrick: Was it understood from everybody at that meeting that each one of these individuals that were giving their statements and sworn testimony knew that it was to be submitted in a proceeding before the FCC?

Mr. Smith: You will have to ask each one.

Judge Fitzpatrick: Did you give them any such instructions?

Mr. Smith: Yes.

Judge Fitzpatrick: Did you instruct Mr. Bogel and West when they went out to get the statements from the public officials as to what it was they were to do. Did you give them guidelines?

Mr. Smith: The guidelines that I gave them were to get people who had personal knowledge of the station and use of the station, not just friends who had just happened to be good friends.

Judge Fitzpatrick: Did you tell them what form . . . ?

Mr. Smith: No, I did not.

Judge Fitzpatrick: The endorsement of the . . . ?

Mr. Smith: Counsel did that.

Judge Fitzpatrick: What form did counsel do that?

Mr. Smith: By telephone and by letter.

Judge Fitzpatrick: But that was between counsel and Mr. West and Mr. Bogel, and you didn't participate?

Mr. Smith: No.

Judge Fitzpatrick: All right. I have no further questions of this witness. Do you have anything, Mr. Hoffart, as a result . . . ?

Mr. Hoffart: Well, I think I'll interrogate Mr. Bogel and West . . .

The author did not question Mr. Smith regarding his knowledge of the illegal notarizations. He had already admitted that he knew that all documents had to be notarized. He showed active indifference in this matter. The statement to counsel: "If you have problems call the radio station," sets some kind of a record in a proceeding. A precedent exists wherein the commission established that active indifference is affirmative to deliberate intent. Quoting from that case:

> In resolving (this issue) a matter to be considered is intent. It is enough for the Commission to find an applicant has evidenced active indifference to his responsiblities. A wanton, gross and callous disregard for (the truth) is equivalent to an affirmative and deliberate intent.[19]

The judge had established that Smith was given directions by counsel by letter and by telephone. It goes beyond the zone of reasonableness that Smith was not aware that all of the documents had to be notarized and that he passed this information along to his employees. When Smith's rebuttal testimony is presented, it will be shown that he denies ever giving instructions that the letters had to be notarized—in conflict with the testimony, *supra*.

Additional damaging testimony elicited from Smith was the fact that he did not review the Direct Written Case exhibits, other than his own, before they were submitted to the judge, the FCC and to Hoffart. Had he done so he should have immediately noticed that nine of the affidavits that were subscribed to by Mr. West and Mr. Bogel were undated, and all were notarized by his employee Ms. Carrie Matthew. In addition, he should have noticed that three out of the five testimonial letters that were notarized by Ms. Matthew also lacked the date of notarization. One more undated notarial act should have caught his attention. Senior KISW notary Ms. Margit Noren had not dated the testimonial letter notarization affixed to the testimonial letter solicited from Mr. John Taylor.

Hoffart had no problem noticing these omissions on his first glance through the Kaye-Smith Direct Case. One "notarial imperfection," however, did escape his notice. After Kaye-Smith filed "corrections" to the nine undated notarial acts of Bogel and West—corrections consisted of

---

[19]*Walton Broadcasting, Inc.*, 83 FCC 2d at 440-441 (1980) "the fact that Walton could not have forseen the misconduct is not relevant because the misconduct could have been prevented." (License revoked)

nine affidavits executed by Ms. Carrie Matthew on November 16th, and subscribed to in front of Ms. Noren, wherein she swore upon oath that all of the nine undated notarial acts were before her on November 9th,—the author noticed that the attachment list to a Bogel affidavit included an affiant that had a testimonial letter notarized on the 10th of November. Bogel's affidavit was also pre-executed, one day early.

And what did the judge conclude in his Initial Decision? He stated that the above acts, and all that is yet to come, should not have happened. Good show. That takes a lot of wisdom. He further ruled that the acts were the result of ignorance on the part of the employees and as such the illegal acts warranted only a "slight demerit," and that there was no intention to mislead the commission. Ignorance is now a mitigating factor in matters before administrative agencies, if Fitzpatrick is on the bench. He believed the self-serving testimony elicited from Lester M. Smith. Hoffart did not.

Smith had testified that he brought Mr. Bailey out of retirement and sent him down "to straighten those young people out." This clearly shows that Bailey became involved only when "corrective actions" were required. There would be no need to straighten anybody out if the author hadn't raised questions. The fact that Mr. Bailey did not report back to Smith in detail goes beyond the "zone of reasonableness." Yet Smith testified that he was not aware of what had transpired until the morning of the hearing. The most damaging aspect of these statutory violations is the fact that Smith did not take charge of the situation, but turned the corrections matters over to the very individuals who tried to deceive Hoffart. This "active indifference" resulted in two more such notarial imperfections in the corrections.

The author, however, did cross-examine Smith regarding the renewal application and some other matters. The renewal application has a section wherein the other business interests of the licensee has to be reported. Smith had reported that Kaye-Smith Enterprises operates Concerts West, an international concert booking agency. Hoffart was aware that Smith had sold this business prior to the execution of the renewal application. This was established in oral deposition.

TR: 224   *Mr. Hoffart*: Did you operate Concerts West when you made your license renewal application?
Mr. Smith: No, sir.
Mr. Hoffart: In 1980?
Mr. Smith: No, sir.
Mr. Hoffart: Does your application say you operate Concerts West?
Mr. Smith: Could have said that. It was an oversight on our application.

Mr. Hoffart: Did you read it before you signed it and certified that it was correct?

Mr. Smith: At the time I signed that application, I signed quite a few and that was an oversight on my part.

Mr. Hoffart: So the application states you operated Concerts West in 1980, but you say you did not operate Concerts West?

Mr. Smith: We did not operate Concerts West. It was sold in 1977.

The reader may agree that this is an oversight, and of no significance. The author, however, suspects all of the other applications that Smith referred to, which were the renewals for their other operations, namely KXL-AM and FM in Portland, Oregon, KJR-AM, in Seattle, and KJRB and KEZE-FM in Spokane, Washington, similarly represented to the commission that Kaye-Smith operated Concerts West. Mr. Bailey, who was assigned to assemble the renewal applications, usually recopied what was in other applications as to business interests and other matters common to the applications. An example of such misrepresentation over some six years and up to nine applications was the statement that Mr. and Mrs. Danny Kaye each owned 50 percent in Belmont Television, when in actual fact that corporation had been dissolved in 1968. Smith had continued to show this Kaye ownership through 1976 renewal applications. The author, however, could not make an issue out of this since the ALJ had limited testimony to the renewal period of 1978 to 1981, and also limited testimony to KISW.

TR: 231   *Mr. Hoffart:* How many hours a week did you devote to KISW during the last license period?

Mr. Smith: I can't tell you.

Mr. Hoffart: Don't you know?

Mr. Smith: I can't tell you how many hour per week.

Mr. Hoffart: You're saying here you're going to devote 30 hours per week. I want to know whether you devoted 30 hours a week during the last renewal period.

Mr. Smith: That's not what I am saying here in this exhibit . . .

Judge Fitzpatrick: I know it isn't, but is that what you did?

Mr. Smith: It could very well be. I don't keep track of my day-to-day hours. As far as I could see, it could be far in excess of that.

Mr. Hoffart: How many hours do you have direct knowledge of that Mr. Danny Kaye spent on KISW during the last renewal period?

Mr. Boros: Irrelevant and immaterial.
Judge Fitzpatrick: Overruled.
Mr. Smith: Danny Kaye Spent no time.
Mr. Hoffart: How many hours did Sylvia Fine Kaye spent during the last license period on KISW?
Mr. Smith: No time.

The author had established that Mr. and Mrs. Danny Kaye, 80 percent owners of KISW, by virtue of 100 percent owners of Dena Pictures, had given *de facto* control of KISW, and all other stations, to minority owner Smith. In actual fact Smith spent very little time at any of his broadcast operations during 1977 through 1980. This is the period of time when Mr. Smith assumed the helm of the American League baseball team in Seattle. Sport fans and particularly Seattle area residents will remember the period of time when the franchise for this major league ball team was assigned to Seattle, and that Mr. Smith and Mr. Danny Kaye each held 1/6th interest in the franchise. It goes without saying that Smith had very little time to devote to the operations of his stations during this period of time. If pressed, author Hoffart could prove this, beyond any doubt with sworn testimony from Lester M. Smith himself.

9.

STEPHEN WEST

Mr. Stephen "Steve" West, was named manager of KISW (FM) by Mr. Smith in 1979. Prior to that Mr. West was program director and assistant manager at KJR, Seattle. West also held various other positions with Kaye-Smith and their predecessors. For a while West was a D.J. and program director at KJRB, Spokane, Washington. As with Mr. Smith, Hoffart will skip testimony not related to the issue at hand, that is, misrepresentations to a federal agency.

TR:339   *Mr. Hoffart*: Now, you are currently on the trust board of the Supersonics, and being on this board, do you know Mr. David Watkins?

Mr. West: Yes, I do.

Mr. Hoffart: What is his job at the Supersonics?

Mr. West: He's just been promoted to Vice President.

Mr. Hoffart: Public relations man, and all that?

Mr. West: Well, he's, I would say, the number two man with that organization.

Mr. Hoffart: And I see that you have an affidavit from him. Did you personally go down and see Mr. Watkins to get this affidavit?

Mr. West: I called him on the phone.

Mr. Hoffart: And you received back a statement that was notarized . . . signature on it?

Mr. West: Yes.

Mr. Hoffart: Now, what was the reason why this had to be renotarized?

Mr. West: It didn't have a date on it originally, and that was before we realized that it goes back to this whole thing of did it have to have dates, and which it does in the State of Washington.

Mr. Hoffart: Are there any other changes between those two affidavits?

Mr. West: No.

Mr. Hoffart: Both are signed by David Watkins?

Mr. West: Yes.

Mr. Hoffart: Did he have you compare the two signatures?

Mr. West: Did he have me compare the two signatures?

Mr. Hoffart: Did you compare them?

Mr. West: No.

Mr. Hoffart: If you were shown those two documents, would you know whether they were both signed by a certain person?
Mr. West: No.

The reader has already had an opportunity to look at the two David Watkins's testimonial letters as they are reproduced in the appendix as pages 13 and 14.

Take another look at the two documents with specific attention to the two David Watkins' signatures. It is obvious that one or the other was not affixed by Watkins. The reader should also note that both were notarized before a Washington State notary public. The author did not know which of the two letters had been signed by Mr. Watkins but he assumed, erroniously as he has already revealed earlier, that the letter with the earliest date had been signed by a person other than Mr. Watkins and that was the reason why a "corrected" letter was filed. Hoffart, then, was fishing in his interrogations.

TR:344   *Mr. Hoffart*: Now, looking at 5 (A), have you both copies there in front of you?
Mr. West: Yes.
Mr. Hoffart: Are those two signatures by Mr. David Watkins the same person, same identical? You're not a handwriting expert, I know that.
Mr. West: I'm not going to comment on that.
Mr. Hoffart: Now, this 5 (A) was notarized in your office by a notary public where you're an employee. Is that right?
Mr. West: Uh-huh.
Mr. Hoffart: Did Mr. David Watkins personally come into your office and have that notarized?
Mr. West: Yes.
Mr. Hoffart: So if this first signature is not David Watkins, on the original page 5, how do you explain that?
Mr. Boros: I object. That assumes a matter not in evidence.
Judge Fitzpatrick: That's a hypothetical.
Mr. Hoffart: All right.
Judge Fitzpatrick: You can ask that question of Mr. Watkins if that's his signature. If it develops that that's his signature, and it's properly notarized . . .
Mr. Hoffart: That's why I'm dropping this. I understand I'll have a chance to talk to Mr. Watkins.
Judge Fitzpatrick: All right.

Hoffart had established that Mr. West personally was acquainted with Mr. David Watkins. He also established that Mr. Watkins had personally appeared at KISW where Mr. West and Ms. Noren witnessed his signing of the "corrected" testimonial letter. This was proven untrue when Ms. Noren, the notary, stated that Mr. Watkins had not appeared before her. Of course the reader will note that this 5 (A) exhibit page shows that Ms. Noren stated, in her notarial attestation: "Subscribed and sworn before me this 17th day of November, 1982." She affixed her signature and her official notary seal. Ms. Noren, then, represented to a federal agency that an affiant, in this case a Mr. Watkins, had personally appeared before her and signed a document. She perjured herself when she so attested on the document. This act was with intent to deceive Hoffart and the judge.

It must be recognized that Ms. Noren had no choice but to tell the truth. She was aware that Mr. Watkins would have to appear as a witness—and with two patently different styles of his signature on two documents, both attested to by notaries as being his signature, Mr. Watkins also had no choice in the matter. He had to be truthful as to which notary he had faced with his letter of commendation that was solicited from him by Mr. Stephen West.

Just what transpired in this matter will become clearer when Ms. Noren testifies. Mr. West's part in the deception will be fully detailed when she is interrogated by the judge and Hoffart.

Ms. Carrie Matthew, the KISW junior notary, will also testify in a manner that supports the author's charges that Ms. Noren and Mr. West violated the statute against making false statements of a material fact before a federal agency.

The author submits that the public should demand that a federal grand jury be empaneled to investigate this case. The author charges that the relevant factors adduced at the hearing were either superficially treated or simply ignored.

The author will present more testimony elicited from Mr. West as this story moves along.

10.

ERIC BOGEL

Appendix page 3 is an affidavit executed by the program director Eric Bogel. The attachment referred to in this affidavit is appendix page 4. The content of the affidavit is untrue. It has already been established that affiant Ms. Judy Balint had not been told that her letter of commendation would be used to bolster a legal case or as testimony before the FCC. Ms. Balint is listed on the Bogel attachment list, as are Julie McCullough, Shawn Taylor, John Taylor and Nina L. Evers. The Julie McCullough and Shawn Taylor letters, in addition to the Judy Balint letter, had been notarized outside the presence of these so-called affiants by Ms. Carrie Matthew.

Testimony elicited from Ms. Matthew and Ms. Noren established that Mr. Bogel affixed his signature to his affidavit sponsoring the testimonial letters on November 9, 1982. The Nina L. Evers testimonial letter shows it was not notarized until the 10th of November. Here we have another case of an apparently pre-executed affidavit. Ms. Nina L. Evers was not an affiant on the 9th, as Mr. Bogel states, under oath. Her letter was authored on the 8th and just why it was not notarized until the day after she was represented to be an affiant is a mystery. Author Hoffart reproduces the Nina L. Evers testimonial letter as proof.[20] The author wishes to expressly state that Ms. Evers appears to be just another innocent victim of Kaye-Smith employees representations and her name appears in this book courtesy of those employees and Kaye-Smith. Hoffart does not question the veracity or sincerity of Ms. Evers. On the surface it appears that counsel may have authored the attachment list in New York. Bogel testimony in the transcript so suggests.

TR. 470   *Mr. Boros*: When, where and how did you come to affix your signature to this page 2?
Mr. Bogel: I was with Steve West and a Carrie Matthew, the station's notary, on the 9th of November.
Mr. Boros: Where were you and Mr. West with Ms. Matthew, in the sense of where physically were you?
Mr. Bogel: Inside Steve's office at KISW.
Mr. Boros: When you affixed your signature, was anyone immediately in your presence when you affixed your signature?
Mr. Bogel: Aside from Steve West and Carrie Matthew, no.

---

[20]Appendix page 31.

Mr. Boros: But they were both there?

Mr. Bogel: They were both there.

Mr. Boros: You signed in their presence?

Mr. Bogel: Yes.

Mr. Boros: Do you know how Exhibit 9, pages 3 and 4 came into being?

Mr. Bogel: Yes, I do. Because on the affidavit that I signed on the 9th, the day was deleted from the affidavit so Carrie had to go back and put another one together that attested to the fact that she was in fact there on that date.

Mr. Boros: What to you mean when you use the term "deleted?"

Mr. Bogel: Well, on the affidavit that I signed it says "subscribed and sworn to before me this blank day," and there was no date.

Mr. Boros: Is that what you mean by the word "deleted," that there was no date?

Mr. Bogel: Yes.

Mr. Boros worked through the exhibits in numerical order until he reached Kaye-Smith exhibit 16. This exhibit was jointly sponsored by Bogel and West and contained some of the testimonial letters that had been affixed with phony verifications by Ms. Carrie Matthew. At this point the judge wanted some answers.

TR:484   *Judge Fitzpatrick*: Mr. Boros, let me tell you, before I'm going to give you a ruling on Exhibit 16, I want to have adduced all of the testimony concerning, one: who it was that contacted all the various people who represent the so-called written testimony listed on page 3, whether these contacts were made by this witness or somebody else. And then I want this witness to explain how it was that these letters were gotten and why we have these corrections to the notarial imperfections, I should call it. You're submitting the corrected pages too, are you not, as part of this exhibit?

Mr. Boros: Yes, your Honor.

Judge Fitzpatrick: Then we're going to have to have a full explanation before this exhibit is received in evidence.

Mr. Boros: Mr. Bogel, I direct your attention to pages 2 and 3 of Kaye-Smith Exhibit 16. Now, with reference to pages 2 and 3, and specifically the description of written testimony which was elicted from Seattle area community members and which is described on page 3, what part did you play in obtaining those written testimonies?

Mr. Bogel: I either personally obtained the letters or delegated to Tamara Kern, my secretary. The letter regarding Charles Royer . . .

Judge Fitzpatrick: Would you do this? Of those listed, tell us of the ones that you personally solicited and obtained, the ones you personally did.

Mr. Bogel: Charles Royer, Nina L. Evers, Shawn Taylor, Patricia Frank, Wanda Harrison, Gene Beal, John Taylor.

Mr. Boros: And with respect to Ms. McCullough and Ms. Balint's testimonies and letters, did you delegate to someone the obtaining of those letters?

Mr. Bogel: I delegated the Judy Balint letter, and Julie McCullough I had no involvement with.

Judge Fitzpatrick: You had no involvement with it?

Mr. Bogel: That was handled by Mr. Paul Sullivan, a salesman for the radio station.

Judge Fitzpatrick: And he didn't do this under your direction?

Mr. Bogel: Not directly under my direction, no.

Judge Fitzpatrick: Then this testimony is incorrect, Mr. Boros. Page 2 says "each of the affidavits were obtained by me or those under my direction."

The judge was overly kind in his statement. He termed the content of the affidavit that had been executed by Mr. Bogel as incorrect. The author calls it perjury with intent to deceive. The reader will recall that Ms. Balint is also on this attachment list to the affidavit, and her letter to Hoffart also proves that Mr. Bogel's affidavit constitutes perjury.

The author quotes from Title 18, Crimes and Criminal Procedure, Chapter 79, section 1621; Perjury generally:

Whoever (1) having taken an oath before a competent tribunal officer, or person, in any case in which a law of the United States authorizes an oath to be administered, that he will testify, declare, depose, or certify truly, or that any written testimony, declaration, deposition, or certificate by him subscribed, is true, willfully and contrary to such oath states or subscribes any material matter which he does not believe to be true; or (2) in any declaration, certificate, verification or statement under penalty of perjury as permitted under section 1746 of title 28, United States Code, willfully subscribes as true any material matter which he does not believe to be true . . . is guilty of perjury.

In addition to the falsity of the Bogel affidavit content, Mr. Bogel could not have had the attachment list before him on the 9th. Bogel's testimony, by a "preponderance of evidence" test, supports the authors conclusion. Bogel had stated, under oath, that he signed his affidavit on the 9th, but the attachment list contains the Nina L. Evers name, and her letter was not notarized until the 10th, again with reference to appendix page 31.

TR:486   *Mr. Boros*: Can you explain and reconcile your testimony on page 2 with your testimony this minute with Mr. Sullivan?

Mr. Bogel: At the time when we were getting letters, it became kind of a community effort as far as getting together and accumulating the letters that we did. So to be quite honest with you, I am probably . . . to kind of re-state regarding Paul Sullivan, I am probably as involved as anybody at the radio station for acquiring that letter, although it was not directly under my designation.

Mr. Boros: You mean it was indirectly under your . . . ?

Mr. Bogel: Well, I mean, I am involved with Greenpeace as the program director of the radio station. I knew that Paul Sullivan had a close relationship with the people from his workings with them as well, and I said, would you do it. But it was he who obtained the letter and made the phone call.

Mr. Boros: Now with respect to the letters which you personally obtained, how did you go about obtaining those letters?

Mr. Bogel: They were all obtained by phone calls from myself to the people involved.

Mr. Boros: Directly to the people involved, whose names are listed here?

Mr. Bogel: With the exception of Patricia Frank. I contacted our contact through the Big Sisters, who in turn spoke to Patricia. But in every other instance, yes, it was a personal contact made by myself.

Mr. Boros: And when you contacted these potential witnesses, what did you say to them?

Mr. Bogel: I explained in essence that KISW's license was up for renewal and being challenged, and that it was important at this time that we go back to community service organizations that we'd worked with and had a good relationship with, and get a testimonial letter from them stating their feelings about the responsiveness of

KISW to their particular needs, and have it notarized, and we'd be able to use it on our behalf.

When the author presents the testimony given by Mr. Shawn Taylor, whose name is on the Bogel attachment list, that testimony will be shown to be in conflict to what Mr. Bogel has just stated. The reader will be referred back to this sworn testimony and then can decide for him or herself if there are any ambiguities in Bogel's testimony.

TR:488   *Mr. Boros*: Did you state what use would be made of these letters?
Mr. Bogel: Other than that we'd be using it in a hearing for our defense. Other than that, no.
Judge Fitzpatrick: Did you tell any of these individuals that they would be subject to being called as witnesses, to be cross-examined concerning what they said in their letter?
Mr. Bogel: No, I didn't.
Judge Fitzpatrick: Did you know that that was the case?
Mr. Bogel: No, I didn't.
Mr. Boros: Did any of them express any willingness to appear personally before the FCC in this case?
Mr. Bogel: In a general statement, many of the, although I couldn't say specifically, because many of the letters that I received or that I obtained are not even listed here. But many of the people in general said, "anything I can do to help I'd be more than happy to."
Mr. Boros: Well, directing your attention to the letter from Mr. Charles Royer, Mayor of Seattle, what did he say to you and what did you say to him about appearing in this case?[21]
Mr. Bogel: There was no gesture on his part to say that he would be willing to appear. There was nothing to the contrary. There was no offer made.
Mr. Boros: Well, what did you say to him and what did he say to you?
Mr. Bogel: I explained to him that what I said prior, that our license is up for renewal and we need to go back to major community leaders or services that we've been involved with. And being that we'd been involved with the Mayor on two food bank drives he said he'd be more than happy to get a letter to us.

---

[21]Appendix page 32.

Mr. Boros: Did you mention to him that a hearing would be held in Seattle before the FCC?

Mr. Bogel: I mentioned to him that it would be used in court.

Mr. Boros: What did he say to that?

Mr. Bogel: He didn't seem to say anything. He said, I'll get you the letter as soon as I can.

Mr. Boros: We have no further questions on direct of Mr. Bogel.

Judge Fitzpatrick: Mr. Boros, you're not going to get this exhibit in. I don't see why I should have to conduct the examination. Well, I will. Never mind, Mr. Boros. I'll do it myself. Turn to page 6, please . . . that letter purports to be from a Julie McCullough?[22]

Mr. Bogel: Yes.

Julie McCullough was one of the affiants on the Bogel affidavit attachment list. Hoffart had written her a letter questioning the authenticity of the notarial attestation. She responded by sending the author a copy of her original letter now showing that it was notarized before a Diana Blane. The original letter, dated October 22nd, and addressed to Paul Sullivan, was affixed with a phony notarization by Ms. Carrie Matthew.

TR:490   *Judge Fitzpatrick*: It's dated October 22nd, 1982. It appears on the right-hand bottom, what purports to be a notarization by Carrie Matthew on October 28, 1982. What do you know about it?

Mr. Bogel: I know very little about that, outside that Paul and I spoke and he said he would take care of obtaining a letter from Julie, and when it came into the station it was his doing. I have no idea what went on once it hit the radio station.

Judge Fitzpatrick: You didn't know whether or not Ms. McCullough did or did not appear before Ms. Matthew to affix her signature to this document?

Mr. Bogel: No, I do not.

Judge Fitzpatrick: Turn to page 7, if you would, and 8. That purports to be a letter from Shawn Taylor dated November 5th, 1982. Now, on page 8, that has a notarization by Carrie Matthew on November 5th, 1982. What, if anything, do you know concerning that notarization?[23]

---

[22]Appendix page 9. The original McCullough letter bearing a phony notarial verification.

[23]Appendix pages 15 and 16. Page 16 is a phony verification of Mr. Taylor's signature.

Mr. Bogel: In this instance Shawn walked into the radio station and had it notarized personally.

Judge Fitzpatrick: On November 5, 1982?

Mr. Bogel: On November 5, 1982. There's two Shawn Taylors.

Judge Fitzpatrick: This is a Shawn Taylor.

Mr. Bogel: I'm sorry. There's a Shawn Taylor and a John Taylor. I'm sorry. Shawn Taylor, again, came into the radio station, and beyond that as far as notary it was not in front of me.

Judge Fitzpatrick: So you're correcting your testimony? He did not come into the radio station?

Mr. Bogel: I'm sorry, no. There's a John Taylor and a Shawn Taylor, and I got them confused. Once he came into the radio station I don't know whether it was notarized in his presence or not.

Judge Fitzpatrick: You never investigated?

Mr. Bogel: No, I did not, I know, inquire.

Judge Fitzpatrick: Did there come a time when you found out there was a problem concerning some of these letters?

Mr. Bogel: Yes. Steve West had called me into his office and said some of these came in unnotarized, you know, without any notary on them, and there's a problem in that we're going to have to get back to some of those people, just to double-check that we did notarize it with their permission, and then do a second one. So it was at this point. . . .

Judge Fitzpatrick: Did you notarize it with their permission? Did you explain what he meant by that?

Mr. Bogel: Many of the people said, "we have no notary in our building. I don't even know where to find a notary. Can I come into your radio station and do it?" And I said fine, like Steve West. And it sounds ignorant, and I feel dumb now. I didn't know it had to be signed in their presence. I thought if I dropped it off it would be OK.

Judge Fitzpatrick: What did you think a notarization was?

Mr. Bogel: I never had to deal with a notarization other than a house lease.

This is an untrue statement. Mr. Bogel, under his professional name of "Beau Phillips," had affixed the name of Beau Phillips to a memo dated July 20, 1982, about four months prior to this testimony. This is the memo referred to earlier relating to his "setting the record straight" regarding the airing of the untrue event that advanced time would start in March of 1982 instead of April. This memo, found in the public file at KISW by the author, was notarized by Ms. Margit Noren.[24] This notarization will also be dealt with later when it is shown that Ms. Margit Noren testified that she had not previously notarized any documents for anyone at the radio station. The Noren testimony will also be shown to be untrue.

TR:492   *Judge Fitzpatrick*: When did you first become aware, if you did become aware, that there was a problem with respect to this letter from Mr. Shawn Taylor to yourself that was dated November 5th?
               Mr. Bogel: Only after we had sent it to counsel in New York and they informed us that the notary was incorrect.

The author raises the question of how counsel knew there was a problem with this particular letter. The letter shows it was dated on the 5th of November and was notarized on the 5th by Ms. Matthew. Nothing wrong here that might lead counsel to raise questions. The author suspected that there might be something wrong (thus triggering his letter to Mr. Taylor) because there were just too many notarial acts by Ms. Matthew—fourteen in fact, and only two were dated. Common sense dictates that KISW told counsel that this Shawn Taylor letter was affixed with a phony verification after Hoffart questioned the notarization.

TR:492   *Judge Fitzpatrick*: And you know nothing about when Carrie Matthew affixed the notarization to Mr. Shawn Taylor's November 5th, 1982 letter?
               Mr. Bogel: No, I don't.

Author Hoffart takes leave here to reproduce his cross-examination of Mr. Bogel as it relates to the Shawn Taylor phony verification. The testimony so far is that Mr. Bogel personally asked Mr. Taylor for a testimonial letter during a conversation relating to another matter. Counsel for Kaye-Smith had filed a "correction" to this letter due to a notarial imperfection, as they called it, but what is actually filing of false information with a federal agency. The affixing of additional wording to a document without the author's knowledge is forgery, a felony.

TR:509   *Mr. Hoffart*: Now in the new affidavit did Mr. Shawn Taylor approach you or anybody at the station, to your

---

[24]Appendix page 33 is a copy of the memo.

knowledge, or did you approach Mr. Taylor for the affidavit?

Mr. Bogel: For the corrected affidavit, is that what you are saying?

Mr. Hoffart: Yes.

Mr. Bogel: No, I called him back when it was pointed out to me by Steve West that there was a problem with the notary seal.

Judge Fitzpatrick: What was the problem?

Mr. Bogel: In this instance I was told that there were two problems, depending on which letters we're going on. Some of them the letter was written on a different date from the notary seal, or as in this case the . . . yeah. To be quite honest with you, I don't see anything wrong with Shawn Taylor's letter at all as far as this . . .

Judge Fitzpatrick: You don't see anything wrong with it? Then what did you tell Mr. Taylor when you called him? Why did you tell him it had to be done over again?

Mr. Bogel: Oh, I know. I think if I remember correctly, there were people we had to call and verify in addition to getting a new letter. Some of the people we called, and I believe Shawn was one, we had to find out from him if in fact he signed it in front of a notary, or whether he had given it to somebody to walk down the hall and sign.

Judge Fitzpatrick: What did you discover?

Mr. Bogel: Shawn said that he had signed it in front of Carrie.

Judge Fitzpatrick: He said hc had signed it in front of Carrie?

Mr. Bogel: Uh huh.

Judge Fitzpatrick: Originally?

Mr. Bogel: If I remember correctly, yes.

Judge Fitzpatrick: Why did you ask him for a new letter?

Mr. Bogel: That was the phone call that was made. I don't know. I don't understand it. Let me look at the second letter. From the looks of the original letter, all I can say is that there was many letters I was dealing with. From the looks of this letter I don't see . . . I don't recall what the exact problem was, over and above what I've said.

The reader may well imagine the chaos that prevailed at KISW and the Bellevue office of Kaye-Smith Enterprises when they became aware, most probably from one of the letter authors, that Hoffart had detected their attempts to deceive him and all other parties, including the judge.

It goes beyond the zone of reasonableness that one or more of the authors of letters did not call KISW when they found their unnotarized testimonial letters returned to them by a stranger, now notarized before a Carrie Matthew or a Margit Noren. (It has not been established that there was anything illegal in the notarizations of original testimonial letters by Ms. Noren.)

Later in this book Mr. Young, Kaye-Smith co-counsel, will be shown to testify from the floor that he perceived something wrong with the verifications on the 12th and called KISW. It will be shown that there is conflicting testimony regarding whom Mr. Young talked to on that date. That raises the question if Mr. Young actually called anyone to ask about the validity of the notarizations.

Regardless, it was the author who detected the second round of phony verifications that were filed in this case by counsel for Kaye-Smith on the 24th of November, and this second round of filing of false information with a federal agency should have resulted in basic disqualification of Kaye-Smith.

The testimony of Ms. Noren, the senior KISW notary, will be forthcoming shortly after Mr. Bogel and Ms. Mathew are finished testifying. The Noren testimony will establish, beyond any doubt, that Mr. West, the KISW station manager, committed perjury when he testified that Mr. Watkins, the subject of one of the corrected letters, had appeared at his office at KISW and Ms. Noren notarized his signature.

Just how the three review board members can class Hoffart's proven charges of falsehoods as a hodgepodge of accusations and allegations . . . typical adversarial puff and much ado about nothing is something only review board members Marino, Jacobs and Blumenthal can answer and the author hopes that the media will press them for an analysis of their findings. What they may have to say should be illuminating. Similarly, the five commissioners should be asked to explain how they arrived at their Order upholding the review board.

TR:511 *Mr. Hoffart*: Well, you had stated you had to get a new affidavit because there was something wrong with the date?

Mr. Bogel: Either the date or the notary, yes.

Mr. Hoffart: I see this letter, November 5th, and I see it notarized on November 5th?

Mr. Bogel: Yes

Mr. Hoffart: What's the problem?

Mr. Bogel: I don't understand the legal thinking. I went back and called the people I was told to call.

Mr. Hoffart: Mr. West told you to call these people to get a new . . .

Mr. Bogel: Exactly. I went back and called them.

Mr. Hoffart: He didn't explain to you that the problem might be it was notarized by a Carrie Matthew?

Mr. Bogel: I went and told the people that I was told to call, saying that there's a problem either with the notary or the lack of a date on the notary, or the fact that the date of the letter and the date of the notary were different, or the fact at that time to call people where the letters were fine just to say, did you in fact sign this in front of a notary at your office or did you have somebody for you. Now, trying to pick out which ones were which, I can't quite recall.

Judge Fitzpatrick: Do you recall what Mr. Taylor told you?

Mr. Bogel: No, I don't.

Mr. Hoffart: Do you know what date he told you to go ahead and get some new affidavits, to call these people?

Mr. Boros: Objection.

Judge Fitzpatrick: Overruled. Mr. West, who else told him to get the affidavits? We've been testifying about this for half an hour now.

Mr. Hoffart: Do you know the date you called Mr. Shawn Taylor and told him you needed a new letter?

Mr. Bogel: Sometime between the 5th and the 23rd, which is the dates of the two letters. Aside from that, more specifically, no, I can't.

Mr. Hoffart: That's like about 18 days?

Mr. Bogel: Right.

Further cross-examination revealed only that Mr. Bogel had occasion to talk with Mr. Taylor on an unrelated matter and that there were no discussions since the corrected letter had been obtained, to the best of his recollection.

Let's drop back now to the interrogations by the judge relating to others on the attachment list of affiants.

TR:493   *Judge Fitzpatrick*: Turn, if you will, to page 13. Now that purports to be a letter from John Taylor?

Mr. Bogel: Right.

Judge Fitzpatrick: And that purports to have a notarization that was undated. Now, what, if anything, do you know concerning that notarization?

Mr. Bogel: As Steve West brought it up, there was a problem with . . . there were two problems we had, and after seeing this it's difficult to remember which was

53

which. Some had a problem where they came in un-notarized, and some of them had a problem where they were notarized but the notary was done on a different day then the letter was written.

Judge Fitzpatrick: Some notarizations weren't dated?

Mr. Bogel: At all, yeah. That's why I'm saying it's difficult to tell from this which is which.

Judge Fitzpatrick: Could you show it to him, page 13?

Mr. Bogel: This is an instance where John Taylor came into the radio station. Meg Noren was present.

Judge Fitzpatrick: Do you know this of your own knowledge?

Mr. Bogel: Yes, I was in the building, and I watched him and saw him and Meg speaking, so I assume that's what happened.

Judge Fitzpatrick: Were you present when he affixed his signature?

Mr. Bogel: No, I know that John came into the radio station with his letter looking for Meg so she could notarize it, and the problem with this letter was simply that Meg's notary seal was undated.[25]

The original John Taylor letter was notarized by Ms. Margit Noren on an unknown date. The corrected letter was also notarized by Ms. Noren. This corrected letter was authored on November 22nd, 1982 and was notarized the following day at KISW, according to the testimony elicited from Mr. Bogel. Mr. Taylor was one of the letters authors who had been sent a letter of inquiry by Hoffart. Mr. Taylor did not respond. The author had asked Mr. Taylor if he had appeared before Ms. Noren for the notarization of his October 25th letter. It appears that a response would have been in the favor of Kaye-Smith if Mr. Taylor had appeared as the document shows.

Hoffart does not question the sincerity of Mr. Taylor as to the content of his letter. His name appears in this book, as all other authors of testimonial letters, by courtesy of Kaye-Smith Enterprises. Later it will be shown that Ms. Noren testified, under oath, that Mr. Taylor had appeared before her on both occasions and there is nothing in the record to indicate otherwise.

The judge did not require testimony from Mr. Taylor, he ruled that any testimony from him would be cumulative. Hoffart stated that Mr. Taylor had not responded to his letter of inquiry. The judge, however, was adamant. The reader should recognize that Hoffart was short-

---

[25]Appendix pages 19 and 20 are copies of the original and corrected John Taylor solicited letters.

changed. The only testimony in the record that supports the fact that Mr. Taylor had his first letter notarized before Ms. Noren is by Ms. Noren herself. *Falsus in uno, falsus in omnibus.*

Mr. Bogel had just testified that one of the problems associated with the notarial attestations was that the date of the letter and the date it was notarized do not coincide. Here, however, we have Mr. John Taylor's letter dated November 22nd and notarized by Ms. Noren on the 23rd. She had no qualms or apparent concern here because the dates did not match. Of course there is nothing illegal with the notarization of a document on a date later than the date it is written, provided it is signed before a notary. Mr. Bogel's reasons why some of the letters had to be renotarized have been gutted by this corrected exhibit dating.

Mr. Steve West, in his testimony, had mentioned that the author was a disgruntled ex-employee. This part of his testimony has not been printed. The author had not cross-examined Mr. West in regards to his statement. Now, however, Mr. Bogel is asked about this characterization.

TR:514   *Mr. Hoffart:* You personally contacted Mr. John R. Taylor?

Mr. Bogel: Right.

Mr. Hoffart: Did you tell John Taylor what you needed in the way of a letter? Did you tell him why it was needed?

Mr. Bogel: Yes.

Mr. Hoffart: Did you explain to him that it was a disgruntled ex-employee was challenging a license renewal?

Mr. Bogel: That wording came up. As far as who exactly I said it to, I made probably in the neighborhood of 40 phone calls. Who I said it to or specifically what wording it is with each person it's difficult to recall, in fact probably impossible. I did make contact with John Taylor and asked him for a letter.

Mr. Hoffart: Do you know who first mentioned the word disgruntled ex-employee to you, disgruntled ex-employee?

Mr. Bogel: I'm not sure anybody did. It seemed to be to me not a detrimental way to mention the situation.

Judge Fitzpatrick: Excuse me, you don't consider the word disgruntled to have some connotations other than complimentary?

Mr. Bogel: Oh, certainly not complimentary. We certainly wouldn't be having our license challenged if there was a complimentary situation.

Judge Fitzpatrick: What do you consider a disgruntled employee?

Mr. Bogel: Someone who's upset enough with the goings of the company to challenge the license.

Judge Fitzpatrick: All right.

Mr. Hoffart: Now, when you were saying disgruntled ex-employee, you knew it was Mr. Hoffart that we're talking about?

Mr. Bogel: Yes.

Mr. Hoffart: Now, to your knowledge, do you know anything about how Mr. Hoffart got terminated and became a disgruntled ex-employee?

Mr. Bogel: No. It was none of my business.

Mr. Hoffart: You just took somebody else's word for it that I was a disgruntled ex-employee?

Mr. Boros: Object. That's argumentative.

Judge Fitzpatrick: Overruled. Let's find out what he thought when he was characterizing this person as a disgruntled ex-employee to members of the public.

Mr. Bogel: Could you restate the question, please?

Mr. Hoffart: Did you know under what circumstances I got terminated by a case that you decided that you had the right to go around and tell people I was a disgruntled ex-employee?

Mr. Bogel: No, I did not understand the circumstances.

Mr. Hoffart: Do you understand the penalties for libel and slander?

Mr. Bogel: Would you care to explain that to me?

Mr. Boros: I object, your Honor. This is intimidation of a witness under these circumstances.

Judge Fitzpatrick: I think maybe he didn't understand it or he might not have used that term, Mr. Hoffart.

The judge's statement was addressed to Mr. Hoffart. This, then, would indicate that it was his opinion that Mr. Bogel did not slander Hoffart. Hoffart, however, disagrees.

Slander is defined as the utterance or spreading of a false statement or statements, harmful to another's character or reputation. Here we have a Kaye-Smith employee characterizing an ex-employee who was discharged for reasons unknown to Mr. Bogel, as being disgruntled, and using this characterization to assist in obtaining testimonial letters supporting the renewal of the KISW (FM) license. Thus Bogel had motive. He also stated he made some forty phone calls but does not recall to whom, or to how many, he made this characterization. The author wonders if any of the readers of this book can recall being told Hoffart was a disgruntled ex-employee of Kaye-Smith Enterprises. Significantly, Bogel made forty phone calls but only filed nine testimonial letters; three of these were affixed with phony verifications. Two others on the list, John Taylor and Nina Evers, are unresolved as to the matters the author raised. It appears that KISW had problems getting notarized testimonial letters. The total filed was twenty-four. At the pre-hearing the judge suggested that he would accept forty-five. Can it be that the Seattle area residents do not think that KISW is programming their station in the public interest?

The author will not go into the reasons why he was terminated. Suffice to say he has three affidavits in his files, all signed by Mr. Lester M. Smith. Each gives a discrete reason as to why Hoffart was fired. Smith filed these affidavits with the FCC, with one exception. One states Hoffart was fired for recommending a female as a station manager. It was called "insinuation into management" and grounds for dismissal.

TR:494   *Judge Fitzpatrick:* Page 14. A letter of Judy Balint. What, if anything, do you know concerning that notarization?[26]
Mr. Bogel: Since yesterday when this letter first came up I spoke with my secretary, who actually did go out under my direction and got this letter.
Judge Fitzpatrick: Her name is?
Mr. Bogel: Tamara Kern. She explained to me that like many of the public service agencies they're staffed by volunteers. The woman that she spoke with is named Ann. Ann is the head person at Focus. Ann was explained the same wording that we told everybody else, that we're going to be going to court to determine our license renewal. Our license is being challenged. It's important to go back and get testimony about community services and leaders that we've worked with, and it must be notarized. Ann heard that, seemed to understand that I assumed from what my conversations with Tamara were, and lo and behold, we got a letter from Focus but it was signed by Judy Balint. So it's not impossible to understand why Judy Balint doesn't know anything about it, because she wasn't the person that was originally contacted but she was the person that wrote the letter.

Bogel lied. The letter before him had not been picked up by Tamara Kern. The preponderance of evidence, as will come later when Ms.

---

[26]Appendix page 1. This letter has a phony verification affixed by Ms. Carrie Matthew.

Balint is on the witness stand, supports the fact that Tamara Kern picked up a corrected letter, but the corrected letter was not filed by Kaye-Smith. Let's look at some of the upcoming Judy Balint testimony:

TR:643   *Mr. Hoffart*: Were you the person that was originally called by KISW, approached . . . ?
Ms. Balint. Yes, I believe so, yes.
Mr. Hoffart: For a letter?
Ms. Balint Right.

The Ms. Balint sworn testimony differs from what Mr. Bogel had to say on the witness stand. Bogel had reason to testify as he did. Ms. Balint had no axe to grind. As the reader, who do you think is the more credible witness? Bogel's testimony also revealed that an effort was made to obtain a "corrected letter" from Ms. Balint, one that was legally notarized. If one was ever obtained, it was not filed by KISW. However, let's move forward again, to some of the Balint testimony:

TR:641   *Judge Fitzpatrick*: Do you have occasion to have your signature notarized frequently or infrequently?
Ms. Balint: Infrequently.
Judge Fitzpatrick: Do you know what the purpose of a notarization is?
Ms. Balint: To verify that the signature is correct.
Judge Fitzpatrick: And that it's done before the notary so they see the person do it?
Ms. Balint: Right.
Judge Fitzpatrick: Did you have that in mind when they called you and said, "do you give us authorization to notarize your signature?"
Ms. Balint: Frankly, what I had in mind was to get out of this whole mess since we were so unaware of whatever was going on.
Judge Fitzpatrick: I can understand that.
Ms. Balint: I really hadn't given it much thought, no. We just wanted to say, "here, get on with it, here it is, leave us alone."

As the reader already knows, the judge, in his Initial Decision concluded that all of the "notarial imperfections" were due to the ignorance of the Kaye-Smith employees and as such warranted only a "slight demerit." Characterizing station employees as "ignorant" individuals in order to mitigate a licensee's shortcomings is without precedent. Perhaps the employees will seek to correct this stigmatization by a federal agency.

11.

CARRIE MATTHEW

Carrie Matthew followed Mr. Bogel on the witness stand. Counsel for Kaye-Smith had filed "corrections" to the five testimonial letters that had been notarized by Ms. Matthew. The judge wanted some answers, as did Hoffart.

Ms. Carrie Matthew was duly sworn upon oath and stated that she lived at 400 West Roy, Seattle. She had been employed by KISW (FM) for a little over a year and had previously been employed by Data Card Computer Supply, and Eucalyptus Records. She had attended Metropolitan Business School. She had worked at J.C. Penney while attending school.

TR:530   *Mr. Boros*: Are you a notary public?

Ms. Matthew: Yes, I am.

Mr. Boros: When did you become a notary public?

Ms. Matthew: Last June. (1982)

Mr. Boros: Before you became a notary public, had you ever taken any training in becoming a notary public?

Ms. Matthew: No, I didn't.

Mr. Boros: How did you happen to become a notary public? Can you describe the procedure?

Ms. Matthew: Well, Meg and Steve told me they wanted me to become one in case it ever came up on this job that I would need to. And then I just went down to the office where they do that and just signed my name.

Mr. Boros: Now, when you say Meg and Steve, could you . . .

Ms. Matthew: Steve West and Meg Noren.

Mr. Boros: And when you say you went down to an office, could you describe what office you went down to and what you did in terms of signing your name?

Ms. Matthew: I can't . . . it was the government office, downtown Seattle, and they just had me sign my name and they gave me instructions with a . . .

Mr. Boros: Did that make you a notary?

Ms. Matthew: Yes, and I filled out some forms that Meg gave me to fill out before I went down.

Mr. Boros: And you handed those forms to the government authorities, is that correct?

Ms. Matthew: I gave them to Meg Noren, and then she sent them in.

Mr. Boros: That's before you went down and signed your name at the government office?

Ms. Matthew: Yes.

Mr. Boros: Now, after you signed your name at the government office, did you understand that you were then a notary?

Ms. Matthew: Yes. I'm not sure.

Mr. Boros: When did you get notification in your own mind that you had the position of notary?

Ms. Matthew: Well, when I had my certificate from the government and had my seal.

Mr. Boros: And after you signed your name, how much time elapsed before you signed your name and you got your certificate and seal from the government?

Ms. Matthew: Oh, a week or two.

Mr. Boros: Now, how old were you at the time you first received your seal and the certificate?

Ms. Matthew: 21.

Mr. Boros: That's your age now, is it?

Ms. Matthew: Yes.

Mr. Boros: Did you understand the term "affidavit" at any time prior to hearing that term today?

Ms. Matthew: Yes, I did.

Mr. Boros: What did you think an affidavit was?

Ms. Matthew: Something that actually happened.

Mr. Boros: Do you know where you got that knowledge of what an affidavit is, the basis of where you learned the meaning of affidavit?

Ms. Matthew: Well, I learned it at KISW.

Judge Fitzpatrick: From whom?

Ms. Matthew: Well I'm the traffic director there, and I have to make sure that everything runs properly with what it's supposed to run. And that's called the affidavit of . . . you know, I go through the log after it's been run, you know, the day after, and I go through and I make any changes that happened. What actually went.

Judge Fitzpatrick: The affidavit is a statement as to what took place, is that correct? The affidavit states that these programs were broadcast as contracted for whatever it says, is that correct? Is an affidavit of performance you're talking about?

Ms. Matthew: Yes.

Judge Fitzpatrick: When you went down to the State Authorities or County Authorities to become a notary, did they give you any instructions as to what the function and role of a notary was?

Ms. Matthew: They gave me some pages with all the instructions on it, all the legal terms.

Judge Fitzpatrick: And did you read and study those?

Ms. Matthew: Yes, I did.

Judge Fitzpatrick: Was it your understanding that you were not to affix your signature as a notary unless the person affixed their signature to the document in your presence?

Ms. Matthew: I didn't understand that, no.

Judge Fitzpatrick: And there was nothing in the instructions that you received from the state or county that told you that that was the case?

Ms. Matthew: Yes, there was.

Judge Fitzpatrick: Well, if the instructions were there, then how was it you didn't understand it?

Ms. Matthew: Well, it had been some months, and I didn't fully understand all the legal terms when I read it.

Judge Fitzpatrick: Did you question anybody else? Now, Ms. Moren, is that her name? (he was close).

Ms. Matthew: Noren.

Judge Fitzpatrick: She's been a notary longer than you. Did you ask her any questions, get any guidelines from her?

Ms. Matthew: Yes. She said it was okay to do that. She instructed me to notarize them.

Judge Fitzpatrick: We'll get to that.

Well, the general public now knows what it takes to become a notary in the State of Washington. All you do is go down to some unidentified building in Seattle and sign your name. You need only be twenty-one years old—no other requirements. You do not need a list of freeholders on your application; you do not need to take an oath of office; you need not be bonded to receive a certificate and seal. The initiated will immediately recognize that the testimony given by Ms. Matthew is suspect, to say the least, and is self-serving. It is clear that counsel's strategy is to impress upon the judge that Ms. Matthew is a lay person, and as such cannot be held responsible for her acts. It would have been idle for Hoffart to object to the leading questions by the judge and by counsel.

It is a well-known precept that an employer is responsible for the acts of his or her employees when they are acting in his or her behalf with actual or apparent authority to do so. It is also well-known that an employer is responsible for training an employee to do their assigned tasks. Here we have Kaye-Smith asking an employee to obtain a Washington state notary commission for the express purpose of executing advertising performance affidavits. They did not train her in her duties as a notary. In actual fact the judge had to prompt her regarding what she was to do—notarize bills or so-called performance affidavits. It is clear that she knew it was necessary for an affiant to appear before her. The instructions she had received stated so. Subsequent testimony will show that she notarized the five testimonial letters on instructions from her superiors. Had she refused, she probably would have been fired.

TR:534   *Mr. Boros*: Did you ever in your career as a notary, beginning last June, have someone come before you from outside the station and ask you to notarize anything for them?
Ms. Matthew: No, I didn't.
Mr. Boros: Did anyone in the station, beginning at the time your career as a notary began in June of 1982, come to you and ask you to notarize something for them?
Ms. Matthew: No, not before those.
Mr. Boros: But there did come a time when you were asked to notarize certain letters by people in the station, is that correct?
Ms. Matthew: Yes, these that we are speaking of.
Mr. Boros: When did that time arise, as best you can remember?
Ms. Matthew: In October, November.
Mr. Boros: And who asked you to do what in terms of notarizations as you can recall, to the best of your recollection?
Ms. Matthew: Meg Noren.
Mr. Boros: What did she say to you? Do you recall?
Ms. Matthew: She told me that the letters needed notarizing and that everything was accurate on it, and then she showed me how to do it and told me to go ahead and do it.
Mr. Boros: When she said the letters needed notarization, are you referring to a certain group of letters?
Ms. Matthew: The letters from the clients that they sent in.
Mr. Boros: She asked you to notarize these letters, is that correct?
Ms. Matthew: Yes, it is.

Mr. Boros: Now, with respect to show you how to do it, what did she show you and what did she say to you when she showed you? Could you state that for the record?

Ms. Matthew: Well, she told me that it needed to say my name, notary public, and the date, and then sign it and put the stamp over it.

Mr. Boros: Did she give you any demonstration of how it was done?

Ms. Matthew: She showed me one that had been done.

Mr. Boros: When you say had been done, was it done in your presence, or did she show you something which already had what appeared to be notarial type writing on it?

Ms. Matthew: It had already been done.

Mr. Boros: What did you say to her when she gave you these instructions and showed you this letter or paper, whatever it was, with certain notarial type writings? Did you say anything to her?

Ms. Matthew: I don't remember.

Mr. Boros: Did you at that time think that you understood the process?

Ms. Matthew: Yes.

With all the preliminaries out of the way regarding her obtaining a notarial commission, her involvement in notarizing testimonial letters, and also regarding the nine undated exhibit verifications wherein she notarized the signatures of Mr. Bogel and Mr. West, Mr. Boros directed his interrogatories to specific acts. But first let's review the Matthew testimony up to this point.

She stated that she had been instructed by Ms. Noren to date her notarial acts and she also testified that the instructions she had read required affiants to appear before her. The Kaye/Smith Direct Case exhibits show that only two of her fourteen verifications were dated and that they were dated one week apart.[27] She had notarized the Julie McCullough letter outside the presence of Ms. McCullough on the 28th of October and the Shawn Taylor letter on the 5th of November. She had a full week, after her initial illegal act, to recant her notarization. She did not. In actual fact she notarized four more in the same illegal manner, three undated as to when she affixed her notarial attestation.

It is a well-known precept that there is no need for a showing of willfullness when an act is repeated, and repeated simply means more than once. In his Initial Decision the judge concluded, in his unending

---

[27]Appendix page 9. The Julie McCullough letter. Appendix page 16. The Shawn Taylor letter.

wisdom, that there was no intent to disregard his orders. Of course not. He had ordered that all exhibits had to be sponsored and supported by an affidavit of the sponsor. So Kaye-Smith merely followed his instructions and filed notarized exhibits. The fact that they were illegally notarized is of no consequence.

Hoffart is not a lawyer. He had never had occasion to cross-examine anyone in a court situation before. He has no legal training. He does know, however, what intent means, as defined in the dictionary. Intent is an act done with a purpose, and the purpose in this case was to pass off unnotarized documents as being legally notarized before the affiant in order to be acceptable in a legal case. Just how a judge can find that there was no intent to deceive anyone defies analysis.

The author again takes leave to move forward in the record to present his cross-examination of Ms. Matthew as it relates to her obtaining a notary commission. Her other direct and cross-examination will follow shortly.

TR:562   *Mr. Hoffart*: Ms. Matthew, now you stated that you walked into a government office. What kind of a government office? Did you get this notary paper, application paper?
Ms. Matthew: I walked in . . . I'm not sure what . . .
Mr. Hoffart: Well, was it downtown?
Ms. Matthew: Yes, it was downtown.
Mr. Hoffart: And you got an application blank to become a notary, is that it?
Ms. Matthew: I got the application blank at where I work, and I filled it out before I went down there.
Mr. Hoffart: What did you have to fill out on this sheet of paper?
Ms. Matthew: Just my name and address.
Mr. Hoffart: Did anyone have to sign on there? Anyone else put a signature on that sheet of paper?
Ms. Matthew: Meg Noren notarized it.

The reader should remember this sworn testimony. Ms. Matthew stated that Ms. Noren had notarized her notary commission application. Subsequently, when Ms. Noren is questioned by Mr. Boros, she will state, without equivocation, that she had never notarized any documents other than performance affidavits. It has also already been brought to light that Ms. Noren had notarized the advanced time memo for Mr. Bogel. When the Noren testimony is presented, the author will present documentary proof that Ms. Noren was an experienced notary—counsel's attempts to prove otherwise notwithstanding.

Mr. Hoffart: There was no list of freeholders certified?

Ms. Matthew: Oh, and I needed ten names of landowners in King County.

Mr. Hoffart: Did you put those names of landowners on there?

Ms. Matthew: I had them sign it.

Mr. Hoffart: Did you explain to them, each landowner, what they were doing?

Ms. Matthew: Yes, I did.

Mr. Hoffart: Did you know what they were for?

Ms. Matthew: I knew it was required.

Mr. Hoffart: Did you get an instruction booklet with it on notarial duties?

Ms. Matthew: Yes, after I went to the office.

Mr. Hoffart: Did any place in that instruction booklet tell you that a person has to appear before you and you have to identify the person before you notarize the statement?

Ms. Matthew: It said that in the instructions.

Mr. Hoffart: Now, is there any place on that application form that you had to be bonded?

Ms. Matthew: I don't believe so. I can't remember.

Mr. Hoffart: You are not a bonded notary?

Ms. Matthew: No.

Mr. Hoffart: You stated that you were a traffic clerk and you notarized documents as to the performance that spots were run?

Ms. Matthew: No, I don't notarize those.

Mr. Hoffart: Isn't that what you received your seal for?

Ms. Matthew: Well, I received it in case something would come up in the job that I would need it . . .

Mr. Hoffart: But you never had to use it?

Ms. Matthew: No, I didn't.

Judge Fitzpatrick: Well, you sign the affidavits as the person with the knowledge that somebody notarizes your signature? Is that how you do it?

Ms. Matthew: No. You mean for the affidavits that go out?

Judge Fitzpatrick: That's correct, yes.

Ms. Matthew: Meg Noren signs those.

Judge Fitzpatrick: Who notarizes her signature?

Ms. Matthew: She notarizes it. I don't understand.

Judge Fitzpatrick: Didn't somebody notarize the signature of the person who's doing the certification, or do they?

65

Ms. Matthew: No.

The cross-examination established, once again, that Ms. Matthew knew affiants were to appear before her before she could affix her notarial attestation. It also established that she stated she was not bonded. It is well-established that bonding is required before a notary commission may be bestowed upon an individual. In actual fact KISW notary Ms. Matthew was bonded at the required ten thousand dollars and that the bond had been posted by Safeco.

What is more important, however, is that Ms. Matthew stated that Ms. Noren notarizes the performance affidavits. Ms. Noren was listed as administrative assistant to the manager. She had no direct knowledge, in all cases, that the commercials had been aired, yet she swore upon her oath, self-administered, that the spots had been broadcast and had done so for three and one-half years. This will be more fully established when Ms. Noren testifies in this regard. Suffice to say, at this time, that advertisers who received notarized bills were being billed on hearsay knowledge that their advertising was run. It will also be shown that Ms. Noren testified that this notarization procedure was in effect at the time she became a notary. This will be proven untrue. The author is not charging Kaye-Smith with billing fraud. What he is saying is that there was potential for fraudulent billings and those billings sent by mail also constituted potential mail fraud. Advertisers who relied upon Kaye-Smith performance affidavits may wish to take note.

Now, what did the judge put in his findings of fact and conclusions of law on this potential fraud? He took the easy way out. He did not mention it in his findings of facts and made no discrete conclusions. In other words, so what? It cannot be denied that the performance affidavits were, in a large part, issued during the renewal period and as such a nexus was established that should have resulted in a finding and a conclusion that such indifference is not in the public interest and reflects upon the character qualifications of a licensee. Smith and the Kaye's could care less. They were laughing all the way to the bank.

Mr. Boros continued, with reference to one of the undated affidavits executed by Mr. West, this one affixed to exhibit 5.

TR:538   *Mr. Boros*: Now, how did you happen to put your signature on this piece of paper?

Ms. Matthew: I signed it and I put when my Commission expires, and I notarized it over the signature.

Mr. Boros: What do you mean when you say you notarized it over the signature?

Ms. Matthew: I put the seal over it.

Mr. Boros: Was someone in the room with you when you did this?

Ms. Matthew: Yes. Steve West and Eric Bogel.
Mr. Boros: Now did Mr. West sign this in your presence?
Ms. Matthew: Yes, he did.
Mr. Boros: And then you wrote your name and then you put your seal? Is that how it happened?
Ms. Matthew: Yes.
Mr. Boros: Now, there is no date between this and the word day. Do you see that?
Ms. Matthew: Yes, I do.
Mr. Boros: Do you know why there's no day written there?
Ms. Matthew: I didn't write it in.
Judge Fitzpatrick: Now, let me ask you a question, It says "subscribed and sworn before me this blank day." What do you understand that to mean?
Ms. Matthew: That this was the truth.
Judge Fitzpatrick: Did Mr. West swear to the truth of what he'd signed before you?
Ms. Matthew: Well, he signed it, and . . .
Judge Fitzpatrick: Did you ask him as a notary as to whether or not the statements in there were true and correct, to the best of his knowledge?
Ms. Matthew: He told me that they all were.
Judge Fitzpatrick: He did?
Ms. Matthew: Yes.
Judge Fitzpatrick: All right.

The Kaye-Smith exhibit to which this questioning related was the bibliography of Mr. West. The content of that exhibit is not an issue here. It should be remembered, however, that this was only a typical exchange. West and Bogel had also notarized, presumably before Ms. Matthew, their affidavits relating to exhibits 16 and West also supported exhibit 17. Those three affidavits were untrue in content. The affiants had not been told, in all cases, that their testimonials would be used as testimony in a proceeding before the Federal Communications Commission.

The judge found that in some cases the affiants had not been so advised, and that, in his opinion, this was just an oversight on their part. No demerits were warranted for this filing of affidavits that contained untruths. Applicants may now knowingly file false information with the FCC and Judge Fitzpatrick may rule that the acts are oversights.

Kaye-Smith counsel had filed nine affidavits on November 23rd to supply the missing dates. In all nine Ms. Matthew stated that the missing dates were all November 9th. The questioning of Ms. Matthew now turned to these nine corrections.

TR:539 *Mr. Boros*: I ask you to turn to page 6 of Kaye-Smith Exhibit 5. At the top of that page it says Affidavit of Carrie Matthew. Could you tell us how that affidavit came into being, what caused you to make that affidavit if indeed you did make it? And first please state, is that your signature there, Carrie Matthew?
Ms. Matthew: Yes, it is.
Mr. Boros: What caused you to make this affidavit?
Ms. Matthew: Because I didn't put the date on this affidavit.
Mr. Boros: Well, who asked you, if anybody, to make up this affidavit and brought to your attention the fact that you left out a date?
Ms. Matthew: Meg Noren did.
Mr. Boros: What did she say to you? Do you remember?
Ms. Matthew: She said that I was supposed to date these and that I didn't, and so that we had to make up a new affidavit saying that I didn't date it.
Judge Fitzpatrick: How did you recall what the date was that you had done it in the first place?
Ms. Matthew: How did I recall?
Judge Fitzpatrick: Yes, how did you remember that you did it on November 9th? Did you have a clear recollection that you did it on November 9th?
Ms. Matthew: Yes. It wasn't that long after.
Judge Fitzpatrick: All right. It was exactly a week?
Ms. Matthew: Yes.

This testimony may appear somewhat superflous to the reader. However, it establishes, under oath, that Ms. Matthew also notarized the West and Bogel affidavits relating to the testimonial letters attachment lists and as such raises the question why the Nina L. Evers letter, notarized on the 10th, appears on the Bogel list. The answer, by a preponderance of evidence test, is that Mr. Bogel did not have an attachment list on the 9th, but that it was typed up on the 10th or later. Bogel had pre-executed his affidavit.

Mr. Boros continued through the exhibits sponsored by Mr. West and Bogel. In all cases Ms. Matthew testified the same. When exhibit 16 was reviewed before being offered into evidence, the questioning moved to the notarizations by Ms. Matthew of the testimonial letters. Exhibits 16 and 17 are the twenty-four letters solicited by KISW employees from area community leaders in support of their renewal application.

TR:550   *Mr. Boros*: I direct your attention to page 6 of Kaye-Smith Exhibit 16.[28] That purports to be a letter from a Ms. McCullough to a Mr. Sullivan. Do you have it before you?

Ms. Matthew: Yes.

Mr. Boros: Now, at the bottom under the date 10/28/82 there is a signature. Whose signature it that?

Ms. Matthew: That is mine.

Mr. Boros: And next to it is that a seal, in the middle?

Ms. Matthew: Yes, there is a seal.

Mr. Boros: And it's yours?

Ms. Matthew: Yes.

Mr. Boros: Could you explain how your signature came to be affixed to that piece of paper?

Ms. Matthew: Yes.

Mr. Boros: How did your signature come to be affixed to that piece of paper?

Ms. Matthew: I was instructed by Meg Noren.

Mr. Boros: What did she say you should do with this letter in terms of putting your signature on it?

Ms. Matthew: She told me to type out my name and notary public and the date, and put my seal on it.

Mr. Boros: Was Ms. McCullough before you when you did this act of putting your name, et cetra, on the piece of paper?

Ms. Matthew: No, She wasn't.

Judge Fitzpatrick: Did you question her asking you to do this?

Ms. Matthew: No, I didn't.

Judge Fitzpatrick: You didn't consider it improper?

Ms. Matthew: Well, if she told me to I thought that it was right, because she'd been a notary.

Judge Fitzpatrick: Did you ask her why she didn't do it?

Ms. Matthew: No, I didn't.

Judge Fitzpatrick: Have you asked her since why she didn't do it?

Ms. Matthew: No, I haven't.

Mr. Boros: Did you think you were doing the right thing putting your name on the paper?

Ms. Matthew: Yes, I did.

Judge Fitzpatrick: Other than asking you to notarize this signature of Ms. McCullough, who did not affix her sig-

---

[28]Appendix page 9.

nature in your presence, did she say that anybody had directed her or asked her to have this done?

Ms. Matthew: I really can't remember.

Judge Fitzpatrick: You have no recollection? She didn't say "do this because Mr. Blank said he wanted you to notarize this?"

Ms. Matthew: I really don't remember. She may have.

Judge Fitzpatrick: What's your best recollection?

Ms. Matthew: Well, I remember that she told me to do it, so I did it.

Judge Fitzpatrick: Did you know that this was being sent to the Federal Communications Commission?

Ms. Matthew: No. I didn't.

Judge Fitzpatrick: What was your understanding as to what use was being made of this letter?

Ms. Matthew: Well, she said it was accurate and it needed a notary seal.

Judge Fitzpatrick: And in all the material you had read or any material you had gotten from either the State or County concerning what your duties as a notary public were, nowhere did you recall reading that it said the person had to affix their signature before you and in your presence?

Ms. Matthew: I didn't remember it.

Judge Fitzpatrick: All right. Is this the first time since you became a notary that you have affixed your notarial attestation to a document and the person had not affixed their signature to the document in your presence?

Ms. Matthew: Yes, This is the first document I have ever notarized.

Judge Fitzpatrick: This is the first document you ever notarized in your life as a notary?

Ms. Matthew: Yes.

Judge Fitzpatrick: This one piece of paper here, on October 28th?

Ms. Matthew: I believe it was.

Judge Fitzpatrick: All right.

The documentation in the appendix shows that Ms. Carrie Matthew also notarized the affidavits signed by Mr. Eric Bogel filed as the sponsor of some of the exhibits. In addition she had notarized the Bogel affidavit wherein he stated that all affiants had been told their letters would be used in a FCC proceeding. This affidavit is untrue, as will be reviewed when the authors of testimonial letters testify. Hoffart,

70

through cross-examination of Ms. Matthew, wanted to establish if Mr. Bogel had sworn upon oath, before her, that the contents of his affidavits were true.

TR:565   *Mr. Hoffart*: Now, you're working at KISW. Do you know any people up there that use more than one name?
Mr. Boros: Object, your Honor. Totally irrelevant and immaterial.
Judge Fitzpatrick: We'll find out. It's cross-examination. Overruled.
Ms. Matthew: Yes, there are.
Mr. Hoffart: Would Mr. Bogel have another name?
Ms. Matthew: Yes, he does.
Mr. Hoffart: What name does he use?
Ms. Matthew: Beau Phillips.
Mr. Hoffart: When you sign something that Mr. Bogel has signed, did you, before you signed, watch him? Did you see his drivers license and identify him?
Mr. Boros: Object. That assumes something not in evidence, that Mr. Bogel has a driver's license.
Judge Fitzpatrick: Did you ask her if you asked to see a drivers license?
Mr. Hoffart: Did you ask to see any identification from Mr. Bogel as to what his name was?
Ms. Matthew: No, but I knew that's what his name was.
Mr. Hoffart: How did you know?
Ms. Matthew: That's what everybody says. Why would he lie about his real name?
Mr. Hoffart: How do you know his real name isn't Beau Phillips?
Mr. Boros: Object, your Honor. That's totally immaterial.
Judge Fitzpatrick: Overruled. Please.
Ms. Matthew: Beau Phillips is just his name he used when he went on the air. It's just a radio name.
Mr. Hoffart: Did you see any sort of identification from Mr. Bogel that his real name is Eric Bogel?
Ms. Matthew: No, I didn't.
Mr. Hoffart: So you did not know when you made the second affidavit that the man before you was really Mr. Eric Bogel by any identification?
Ms. Matthew: No.

71

Judge Fitzpatrick: What did you think it meant when it said "subscribed and sworn to before me this blank day?" What did you think it meant?

Ms. Matthew: That they were saying that what the document said was accurate.

Judge Fitzpatrick: Did he in each case swear to you that the document was accurate? Did he raise his hand and swear that. "I swear that the document is accurate?"

Ms. Matthew: No, but he didn't raise his hand and swear, but he told me that everything was accurate.

Judge Fitzpatrick: Why did you attest to the fact that it had been sworn to before you?

Ms. Matthew: Well, I didn't know that was the routine, that he had to do that.

Judge Fitzpatrick: Well, you didn't type up the form. The form was already there, and it does say "subscribed and sworn to before me this blank day of" . . . what did you think that meant?

Ms. Matthew: Well, that was their signature and they told me.

Judge Fitzpatrick: What does the word subscribed mean?

Ms. Matthew: Authorized and signed.

Judge Fitzpatrick: Subscribed means he signed his name, subscribed?

Ms. Matthew: Right.

Judge Fitzpatrick: What does the word sworn mean? It means something more than just signing his name, doesn't it?

Ms. Matthew: Yes. Well, he told me they were true.

Judge Fitzpatrick: In what form did he tell you that they were true? How did he say that?

Ms. Matthew: Well, he said "everything that I'm signing here is the truth."

Judge Fitzpatrick: He said that in each case?

Ms. Matthew: No. He said it at the beginning. He said, "everything that we are signing is the truth."

Judge Fitzpatrick: All right.

The author's purpose behind his cross-examination was to establish that Mr. Bogel also used the name of "Beau Phillips." This is significant because, as appendix page 33 shows, Ms. Noren had notarized the "Beau Phillips" name in that form on the advanced time memo Hoffart located in the KISW public file. Apparently Ms. Noren had no aversions to notarizing a document bearing a phony signature.

When the authors of testimonial letters appear it will be established that in each case where Ms. Matthew affixed her notarial attestation outside the presence of the author of the letter she was instructed to do so by Ms. Noren. In the case of the Blacksmith letter,[29] however, Mr. West had testified that it was he that called Ms. Matthew into his office and had her notarize the Charles Blacksmith document. Let's pick up this testimony by Mr. West:

TR:307   *Judge Fitzpatrick*: Do you know how it came about that Carrie Matthew had notarized Mr. Blacksmith's signature?

Mr. West: Yes, Mr. Blacksmith didn't have a notary and he asked if we would do it.

Judge Fitzpatrick: Who?

Mr. West: Me.

Judge Fitzpatrick: You dated it October . . . just explain to me what happened.

Mr. West: In the case of Mr. Blacksmith, and a few others, they didn't have a notary that they could use. And we were in a timeframe where we were in a hurry. They asked if we would notarize it. (moving forward in the testimony)

TR:308   *Judge Fitzpatrick*: Now, you got Mr. Blacksmith's letter and it wasn't notarized and you talked to Mr. Blacksmith about that?

Mr. West: Yes.

Judge Fitzpatrick: Before . . .

Mr. West: Yes.

Judge Fitzpatrick: Mr. Blacksmith asked you to have somebody notarize it?

Mr. West: Yes.

Judge Fitzpatrick: Then you asked Ms. Matthew to come in and affix notarization?

Mr. West: Yes.

Judge Fitzpatrick: Did she tell you that that's not the way you do it?

Mr. West: No.

To establish that either Mr. West or Ms. Carrie Matthew stated untruths, lets go back to Ms. Matthew's testimony on the witness stand:

---

[29]Appendix page 24. The original Blacksmith letter notarized outside the presence of Mr. Blacksmith by Ms. Carrie Matthew.

TR:557   *Mr. Boros*: Now, with respect to page 24 of Kaye-Smith Exhibit 16, could you turn there, please. Do you have that before you? (The original Blacksmith letter)
Ms. Matthew: Yes.
Mr. Boros: At the bottom of the page above the words "notary public" appears a signature. Is that your signature?
Ms. Matthew: Yes, it is.
Mr. Boros: How did your signature happen to come to be put on that page?
Ms. Matthew: I was instructed by Meg Noren.
Mr. Boros: To do what?
Ms. Matthew: To notarize it.
Mr. Boros: Was Charles E. Blacksmith before you at that time?
Ms. Matthew: No, he wasn't.
Judge Fitzpatrick: Did you know what use was to be made of this document?
Ms. Matthew: No, I didn't.
Judge Fitzpatrick: You didn't know it was being submitted to the FCC?
Ms. Matthew: No, I didn't.
Judge Fitzpatrick: Mr. Blacksmith wasn't before you when you notarized that?
Ms. Matthew: No, he wasn't.

The reader now has the two versions of how Ms. Carrie Matthew happened to affix a phony notarization to the letter solicited from Mr. Blacksmith. You can well imagine the predicament the judge found himself in. Here a case before him was going sour for the incumbent, an influential broadcaster. No challenger, to the best of the author's knowledge, had prevailed in a comparative renewal case since the early sixties. His questioning already shows signs of bringing into the record mitigating circumstances. In this case, again, he asks Ms. Matthew if she knew that the illegally notarized testimonial letters would be submitted to the FCC. It is irrelevant and immaterial if she did or did not know that fact. What is relevant and material is that she was executing orders from superiors, including the station manager and that *they* knew what was going to happen to those letters. Ms. Matthew was just a pawn used by her immediate supervisors and her employers to assist them in a botched attempt to have illegally notarized documents filed in support of their renewal application.

12.

MARGIT E. NOREN ‑

Margit E. Noren, senior notary for Kaye-Smith at KISW was sworn upon oath by the judge. She stated that she went to work for KISW after attending Skagit Valley College in Mount Vernon. At first she was a part-time employee in the promotion department. Shortly thereafter she became a receptionist and ten weeks later administrative assistant to the manager, who at that time was Harry Caracco. She continued working as administrative assistant to the manager when Mr. Stephen West became manager in August of 1979. At that time Ms. Noren had been employed about thirteen months.

TR:585   *Mr. Boros*: Did a time come when you became a notary?
Ms. Noren: Yes.
Mr. Boros: When was that?
Ms. Noren: In June of 1979.
Mr. Boros: And at the time you became a notary, was that your own idea or did someone suggest it to you?
Ms. Noren: It was suggested to me.
Mr. Boros: By whom?
Ms. Noren: I don't recall.
Mr. Boros: Was it someone at KISW?
Ms. Noren: Yes.
Mr. Boros: Do you recall what was suggested to you about becoming a notary?
Ms. Noren: I was needed to become a notary for billing purposes.
Mr. Boros: Would you describe more specifically further what was involved in your becoming a notary for billing purposes?
Ms. Noren: When we send out our billing there's a statement and an affidavit of performance which shows the times that the commercials were run, and frequently advertisers request that those be notarized for co-op purposes.
Mr. Boros: How did you undertake to become a notary when it was suggested to you that you should become a notary?
Ms. Noren: I was sent forms from our home office by Anne Curtis which I had to get ten land owners to sign this form, and then take it to the courthouse and pay a $2.00 fee and be sworn in, and receive my seal.

Mr. Boros: And after that were you told by any people at the courthouse that you were a notary?

Ms. Noren: They said I would officially become a notary when I received my certificate from the Capital.

Mr. Boros: Did a time come when you received such a certificate?

Ms. Noren: Yes.

Mr. Boros: Did you thereafter enter into performing certain notarial duties?

Ms. Noren: Yes, I did.

Ms. Boros: What sort of notarial duties did you perform?

Ms. Noren: As I said before, for the billing. I notarized the bills that went out.

Judge Fitzpatrick: Did you notarize the bills, or did you notarize the signature of someone?

Ms. Noren: No, I notarize the bills, stating that to the best of my knowledge these commercials and tapes are what ran.

Mr. Boros: When you notarized the bills, what did you do in a physical sense in terms of either putting your name on the bills, or a stamp, or a certificate and the date. Could you state what your routine was, and was the routine the same all the time?

Ms. Noren: Yes.

Mr. Boros: What was the routine?

Ms. Noren: That we have a rubber stamp that says that according to the best of my knowledge in accordance with our laws, that on this date and this month, and then I sign it, that according to our logs this is what ran to the best of my knowledge, and I date it and sign it and then affix my seal over it. And that had been the same routine prior to when I came.

Ms. Noren was the first witness on the third day of the hearing. The previous day Ms. Matthew had testified that she was the traffic clerk and she checked the logs, but that Ms. Noren notarized the billings. This accounts for counsel's questioning of Ms. Noren along this line the first opportunity he had. It is clear that he was aware that the notarizations of the bills by Ms. Noren do not satisfy the law. She was notarizing the billings upon hearsay from Ms. Matthew, or even possibly notarizing off the contracts without benefit of any knowledge that the commercials were aired. She testified that she had been doing this routine for four years even though she had not been a notary for that long. She said, under oath, that the routine had not been changed when she became a notary. This is true insofar as affixing a stamp on the bills. It is not true as far as having someone other than the traffic clerk, who checks the logs, telling some other person to notarize the bills.

First, as to the wording of the billing verification: the author obtained a billing that has the wording on it. It happens to be a bill for the Slade Gorton Election advertising in September of 1980. The rubber stamp imprint reads:

> We warrant, that in accordance with certified station logs, the programs and/or announcements as indicated were broadcast. Subscribed and sworn to me this 3rd day of October in and for the county of King, State of Washington.
>
> (s) Margaret E. Noren, notary public
State of Washington.
>
> My Commission expires 6-15-83.[30]

Nothing in this rubber stamp notarial verification says that the advertising was run to the "best of her knowledge." It says nothing about being in accordance with our laws. It simply states that Ms. Noren warrants that the commercials were aired. It says the information was subscribed and sworn to her. In actual fact nobody appeared other than herself, and she could not have had actual knowledge, in all cases, that her self-serving affirmation was true. Her sworn testimony, at the hearing is not true.

Ms. Noren had stated, under prodding by counsel, that the routine had not been changed. While the same stamp may have been used by the notary before her, that notary was the traffic clerk. Since the traffic clerk checks the logs, a different set of facts are at hand. A notary that checks the logs may well warrant that the commercials were aired.

Prior to Ms. Noren notarizing the billings, a Ms. Christine A. Woolson was traffic manager. Her name appears in the roster of employees filed by Kaye-Smith with their Direct Case. The roster shows that Ms. Woolson departed KISW in May of 1979. Ms. Noren testified that she was commissioned in June of 1979. The roster also shows that a Karen T. Raines was hired as traffic director. She was not commissioned as a notary according to the records at the Secretary of State. It becomes apparent, then, that Ms. Noren, the administrative assistant, took over the verification of the billings at the time Ms. Woolson departed. Proof exists, in the form of Kaye-Smith Direct Case exhibit 17, page 8, that Ms. Christine Woolson was a notary. She had notarized this testimonial letter, one solicited from Mr. C. Clark Griffin, on October 29, 1982. By a preponderance of evidence, then, the Ms. Noren testimony that the routine had not been changed is untrue.

---

[30]Appendix page 34. Slade Gorton advertising schedule with rubber stamp verification and superimposed transcript testimony affixed by the author.

The author will, subsequently, review the C. Clark Griffin letters and suggest that this letter is another one with a phony verification. Several factors point in that direction. Incidently, Mr. Smith, in his oral depositions, stated that Ms. Karen T. Raines, a black female, was an excellent employee and he was sorry to see her leave. He stated she left to seek a career in video. The author does not know why she was not asked to become a notary or her whereabouts at this writing. It also goes beyond the zone of reasonableness that Smith did not know that the routine had been changed to the scenario suggested by Hoffart; a routine he developed through an association of facts.

The commission has, in the past, revoked licenses when proof of fraudulent billing surfaced. They also have case precedents relating to the licensee's responsibility in matters of billings. For example:

> Licensees are reminded of their responsibility of stations bills, invoices, etc., by checking the relevant program logs or equivalent stations records . . .
>
> . . . a licensee was admonished by the Commission when they held that the licensees conduct fell below that expected from a Commission licensee due to deficiencies in monitoring billings by the home office. (EZ Communications v. FCC., 86 2d, page 120, quoting from Public Notice entitled "Fraudulent Billing—Licensee Responsibility to Verify Accuracy of Station Invoices, etc., 56 FCC 2d 371, 1975.)

Under the deregulation of the broadcasting industry, Chairman Mark S. Fowler initiated a docket in which he and his fellow commissioners decided that fraudulent billings and other so-called underbrush are of no concern to them and a burden on the licensee. They ruled that such fraud, as may be involved in double billings, should be handled by the civil courts. It appears to this author that it is not in the public interest to engage in fraudulent billings since the public ultimately is defrauded in the form of higher prices for the goods they buy.[31]

The Communications Act of 1934, as amended, specifically states that a license cannot be issued unless the public interest is served thereby, and that the commission is charged with this responsibility in selecting licensees. What has happened to this responsibility of the commission to act in the public interest?

Other so-called "underbrush" rules and regulations that have been eliminated by Mr. Fowler in the private interests of the broadcasters are the strictures against distortions of audience ratings, conflicts of interest, promotion of non-broadcast interests, concert promotions, failure to perform sales contracts, and false, misleading and deceptive commercials. Are these actions in the public interest, or in the private interests of the broadcasters?

---

[31]Appendix pages 35 and 36. Underbrush deregulation news release.

The media has reported two cases of false, misleading and deceptive commercials since this deregulation has been put into effect. First, it has been reported that radio stations in the Cincinnati, Ohio area promoted a fictitious shopping center in order to test audience reaction and see how many would seek more information. The broadcasters could then assess the effectiveness of radio advertising.

Clearly such deceptive advertising, if true, is in the interests of the broadcast licensee and not in the interest of the public—the victims.

Second, the media also reported that ten radio licensees in Portland, Oregon conducted a similar campaign to test the effectiveness of radio advertising. In this West Coast campaign it was alleged that a fictitious automobile was advertised as being available on February 1, 1986. This was untrue. Again the public was the victim of hoax broadcasts designed to be in the interest of the broadcaster. Allegedly two of the stations involved were owned by Mr. Lester M. Smith. It will be shown later in this book that KISW was admonished by the FCC in 1982 for airing untrue information and Mr. Smith was told that he had a responsibility to monitor the performance of the stations under his control.

This case of notarial imperfections demonstrates just how effective warnings from the commission are. They are nothing but lip service and are no cause of concern to influential broadcasters. No broadcast licensee will lose a license under the commission, as presently constituted. The public may now be deceived by broadcasters with the blessings of the very agency that Congress, by statute, charged with the mandate to protect the public from such acts.

It should be obvious that FCC news releases, such as the cutting of the underbrush, are not distributed to the general public. The general public docs not know that hoax broadcasts and untrue information may be aired with the blessings of the commission.

TR:587   *Mr. Boros:* Did you ever do any other notarial work that you can remember for people at KISW?
Ms. Noren: No.
Mr. Boros: Did anyone at station KISW ever previously ask you to swear to any document which they, he or she, may have signed, and asked you to witness their signature or take their signature and notarize it?
Ms. Noren: No.

Now, the author takes exception to Ms. Noren's unequivocal testimony that she had not notarized any documents for anyone at KISW. Subsequent to the hearings, the author brought three documents to the attention of the FCC that proved, beyond any doubt, that Ms. Noren had notarial experience, that was connected with KISW.[32]

First, Ms. Matthew had stated that Ms. Noren had notarized her notarial commission application. In order to establish that this testimony is true, Hoffart obtained the notarial applications of both Ms. Noren and Ms. Carrie Matthew from the office of the Secretary of State. The application does show that the application was notarized by Ms. Noren, and on the 18th day of May, 1982. Ironically, this same document purports that Ms. Noren administered an oath of office to Ms. Matthew, as required from a notary. In this case the very person who administered the oath, if indeed one was executed, caused and coerced the applicant to violate her oath of office. The notarial documents obtained from the state also verified that Ms. Matthew was bonded. In her testimony Ms. Matthew said nothing about taking any oath of office as a notary, and said that she was not bonded.

Second, the author had obtained the notarized advanced time memo from the KISW public files. On this memo Ms. Noren is shown to have notarized the name of "Beau Phillips" on July 20th, 1982. In actual fact she notarized a document wherein the affiant used a fictitious name. This alone is a notarial violation.

Third, Hoffart researched his files and located a document notarized by Ms. Noren that purports to show the times that KISW aired their required announcements about the hearing notice. Ms. Noren had notarized this document on an unknown date. The last date on which the hearing notice announcements were aired is shown to be June 30, 1982. This document had to be filed with the FCC, probably by counsel. Counsel should have known, then, that Ms. Noren had performed notarial acts prior to the hearing and was an experienced notary public.

It is clear that counsel's questioning was aimed at impressing upon the judge that Ms. Noren was a lay person. Admittedly she may not have remembered three of her notarial attestations, all within six months of the hearing, and as such, testified to the best of her recollection. This loss of memory, if there was a loss, does not by itself erase her notarial experience. Ms. Noren was an experienced notary, her testimony to the contrary notwithstanding.

This untrue testimony by Ms. Noren, as many other untrue statements in the official hearing record, were swept under the rug. Misrepresentations before the judge are disqualifying; therefore, the way to handle these matters is to resort to quiescence.

The author cites three precedents set in FCC proceedings relating to false statements:

---

[32]Appendix pages 33, 37 and 38. Three documents notarized by Ms. Noren prior to the hearing.

... an applicant that deliberately lies in its testimony before the Commission will be disqualified. Quoted from *Grenco, Inc.*, 39 FCC 2d, 26 RR 2d, 1973.

... untruthfullness in an applicant's affidavits or responses to an adversary's interrogations is as much to be condemned as deception at a hearing. Cited from *WNST Radio*, 70 FCC 2d, 44 RR 2d, (Review Board, 1978).

... The Commission must depend on the integrity and representations of its licensee's and a breach of that trust or willfull false statements may be grounds for revocation of licenses and character disqualifications. Cited from *Password, Inc.*, 76 FCC 2d, page 465.

Perhaps the commission's new policy of assessing only a slight demerit on willfull and repeated misrepresentations, as in this Kaye-Smith case, is grounds for reopening the record on the cited Grenco, WNST Radio and Password cases. Like cases demand like treatment, or at least an explanation as to why disparate treatment is warranted.

TR:588   *Mr. Boros*: But a time did come, didn't it, in the fall of this year, October or so, when you were asked to notarize some letters?
Ms. Noren: Yes.
Mr. Boros: Would you describe when in the fall of 1982 you first were asked to notarize some letters? Could you fix the date in terms of the month?
Ms. Noren: No.
Mr. Boros: It was prior to the beginning of this week, though, wasn't it?
Ms. Noren: Yes.
Mr. Boros: Do you recall how or under what circumstances you were asked to perform certain notarial duties with respect to letters?
Ms. Noren: Some of the letters that we'd received and had requested that they be notarized came in unnotarized, and we felt ... well, my understanding was that they, in order to be legal or to up hold in court, they had to be notarized, so I went ahead and notarized them.

The author interrupts the testimony at this point since Ms. Noren appears to state that she notarized some of the letters outside the presence of the affiants. The list of original letters shows only two that were notarized by Ms. Noren: that authored by Bob Curran and that by John Taylor. Later on she testifies that both of these affiants appeared before her in person and she legally notarized their signatures. The question arises, which letters did she notarize outside the presence of the affiants? Ms. Matthew testified that Ms. Noren had shown her as an example, a document that she had already notarized. The document had to be a letter since Noren testified, albeit untruthfully, that she had not notarized any documents other than letters. It will be shown, as it already has been revealed to the reader, that Ms. Noren willfully and knowingly notarized two of the corrected letters outside of the affiant's presence; however, those letters were not in existence when she showed a letter to Ms. Matthew on October 28th, or earlier. The author was denied cross-examination of Mr. Curran and Mr. John Taylor in this matter, more fully explored later.

TR:588   *Judge Fitzpatrick*: Well, let me ask you a question. You said some of the letters that came in which were supposed to be notarized were not notarized. Now, how did you know that the letters were supposed to be notarized? Who told you that?

Ms. Noren: Well, I was in the meeting when Steve spoke with Beau and myself and some of our salesmen who needed to go out and get the letters.

Judge Fitzpatrick: Tell me what happened at that meeting. Tell me to the best of your recollection when that was.

Ms. Noren: It was in October, towards the middle of October, and he told us that we had been told by counsel that we needed to get letters from leaders of the community and different business associates, and that the letters were to be used at this hearing, and that they should be notarized.

Judge Fitzpatrick: Who was present at that meeting?

Ms. Noren: Steve, myself, Beau and some of our salesmen.

Judge Fitzpatrick: Could you identify those individuals?

Ms. Noren: Neil Maybery, Steve Montgomery and Susan Phillips.

Judge Fitzpatrick: Did Mr. West say anything as to whether or not these individuals that were going to be requested to give these letters would have to be made available for cross-examination in an FCC proceeding?

Ms. Noren: I don't recall those exact words.

Judge Fitzpatrick: Well, in any way were the people who were to solicit these letters to inform the people that if they gave a letter, that they might have to appear someplace and testify concerning what they said?

Ms. Noren: That was my understanding.

Judge Fitzpatrick: What was the basis for your understanding?

Ms. Noren: I don't know. I guess because the letters were going to be used in the hearing, that it was as evidence they might have to come in.

Judge Fitzpatrick: Did anyone ask any questions as to how they were supposed to do this?

Ms. Noren: I think they asked whether it was all right to call them on the telephone or if they had to go personally and get them, and it was determined it was fine to call them on the telephone.

Judge Fitzpatrick: Was any explanation given as to why these letters were to be notarized?

Ms. Noren: Because they would be in a court situation and the notary makes it a legal document.

Judge Fitzpatrick: Who said that?

Ms. Noren: I don't think anybody did.

Judge Fitzpatrick: That was your understanding?

Ms. Noren: Yes.

So it is established that Ms. Noren knew that a notarization makes a document legal. It follows, therefore, that the phony verifications were affixed to make the letters legally admissible in a federal proceeding. Intent to file false documents with a federal agency is obvious beyond any doubt.

TR:591   *Judge Fitzpatrick*: Did you solicit any such letters?

Ms. Noren: I got the one from Bob Curran.[33]

Judge Fitzpatrick: Tell us how you went about getting that letter from Mr. Curran.

Ms. Noren: I called him on the telephone at his work and explained the situation, that we were going to have a hearing which I think he was aware of, and that I needed a letter stating how we were, how he had been involved with us during Seafair and different community events during the license period in question, and that the letter needed to be notarized, and that I needed it by a certain date.

Judge Fitzpatrick: Then what happened concerning Major Curran's letter?

Ms. Noren: A couple of days later he came into the station, and I notarized his letter for him and he signed it in front of me.

Judge Fitzpatrick: But he affixed the signature in your presence?

---

[33]Appendix page 21. Letter solicited from Mr. Bob Curran by Ms. Margit Noren.

Ms. Noren: Yes.

Mr. Boros: What difference did you think, if any, existed between someone signing before you and not signing before you?

Ms. Noren: Well, I don't know. In the case of the letters, I thought . . . I didn't even realize that they had to be signed in front of me. I thought it was all right because we needed the notary seal and signature on it, that that was fine to do it, with their approval.

Well, Ms. Noren, why is it, then, as the testimony from some of the affiants will establish, that some of the letters were notarized without their approval? While some of the letters authors did say their approval was sought, you, as a commissioned notary, knew, or should have known, that it is illegal to state "subscribed and sworn to before me on this blank day" when in actual fact this was untrue. Is that what they taught you at Skagit Valley College?

TR:592   *Judge Fitzpatrick*: What was your understanding as to what the notarial seal was representing to the public, somebody that read it? What were they supposed to conclude from that?

Ms. Noren: That it was a true and legal document. When you seal something it makes a print on the paper that is, you're unable to xerox it to duplicate it for any reason. That's my understanding of why you put a seal on it.

The Xerox people will be glad to know that their machines will not pick up the impression of a notary seal. It is the author's understanding that seal impressions were in existence long before the Xerox copying process was invented.

TR:592   *Judge Fitzpatrick*: Now, there came a time when these various people at the meeting went out and solicited letters and the letters started coming back to the station. Was there anybody responsible for receiving and handling these letters, or did they just go to whomever they were addressed? How was that handled?

Ms. Noren: Usually they came to me, and I either kept them in a file, or I usually showed them to Steve West and then put them in a file and kept them all together.

Judge Fitzpatrick: Well, how did they come to you if they were addressed to somebody else? That's what I want to know.

84

Ms. Noren: Well, the salesman who came to me or Steve would get them and give them back to me, to be kept in one place.

Judge Fitzpatrick: Do you have Exhibit 16 in front of you, page 6?[34]

Ms. Noren: Yes.

Judge Fitzpatrick: Now, that's a letter from a Ms. McCullough, addressed to Paul Sullivan. Now, could you just tell me when you first learned that this letter existed and how you learned about it?

Ms. Noren: I believe Paul gave it to me, and I then gave it to Steve.

Judge Fitzpatrick: Now, at the time that Paul gave it to you it didn't contain any notarization, is that correct?

Ms. Noren: No.

Judge Fitzpatrick: Now, when you gave it to Mr. West, did it contain a notarization?

Ms. Noren: No.

Judge Fitzpatrick: Did you and Mr. West or you and Mr. Sullivan have any conversations concerning the fact that there was no notarization on this letter?

Ms. Noren: Yes.

Judge Fitzpatrick: Tell me what was said and by whom.

Ms. Noren: On the, when we were compiling all the letters and had them together and were going to send them out, we realized that there were some that were not notarized.

Judge Fitzpatrick: Do you mean send them to counsel?

Ms. Noren: Yes.

Judge Fitzpatrick: You realized that some of the letters were not notarized?

Ms. Noren: Yes.

Judge Fitzpatrick: Who realized that? All of you?

Ms. Noren: Steve and myself.

Judge Fitzpatrick: You went over the letters together?

Ms. Noren: Yes.

Judge Fitzpatrick: And you recognized that some of them did not contain notarizations?

Ms. Noren: I was in the process of making copies of them.

Judge Fitzpatrick: So then what did you do?

---

[34]Appendix page 9. The Julie McCullough original letter, affixed with a phony verification.

Ms. Noren: We had Carrie and in our station notarize them.

Judge Fitzpatrick: Whose idea was that?

Ms. Noren: Well, at the time I was busy doing something else, so Steve said, "well, Carrie is a notary so let her go ahead and do it."

Judge Fitzpatrick: Well, who was it that suggested that if the letters had not been notarized before they were received at the station, that a notarial seal should be affixed to them at the station? Whose idea was that? Somebody had to suggest it, I assume.

Ms. Noren: Uh-huh, I don't recall, but it was understood that they had to be notarized before they went out. But I don't recall who.

Judge Fitzpatrick: But Mr. West was aware that these letters did not contain the notarizations, and that Ms. Matthew was going to affix her notarial seal to them at the station?

Ms. Noren: Yes.

Judge Fitzpatrick: And he approved that?

Ms. Noren: Yes.

Judge Fitzpatrick: Did you have any discussions with him as to whether that was appropriate or not?

Ms. Noren: No, I don't recall.

Judge Fitzpatrick: Did you have any questions in your mind as to whether that was appropriate or not?

Ms. Noren: I did.

Judge Fitzpatrick: What were the questions that were in your mind?

Ms. Noren: Well, it came to mind that it should be before the person that signed it, or with their approval.

Judge Fitzpatrick: And did you express this view that you had to anybody?

Ms. Noren: I don't recall.

Judge Fitzpatrick: You have no recollection?

Ms. Noren: No.

Judge Fitzpatrick: Weren't you concerned?

Ms. Noren: Yes, I was.

Judge Fitzpatrick: You felt that what was being . . .

Ms. Noren: But I felt that it had been told to me that is what should be done, so . . .

Judge Fitzpatrick: Told to you by whom?

Ms. Noren: By Steve.

Judge Fitzpatrick: He said, "Get this done," is that it?

Ms. Noren: He said get these notarized so that's what I thought we should do.

Judge Fitzpatrick: And you felt that wasn't proper?

Ms. Noren: I had a question in my mind about it.

Judge Fitzpatrick: But you didn't express this question to Mr. West?

Ms. Noren: I don't recall if I did or not.

Judge Fitzpatrick: Is that why you had somebody other than yourself do it?

Ms. Noren: No.

Judge Fitzpatrick: Why didn't you do it?

Ms. Noren: Because I was in the process of getting other papers together and getting other letters at that time, and we were . . . Federal Express was on its way to pick up our package, and I was getting it together for them.

Judge Fitzpatrick: When you asked Ms. Matthew to do this, 6 or 7 of these, whatever the numbers are . . . did you tell her that you had this question in your mind as to whether this was proper to be done?

Ms. Noren: I don't recall.

Judge Fitzpatrick: Did you think you owed that much to her as a fellow notary?

Ms. Noren: I don't know.

Judge Fitzpatrick: I guess what I'm trying to determine is, what was your recollection when Mr. West said, "Oh, look, we have five or six or seven of these letters that haven't been notarized. Let's get it here at the station before we send them on to counsel." What was your reaction when he suggested that?

Ms. Noren: I don't know. I knew also that they had to be notarized.

Judge Fitzpatrick: Yes, but you knew that it should have been in their presence, right, that the signature should have been affixed in the presence of the notary?

Ms. Noren: Or with their approval.

Judge Fitzpatrick: You mean somebody can sign something on Tuesday and call you up on Thursday and say, "That's my signature, notarize it today?" Do you think that's proper?

Mr. Boros: Your Honor, may I suggest respectfully, the real question is not what she thinks is proper today but what she thought was proper then.

Judge Fitzpatrick: What she thought was proper at the time.

Ms. Noren: At that time I thought that was all right, to get their approval over the telephone.

Judge Fitzpatrick: Do you think that today?

Ms. Noren: No.

Judge Fitzpatrick: But at the time you felt in your own mind that it was *improper* to just notarize these things, these letters, without people knowing about it. Is that correct?

Ms. Noren: Yes.

Judge Fitzpatrick: All right. Did you call any of these people?

Ms. Noren: After I did it, yes.

Judge Fitzpatrick: After they were sent to counsel?

Ms. Noren: Yes.

The Ms. Noren testimony establishes that Mr. Stephen West orchestrated the illegal notarizations of the testimonial letters. Since Mr. West is the manager of the station and Ms. Noren his administrative assistant, we are not dealing with low echelon personnel. The culpability is well established. It also shows intent. West gave his orders to have the illegal attestations affixed to the testimonial letters that lacked notarizations. Now, Ms. Noren appears to again state that she was involved in some of the phony notarizations; a fact which further supports a conclusion that one or more of the letters she notarized before the corrections were phony. She also is evasive when asked who might have suggested that the letters should be notarized. This may lead to a conclusion that persons other than West were also involved in making that decision. Since time was a factor, the possibility that counsel or Mr. Smith may have been involved cannot be discounted.

Noren also makes some other puzzling statements. She states that she and Steve noticed that some of the letters were not notarized when she was getting them ready to hand them over to Federal Express, so they had Carrie Matthew notarize them. The first letter Ms. Matthew notarized was on the 28th, that by Ms. McCullough, so if the testimony is true, the phony notarizations started on the 28th. The package of documents, however, must have included the Shawn Taylor letter, dated the 5th of November. Subsequently, in their proposed Findings of Facts and Conclusions of Law, Kaye-Smith counsel stated that the exchange was by *mail*. This switch from sworn testimony is further support that the Noren testimony falls short of being fully candid. Federal Express would be the first to object to their express carrier service being equated with a mail service. The Noren testimony also shows that permission to notarize the letters was after the fact, that is, after they had been sent to counsel and after the author had detected the felonious conduct.

Sure, they called the letter authors after Hoffart discovered their unlawful acts. They had no choice in the matter so they called for permission to notarize the letters, but this was after they had been filed upon the commission and Hoffart. The Judy Balint testimony, part of which has already been revealed, proves this. She was apparently being badgered into giving KISW a properly notarized letter and finally told them to get off her back. Others were more obliging, and some apparently did give permission to KISW to notarize their letters outside of their presence; but this only establishes co-conspiracy to file fraudulently notarized documents with a federal agency, a felony. The author will, as this story unfolds, bring in excerpts from Manager Stephen West's testimony to more fully support his charges that: 1. There was intent to deceive Hoffart, the commission, and the public; and 2. The judge's findings and conclusions that there was no intent are arbitrary, capricious, an abuse of discretion, contrary to the intent of Congress, when they enacted the statute against filing misrepresentations with a federal agency, and contrary to Congressional intent that broadcast licenses be granted only to applicants who will operate in the public interest, convenience or necessity. Furthermore, the evidence and testimony adduced in this case support a finding that the licensee's conduct in this matter falls on the distant side of an abuse of the commissions processes. New standards have now been set by this agency. Clear abuse of processes warrant only a slight demerit which can be erased by a meritorious programming finding.

The fact that Ms. Noren, and others in the employment of Kaye-Smith, did not call or obtain approval to notarize the letters outside the presence of the so-called affiants prior to the submission to counsel, and all other parties, is further established when Mr. Boros asks questions:

TR:600   *Mr. Boros*: Did counsel directly call you about these letters and raise questions about them?
          Ms. Noren: No. They called Steve West.

This testimony will be further explored when counsel Stuart Young testifies, as an officer of the court, from the floor. Mr. Young will testify he called on the 12th of November, the exchange date. Ms. Noren will testify that Mr. West was not there on that date, and West will testify that it was Ms. Noren that was called. This raises the question: Was anybody called on the 12th from New York?

TR:600   *Mr. Boros*: Now, with respect to letting people know their letters had been notarized, did you intend to tell everyone whose letter had been notarized that his or her letter had been notarized and seek their okay?

89

Ms. Noren: The people that got the letters were to go back to those in question and explain the situation.

Mr. Boros: When you say they were to go back, was that your idea?

Ms. Noren: No. That came to me from Steve.

Mr. Boros: Do you know whether this was before or after Veteran's Day, November 11th, 1982?

Ms. Noren: No, I don't.

Mr. Boros: Did Mr. West instruct you to make sure that you or people under your direction or working with you went back to the people whose signatures had been obtained?

Ms. Noren: Yes.

Mr. Boros: What did he say to you?

Ms. Noren: That in some cases we needed to get a new letter; that there was a problem with the dates, either no date on the letter, or they were conflicting with the notary, or there was no date on the notary.

Mr. Boros: Is that all he said to you?

Ms. Noren: Uh-huh.

Mr. Boros: Did you say anything to him?

Ms. Noren: No.

Mr. Boros: Did you undertake to carry out any instructions he gave you?

Ms. Noren: Yes, I did.

Mr. Boros: How did you undertake to do that?

Ms. Noren: I telephoned the people that I was to call back.

Mr. Boros: Was there a group of people you were to call back and a group of people, to your knowledge, that someone else had to call back?

Ms. Noren: The people that I spoke to were after a time when we were waiting to get letters. They would not come and I called them after whoever was supposed to call them was unable to contact them, and I took it upon myself to get ahold of them.

Mr. Boros: Is it fair to say you followed up to clean up loose ends? Is that what happened?

Ms. Noren: Right.

Judge Fitzpatrick: Would you turn to page 13 of Exhibit 16, please. Now that purports to be a letter of October 25, 1982 from a John R. Taylor, and that bears your notari-

90

zation on the lower right-hand side. Is that correct? Is that your signature?[35]

Ms. Noren: Yes.

Judge Fitzpatrick: Did you affix that signature, that notarization, at a time when Mr. Taylor was present and affixed the signature to this letter?

Ms. Noren: Yes, I did.

Judge Fitzpatrick: All right. And the reason for having Mr. Taylor submit a letter of November 22, which is now page 13 (A), and has your notarization of November 23rd, is because your earlier notarization was not dated. Is that correct?[36] (leading question by the judge.)

Ms. Noren: Right.

Judge Fitzpatrick: Just wanted to be sure I understood that.

Mr. Boros: At the time you did your earlier letter for Mr. Taylor and did not date that signature, what was your state of mind? What did you think about whether it was necessary to date?

Ms. Noren I didn't know it was necessary.

Mr. Boros: Is it necessary in the State of Washington?

Ms. Noren: No.

Mr. Boros: That's your understanding, that it's not necessary?

Ms. Noren: Yes.

Judge Fitzpatrick: Is it your understanding that the notary doesn't have to date it if the date appears somewhere else on the document and it's the same date as the notarization?

Ms. Noren: No.

Judge Fitzpatrick: In other words, you could have a document that's totally undated, and you could notarize it without any place indicating the date? Is that your understanding?

Ms. Noren: Yes.

Judge Fitzpatrick: All right.

The author will devote a chapter to this John R. Taylor letter subsequently. For the time being, the reader should remember that one of the reasons given for re-notarizations was to obtain a verification on the same date that the letter was dated. In this correction, as the two appendix exhibits show, the attestation by Ms. Noren was one day after the

---

[35]Appendix page 19. John Taylor original letter
[36]Appendix page 20. John Taylor corrected exhibit.

date of the John Taylor corrected letter. Ms. Noren had no aversions to ignoring West's orders in this regard. There is, of course, nothing wrong with dating a notarial attestation on any date after it is authored, provided the author's signature is affixed before the notary and the notary obtains proper identification.

TR:605   *Mr. Boros*: I'd like you, Ms. Noren, to direct yourself to Exhibit 17. Do you have that before you?
Ms. Noren: Yes, I do.
Mr. Boros: Please turn to page 5 (A). On page 5 (A) there appears to be two signatures on that letter. Could you describe, if you know, how those signatures came to be on that letter?[37]
Ms. Noren: The letter came from Dave Watkins, I did not see him sign it, but I affixed my notary signature and seal to it after speaking to him on the telephone.
Mr. Boros: Well, how did it happen that you spoke to him on the telephone? Did he call you or did you call him?
Ms. Noren: I called him.
Mr. Boros: What did you say to him?
Ms. Noren: I told him that I had been handed the letter from him but it was not notarized, and he said that his notary was out ill that day. And I asked him, would it be with his approval if I notarized it for legal purposes, and he said yes.
Judge Fitzpatrick: Now, this conversation took place on November 17th?
Ms. Noren: Yes.
Judge Fitzpatrick: This was after all of the difficulties had already come to your attention?
Ms. Noren: Yes.

The author has reproduced the two Watkins' letters in the Appendix as pages 13 and 14. In all cases, the suffix (A) behind the page number is an indication that that page is a "corrected" page. The testimony given by Ms. Noren has reference to the corrected David Watkins testimonial letter. The original had been notarized by a Mr. Anthony Tucker and the corrected letter was filed because Mr. Tucker did not date his notarial attestation.

The author does not know if Ms. Noren was referring to Mr. Tucker when she stated that Mr. Watkins told her his notary was ill. When Mr. Watkins will be featured later in this book, verbatim testimony from

---

[37]Appendix page 14. The corrected David Watkins exhibit bearing a phony notarization by Ms. Noren.

Mr. Watkins will show that he said "our notary was not there, and he was in fact out of town for several days."

The damaging testimony by Ms. Noren, up to this point, is that she admitted her notarization of the Watkins letter came after all the difficulties had already come to her attention. The author now goes back and picks up sworn testimony elicited from Station Manager Stephen West when he was questioned by the judge relating to the phony notarial attestation affixed to the Charles Blacksmith testimonial letter:

TR:309   *Mr. West:* We got a letter or phone call from Stu Young the following Friday because I wasn't at work and he talked to Meg Noren and I then talked to him first thing Monday morning and he instructed me to go back out.
Judge Fitzpatrick: You better tell me what was said.
Mr. West: He explained to me basically what you just said, what I have learned in the process that the signature has to be done in front of the notary.
Judge Fitzpatrick: How did he know it wasn't?
Mr. West: Because he questioned, I guess, the fact, that there was more than one that was notarized by Carrie Matthew. There was another thing that he brought up, too: He questioned that in some cases the notary itself was a day or two days after the actual letter was written and he requested those people and instructed me to go back to them and have me stand in front of the notary when they did it, which I did.
Judge Fitzpatrick: Did you tell Mr. Young that you told us today; is that how it happened?
Mr. West: Yes.
Judge Fitzpatrick: And he told you . . .
Mr. West: It doesn't work.
Judge Fitzpatrick: Can't do that?
Mr. West: No.

The West testimony established that he was told, purportedly on the 15th of November, that you cannot affix a notarial attestation to a document unless the affiant appears before the notary. He also stated that he was instructed to stand in front of the notary when they did it . . . "which I did." This will be proven untrue as we pick up the Noren testimony:

TR:606   *Mr. Boros:* Did you think it was all right to put your signature on the letter when you put your signature on on the 17th?
Ms. Noren: Yes, I did.

Mr. Boros: Do you know Mr. Watkins' voice?

Ms. Noren: Yes, I do.

Mr. Boros: You knew his voice on the 17th? Had you ever spoken to him before?

Ms. Noren: Several times. I deal extensively with him with the Seattle Supersonics advertising.

Mr. Boros: When you called him, where did you call him at? Do you know?

Ms. Noren: At his office.

Mr. Boros: You dialed the number yourself?

Ms. Noren: Yes, I did.

Judge Fitzpatrick: Did you tell anybody you did this?

Ms. Noren: I told Steve. He was gone at the time, and I was mailing out this letter that afternoon and he was not in that day. And I told him when he did come in what I had done.

Mr. Boros: What did Mr. West say to you?

Ms. Noren: That was fine.

Judge Fitzpatrick: Can I ask a question? The reason that some of these had to be redone, that was your understanding as to why the Watkins' letter had to be redone? Was it because the notary who did it originally didn't put a date on it?

Ms. Noren: Yes.

Judge Fitzpatrick: Did you check with counsel as to whether the procedure of notarizing signatures that you didn't see the person affix to the document was appropriate?

Ms. Noren: No, I didn't.

Mr. Boros: When his Honor asked you about counsel, did you check with counsel in the State of Washington about notarial duties at any time before you came here today to testify?

Ms. Noren: I read the material that I had that I received when I became a notary. And after reading that, to my understanding it was all right if it was acknowledged by telephone by the person who signed it, the notarization was approved.

The reader's attention is directed to the two Watkins's letters and to the fact that the two letters were not signed by the same hand. The corrected letter, bearing the suffix (A), was actually signed by Mr. Watkin's secretary, with his permission, and was then notarized by Ms. Noren at KISW without anyone appearing before her. In the chapter

94

devoted to Mr. Watkins, his testimony will show that Ms. Noren, or someone at KISW, asked that the unnotarized corrected letter be sent over to them so that they could notarize it there. This sworn testimony makes it all the more sickening to find the judge ruling that there was no intent to deceive anyone, and that the review board called Hoffart's revelations a hodgepoge, typical adversarial puff, and much ado about nothing.

Ms. Noren stated that she informed Mr. West that she had notarized a "corrected" letter outside the presence of Mr. Watkins, and he said "it was fine." How can anyone find that there was no intent to deceive Hoffart or that Mr. West did not perjure himself at the hearing?

TR: 608   *Mr. Boros*: Has any lawyer . . .

Judge Fitzpatrick: I'm not going to accept this witness as any kind of a qualified person to tell me what the laws are to notarizations in the State of Washington, Mr. Boros, not in the view of what's happened here.

Mr. Boros: Oh, we certainly don't intend to argue that she is an expert, it's just the opposite.

Judge Fitzpatrick: Is it your contention that the procedure followed with respect to page 5 (A) is appropriate?

Mr. Boros: It certainly is not any contention because I'm not licensed in the State of Washington, and I don't know. I know what the law is in the State of New York.

Judge Fitzpatrick: Do you think it is appropriate under any circumstances for anybody to say that "subscribed to and sworn to before me this same day" when in fact it's the result of a phone call?

Mr. Boros: My personal position?

Judge Fitzpatrick: Yes, I want to know what your position is.

Mr. Boros: You mean the position of Kaye-Smith?

Judge Fitzpatrick: Your position as counsel representing Kaye-Smith.

Mr. Boros: Well, our position as counsel representing Kaye-Smith was as was set forth in conversations, that it should be done according to the law we are only familiar with, which is New York State law, and New York law you're supposed to appear before a notary public before a document is notarized. That's the law in New York State.

Judge Fitzpatrick: Well, any document that represents that it was subscribed and sworn before the person who's notarizing it, that's a representation that it was done

95

before them, not that it was done on the telephone, Mr. Boros, all right?

Mr. Boros: I have no problems.

Judge Fitzpatrick: As long as we understand each other.

Mr. Boros: I know what the law is in New York State.

Judge Fitzpatrick: I'm not talking about the law. I'm talking about the english language. The english language says, "subscribed and sworn before me."

Mr. Boros: Well, I have no problems with . . .

Judge Fitzpatrick: It doesn't say, "subscribed at another date and sworn to me over the telephone at a later date."

Mr. Boros: I have no problems with that, your Honor. I must say the english language is not necessarily vibrant and vital in all parts of the communications industry.

Judge Fitzpatrick: It should be.

Mr. Boros: I agree with you one hundred percent. Now there I would one hundred percent endorse what you said, not that I don't endorse everything else 99 and 1/10th percent.

Judge Fitzpatrick: I just wanted to know if there was a contention being made.

Mr. Boros: Not on our part, not under New York State law.

Judge Fitzpatrick: I'm not talking about New York State law. I know you are a preeminent attorney called to practice in the State of New York, Mr. Boros, and I happen to be a Judge who's qualified to practice in the State of New York. So we're both New York lawyers and we can kiss each other's hands, but we're not concerned with New York law in this case.

Mr. Boros: As long as we can instruct that we're supposed to notarize with somebody present, at least that's my knowledge.

Mr. Boros: But I want to ask you this, Ms. Noren, did you ever speak to a lawyer in the State of Washington before coming here today about being a notary and what a notary's duties are?

Ms. Noren: No.

Mr. Boros: Now, at any time when you were engaging in these notarial activities, did you think you were doing something which you shouldn't do or that you were cutting corners?

Ms. Noren: No.

Mr. Boros: Now, when you spoke to someone like Mr. Watkins or any outside person outside of KISW, did any of them tell you that there was something wrong or amiss, that you shouldn't be doing what you were doing and putting your name on their signatures without seeing them?

Ms. Noren: No.

The author will recite more direct testimony by Ms. Noren when some of the affiants testify, to show that there is conflicting testimony between the affiants and the Ms. Noren statements. Hoffart cross-examined Ms. Noren regarding the David Watkins phony verification on the corrected letter:

TR:621 *Mr. Hoffart*: . . . and you notarized the David Watkins signature?

Ms. Noren: Yes, I did.

Mr. Hoffart: When Mr. Watkins came in to KISW?

Ms. Noren: No, I did not.

Mr. Hoffart: When you went down to his office?

Ms. Noren: No, I didn't.

Mr. Hoffart: How did it happen, then?

Ms. Noren: I called him on the telephone.

Mr. Hoffart: Oh, that's the one you called on the phone?

Ms. Noren: Yes.

The author's cross-examination was to establish, beyond any doubt, that Mr. Watkins had not appeared before her at any time. The reader may recall that Mr. Stephen West, the station manager, had testified, under oath, that Mr. Watkins had appeared. Let's review that testimony again:

TR:344 *Mr. Hoffart*: Now, looking at 5(A), have you got both copies there in front of you?

Mr. West: Yes.

Mr. Hoffart: Are those two signatures by Mr. David Watkins the same person, some identical? You're not a handwriting expert, I know that.

Mr. West: I'm not going to comment on that.

Mr. Hoffart: Now, this 5 (A) was notarized in your office by a notary public where you're an employee. Is that right?

Mr. West: Uh-huh.

Mr. Hoffart: Did Mr. David Watkins personally come into your office and have that notarized?

Mr. West: Yes.

The author made a point in his Proposed Findings of Fact and Conclusions of Law filed with the judge after the hearing that Mr. West had testified to untruths. In his Initial Decision the judge made no findings or conclusions relating to this perjury. In exceptions to the Initial Decision, Hoffart pointed out to the review board that West had lied in this matter. The review board ruled that West's testimony, under oath, did not rise to the level of perjury. They stated:

> ... the charge that West, Bogel and Noren gave perjured testimony is overblown on the part of Hoffart. Perjury generally connotes a knowingly false statement made under oath. Mere mistakes in recollection or isolated incidents of foregetfulness do not rise to this level.
> (s) Joseph A. Marino, Chairman, Review Board.

Mr. Marino finds that there probably was an error in the recollection of events. The testimony proves otherwise. Mr. West knew that Mr. Watkins had not appeared at KISW. The event was quite recent. Mr. West testified on December 1, 1982 to an event that happened on the 17th of November, a mere two weeks previous to his testimony. It goes beyond the zone of reasonablness that West did not know he was lying. And what about Noren? She stated, in notarizing the Watkins corrected letter, "Subscribed and sworn before me this 17th day of November, 1982". (s) Margit Noren, notary public. Is this a knowingly made false statement? Is this an isolated incident of forgetfulness? Or was it a deliberate attempt to *deceive* all other parties in order to enhance the KISW renewal application? Was there intent to mislead involved?

Just what kind of a judge can reach such conclusions based upon the record evidence? And how can three review board judges and five commissioners agree with that decision?

Preferential treatment, that's how.

13.

JUDY BALINT

Ms. Balint was the next witness called. The reader may recall that Ms. Balint responded to Hoffart's letter of inquiry as to whether or not she had appeared before Ms. Carrie Matthew. The author had enclosed a copy of her testimonial letter showing the Carrie Matthew notarization.[38] It was her response that opened this can of worms. She had stated she had not appeared before Ms. Matthew and did not know that the letter solicited from her would be used by KISW to bolster a legal case.[39]

Ms. Balint was duly sworn upon oath and stated where she lived. She also stated she was office manager and volunteer coordinator for Focus.

TR:630   *Mr. Boros:* I'd like to direct your attention to a document which is before you, and which in the upper right-hand corner has the legend Kaye-Smith Exhibit 16, and then it also has a pagination, page 14, in the upper right-hand corner. Do you have that before you?

Ms. Balint: Right.

Mr. Boros: Now, Ms. Balint, do you know how that document came into existence?

Ms. Balint: I believe, and I really can't recollect whether somebody wrote us a letter or whether we were called on the telephone originally. I really can't quite recall that. We get a lot of requests like this. In any event, we were either called or contacted by mail to send in a letter supporting the public consciousness, I guess, of KISW. And we get requests like that fairly often. It's somewhat routine for us to fill those out because we are a non-profit organization.

Mr. Boros: Now, with respect to the signature which appears on that page. Is that your signature?

Ms. Balint: The Judy Balint one? Yes, that is.

Mr. Boros: When you put your signature on that page, did you do it knowing that KISW was going to make use of the letter with your signature?

Ms. Balint: Not in a legal proceedings, no. I had no idea of that.

---

[38] Appendix page 1. Balint letter with phony notarization.
[39] Appendix page 2. Balint's response to Hoffart.

Judge Fitzpatrick: What was your understanding as to what use was to be made of the letter that had been solicited?

Ms. Balint: Well, as I said, we get these requests quite routinely. My impression was usually the FCC has requirements that stations air a number of PSA's and they ask non-profits to support that, and that's what I thought this was. So that's why I don't recollect it that well, because we get a large number of these coming in and we sort of write them out and put them in. That's my impression of what it was for.

Judge Fitzpatrick: Was it your impression it was to be used before the FCC?

Ms. Balint: Not clearly stated, no. But that was my . . . I mean, that was my inference, I guess. That's what I presumed these things are normally used for, but it wasn't stated.

Judge Fitzpatrick: Can we establish your communication with the person that requested this letter?

Ms. Balint: I believe so, yes.

Judge Fitzpatrick: What's your best recollection as to what was said by them as to what they were requesting you to do, and what use was to be made of the document that you sent to them?

Ms. Balint: I don't think that there was ever any mention made of what it was to be used for. I think the request was made, you know, please send us a support notice saying that we've served the public. And to the best of my recollection, I don't recall any mention being made of what it was going to be used for, whether it was an FCC or a legal. My inference from that was that it was an FCC type of thing but that was not stated.

To this point in the Ms. Balint testimony it is fairly well established that she was not told what use would be made of her letter. She was not told it would be used in an FCC proceeding and obviously not told she would be subject to cross-examination by Hoffart. With reference to the affidavit filed by Kaye-Smith wherein Mr. Bogel swore, under oath, that all affiants had been told their letters would be so used,[40] the Balint testimony establishes that Mr. Bogel perjured himself in that affidavit.

The judge, in his initial decision, found that "in a couple of cases" Mr. Bogel and Mr. West did not inform the affiants that they would be

---

[40]Appendix page 3. Bogel affidavit which Hoffart charges is perjury.

subject to cross-examination, but he ruled that this was an oversight and as such the affidavits do not constitute willful filing of false information with a federal agency.

TR:632   *Mr. Boros*: Was it your impression at the time you put your signature there that there was any limit as to what use could be made of this letter?
Ms. Balint: No, I didn't really think about that, to tell the truth.
Mr. Boros: Now, when you put your name on the letter, was there a Ms. Carrie Matthew in the office at the time you signed the letter?
Ms. Balint: No, No, I wrote this and signed it in my office. And as I recall, I remember thinking at the time there was a request made to have it notarized and I thought to myself, "That's strange. We never usually get that requested." So I, you know, turned a blind eye to that and sent it back unnotarized.
Mr. Boros: And when you sent it back in, do you recall to whom you sent it?
Ms. Balint: No.
Judge Fitzpatrick: Let me ask you a question. You don't recall who it was that contacted you from the station?
Ms. Balint: Not originally. We've had several phone calls since then.
Judge Fitzpatrick: Prior to your sending the letter?
Ms. Balint: No, I really cannot recollect that.
Judge Fitzpatrick: Do you have any recollection as to whether you were informed that were you to send such a letter, you would be expressing a willingness to be subject to cross-examination and be at a hearing concerning its contents?
Ms. Balint: No.
Judge Fitzpatrick: That was not said?
Ms. Balint: No.
Mr. Boros: Are you appearing here this morning of your free will?
Ms. Balint: I was contacted this morning and asked to, if I would come down.
Mr. Boros: And it's fair to say that you were willing to come?
Ms. Balint: Oh, yes.
Mr. Boros: You're not being paid to come down here, are you?

Ms. Balint: No.
Mr. Boros: You're here as a citizen, are you not?
Ms. Balint: Right.

Before Hoffart goes into his cross-examination of Ms. Balint, the reader is reminded that Ms. Balint would have had to appear by subpoena, as has been revealed earlier. The author does not know if she had been told this fact by Kaye-Smith when they asked her to come down to be a witness on their behalf. Mr. Boros made a point with all the witnesses to ask if they were just doing a civic duty by voluntarily appearing to testify. Perhaps none were told that the judge had ordered Kaye-Smith to produce all the witnesses connected with the notarial imperfections.

TR:634   *Mr. Hoffart*: Ms. Balint, when did you first get any information that there may be something wrong with the letter you sent to KISW?
Ms. Balint: It was I think about a week after I had sent it in. Maybe a little bit less, maybe between four or five days and a week after. And again, I honestly can't recollect if it was by mail or telephone call. Somebody called and said, you know, please, would it be okay . . . let me get this right here. Would it be okay if since I hadn't notarized it they had it notarized. Would it be okay if, I believe it was somebody from the station had it notarized, you know, and would that be okay with me, and I said sure, again still not knowing that it was going to be used in any legal proceedings. I really didn't. I didn't ask, either, what it was going to be used for.
Mr. Hoffart: You're talking about after the letter went in. When did you first find out there was something wrong with it and from whom?
Ms. Balint: Well, something wrong with it in the sense that it wasn't notarized. That was what I was told, which was about a week later, and I believe it was a phone call from somebody at the station.
Mr. Hoffart: From KISW?
Ms. Balint: I believe so.
Mr. Hoffart: You don't remember the date?
Ms. Balint: No. As I said, we get a lot of these things coming in and out, and it was somewhat of a routine type of thing so I don't recall.
Mr. Hoffart: Did you receive a letter dated November 13th regarding this letter?

Ms. Balint: Do you have a copy of that, because I might recollect having seen it. Could I take a look at that?
Judge Fitzpatrick: That's fine. When you were called and asked if it would be all right to notarize your signature by somebody at the station, did they tell you at that time that it was to be used in a proceeding and you would be subject possibly to cross-examination?
Ms. Balint: No. Yes, I did see this letter. This is the one that was sent to me.
Mr. Boros: May we have that letter identified for the record, your Honor?
Judge Fitzpatrick: Well, no, you may not. Why would you want to identify it for the record?
Mr. Boros: I don't mean marked for identification. I mean just described.
Judge Fitzpatrick: Oh, I thought it was. It's a letter from Mr. Hoffart to yourself dated what?
Ms. Balint: What's the date on there? November 13th.
Judge Fitzpatrick: You may certainly look at the letter, Mr. Boros, and read it. But I don't see any need to put it in the record unless it's established. I think this record's been burdened enough with letters.
Mr. Boros: I don't want to put it in the record.

In actual fact the letter, and all other letters that the author had written to the affiants were filed with the judge and all parties, including Mr. Boros, in Hoffart's rebuttal to the Kaye-Smith Direct Written Case. So while the letter was not introduced into the record at the hearing, it is still in the records of this case. The official FCC records show that they received this rebuttal on the 22nd of November.

TR:636   *Mr. Hoffart:* Did you receive that letter?
Ms. Balint: Yes, I did.
Mr. Hoffart: Did you receive that letter on November 15th?
Ms. Balint: I presume so. I don't know for sure, but I presume it was around that date.
Mr. Hoffart: You received a letter dated November 13th which happens to be a Saturday, and return receipt requested is dated Monday, November 15th. Do you assume you received it on Monday?
Ms. Balint: Right. As I recall, I don't know if it's important, but I wasn't in the office that day. I don't recognize the signature of the person who signed it.
Mr. Hoffart: Were you in on Tuesday?

103

Ms. Balint: Yes, so I probably got it Tuesday.

Mr. Hoffart: Since you received this letter on a Tuesday, then, that would be on November 16th?

Ms. Balint: Right.

Mr. Hoffart: And KISW called you before the 16th?

Ms. Balint: In regard to this notary?

Mr. Hoffart: Yes.

Ms. Balint: To the best of my recollection, yes. I can't be one hundred percent sure.

Mr. Hoffart: Now, you weren't in on Monday?

Ms. Balint: I was not in on that Monday, the 15th, no.

Mr. Hoffart: And you were not in on a Saturday, obviously?

Ms. Balint: No.

Mr. Hoffart: And you still state that you got . . .

Judge Fitzpatrick: She said she couldn't be sure. Is that what . . .

Ms. Balint: Right. I really don't recall. To the best of my recollection, it did happen before that.

Judge Fitzpatrick: That's your best recollection that the phone call from KISW . . .

Ms. Balint: Yes, must have happened before that.

Mr. Hoffart: In response to my letter, did you respond?

Ms. Balint: No, I don't believe I did. No. See, that was the first time I realized that there was some legal proceedings going on, and I was quite shocked by that.

Mr. Hoffart: You did not send me a return letter?

Ms. Balint: Not to my recollection.

The reader has already been exposed to the letter as it is reproduced in the appendix on page 2. It is dated as having been written on Tuesday, the 16th of November. Ms. Balint was testifying on December 2nd, just about two weeks after the date of the letter. Hoffart had sent her a copy of her testimonial letter, notarized by Ms. Carrie Matthew. Question: Would you, the reader, recollect having sent such a letter after receiving a copy of a testimonial letter you had authored, and had not notarized, but which now supports a notarial verification? The letter, without equivocation, states that she was not aware that this was a legal proceeding. It goes beyond the zone of reasonableness that she knew the letter had been notarized prior to receiving a copy of it, presumably on the 16th. She changes her mind abruptly. Hoffart had the letter in hand.

TR:639   *Mr. Hoffart:* May I approach the bench, your Honor?

Ms. Balint: Maybe I did. Oh, yes.

Judge Fitzpatrick: Please let counsel see whatever you're showing the witness.

Ms. Balint: Yes, you're absolutely right.

Mr. Hoffart: And the letter is dated the 16th?

Ms. Balint: That's right.

Mr. Hoffart: And the letter states "in response to your letter of November 13th, 1982, I did not appear in front of a notary with regard to my letter in support of KISW. I was also not aware that the purpose of these testimonials was to bolster a legal case."

Ms. Balint: Right.

Mr. Hoffart: And you signed it?

Ms. Balint: Correct.

Mr. Hoffart: And you sent me that letter?

Ms. Balint: Right.

Mr. Hoffart: And this is it?

Ms. Balint: This is it.

Mr. Hoffart: Did you subsequently receive another letter from me?

Judge Fitzpatrick: If you don't recall, just say so.

Nice going, judge. While it is proper for a presiding judge to ask probing questions to get at the truth, suggesting answers is not one of their prerogatives. The reader may well know what the response received from Ms. Balint was.

TR:640   *Ms. Balint*: I don't recall. We have so much mail coming out, and this was such a minor thing in our office I don't recall. I might have done it, but I don't recall.

                 Mr. Hoffart: Counsel, do you want to look at this?

Hoffart was trying to introduce a second letter he had written to Ms. Balint. This letter, written immediately after she had advised him that she had not appeared before Ms. Carrie Matthew, or any notary, to have her signature verified, asked her to support her previous response by affidavit. She had not responded to this second letter, and as such Hoffart had only her unnotarized letter to support his allegations that KISW was engaging in illegal notarizations. Not only did the judge prompt Balint on how to respond, he now took over the questioning and denied Hoffart his rights to interrogate Ms. Balint regarding the second letter he had mailed to her.

TR:640   *Judge Fitzpatrick*: After you received the letter from Mr. Hoffart that was dated November 13th, did you get in touch with KISW in any way?

                 Ms. Balint: No.

Judge Fitzpatrick: And after you wrote your letter to him on the 16th, did you get in touch with KISW?

Ms. Balint: No.

Judge Fitzpatrick: Did they get in touch with you?

Ms. Balint: Yes.

Judge Fitzpatrick: When was that?

Ms. Balint: About a week to ten days ago, right before Thanksgiving. (Thanksgiving in 1982 was on the 25th)

Judge Fitzpatrick: Could you tell me what the communication was, who it was that contacted you, what was said?

Ms. Balint: I got a call from Tamara at KISW who said the original letter wasn't notarized. Please, could I send them another letter, because this notarization wasn't satisfactory. Please, could I send them another letter, I believe, and give them my okay to have it notarized.

Judge Fitzpatrick: And give them your okay to have it notarized?

Ms. Balint: Right. That's again to the best of my recollection what happened. And I at that point had already left the office so my co-worker wrote a letter and I believe she signed it on to her signature, Ann Burnes. And the person actually came to our office to pick that up, and I believe she gave that to whoever it was that came to pick it up.

The testimony by Ms. Balint establishes that KISW sent a representative to Focus to pick up a corrected letter and that one was supplied and signed, presumably, by Ann Burnes. No corrected letter was filed by Kaye-Smith in this matter. It should be obvious that a corrected letter signed by another person would not be acceptable. The testimony further establishes that Ms. Tamara Kern, Mr. Bogel's secretary, asked for permission to notarize this second letter. This is at a time when all of the difficulties and felonious conduct had been brought to the attention of their counsel and Mr. Smith.

The Balint testimony up to this point does not square up with that given by Mr. Bogel when questioned about the Balint original letter.

TR:494 *Judge Fitzpatrick*: Page 14. A letter of Judy Balint. What, if anything, do you know concerning that notarization?

Mr. Bogel: Since yesterday when this letter first came up I spoke with my secretary, who actually did go out under my direction and got this letter.

Judge Fitzpatrick: Her name is?

Mr. Bogel: Tamara Kern. She explained to me that like many of the public service agencies they're staffed by volunteers. The woman that she spoke with is named

Ann. Ann is the head person of Focus. Ann was explained the same wording that we told everybody else, that we're going to be going to court to determine our license renewal. Our license is being challenged. It's important to go back and get testimony about community services and leaders that we've worked with, and it must be notarized. Ann heard that, seemed to understand that I assumed from what my conversation with Tamara were, and lo and behold, we got a letter from Focus but it was signed by Judy Balint. So it's not impossible to understand why Judy Balint doesn't know anything about it, because she wasn't the person that was originally contacted but she was the person that wrote the letter.

The Ms. Balint testimony is not on parallel tracks with that given by Mr. Bogel earlier. It is now clear that it was Tamara Kern who picked up a second letter, one that was not filed in the case. The first letter had been sent to KISW by Ms. Balint, as she testifed, under oath.

It is also clear that Mr. Bogel testified untruthfully when he stated that Tamara Kern actually went out under his direction and got this letter. With only one Judy Balint letter in the official record it is obvious that Mr. Bogel was trying to cover up the fact that a second letter had been solicited and apparently signed by an Ann Burnes. It was this second letter that was picked up by Ms. Kern after the badgering by KISW for a corrected letter.

TR:641   *Mr. Hoffart*: This second letter, did you send Mr. Hoffart a copy?
Ms. Balint: No.
Judge Fitzpatrick: Do you have occasion to have your signature notarized frequently or infrequently?
Ms. Balint: Infrequently.
Judge Fitzpatrick: Do you know what the purpose of a notarization is?
Ms. Balint: To verify that the signature is correct.
Judge Fitzpatrick: And that it's done before a notary so they see the person doing it?
Ms. Balint: Right.
Judge Fitzpatrick: Did you have that in mind when they called you and said, "do you give us authorization to notarize your signature?"
Ms. Balint: Frankly, what I had in mind was to get out of this whole mess since we were so unaware of whatever was going on.
Judge Fitzpatrick: I can understand that.

Ms. Balint: I really hadn't given it much thought, no. We just wanted to say, "Here, get on with it, here it is, leave us alone."

Judge Fitzpatrick: All right.

Hoffart has charged that KISW personnel appeared to have badgered the Focus people into supplying them with a corrected letter. The testimony establishes that Tamara Kern picked up a corrected letter, but it was not filed by counsel for Kaye-Smith. Up to now this Judy Balint testimony compared with that given by Mr. Bogel is a hodgepodge of conflicting testimony. It is clear that Mr. Bogel is stretching the truth in this matter. Perhaps an investigative reporter will call upon Ms. Ann Burnes and also on Ms. Tamara Kern and sort out the truth from the fiction. Perhaps Ms. Balint has more to offer. Her name was raked through the mud by KISW personnel and specifically by Mr. Bogel whose sworn testimony appears to establish that it is Ms. Balint who is untruthful. The author now returns to his questioning of Ms. Balint at the point where he was cut off by the judge.

TR:642   *Mr. Hoffart*: I'll show you this letter of November 18, 1982, addressed to you and signed by . . .

Judge Fitzpatrick: Have you shown it to counsel?

Mr. Hoffart: I showed him. He read it.

Mr. Boros: That is the letter I've read, yes.

Mr. Hoffart: Did you receive that letter from Mr. Hoffart?

Ms. Balint: Again, I must say I'm not sure. This was the second letter?

Mr. Hoffart: Yes.

Ms. Balint: I don't recall having seen this, no.

Mr. Hoffart: Did you receive any reembursements in the way of postage or anything for your letters?

Ms. Balint: No.

The author had enclosed self-addressed stamped envelopes in each of the two letters he wrote to Ms. Balint. Her response to his first letter made use of the envelope and postage supplied by Hoffart. She did not respond to the request by Hoffart that she support her first letter by affidavit, a request made in a second letter to her. She states she did not receive the second letter.

TR:643   *Mr. Hoffart*: Were you the person that was originally called by KISW, approached . . .

Ms. Balint: I believe so, yes.

Mr. Hoffart: . . . for a letter?

Ms. Balint: Right.

Mr. Hoffart: And what were you told was the need for this letter?

Ms. Balint: To the best of my recollection, again I don't recall whether it was by mail or by phone. There was no explanation given. It was just, you know, would you mind writing a letter supporting our public service type stuff.

Mr. Hoffart: You don't recall whether you got a letter or by phone?

Ms. Balint: No.

Judge Fitzpatrick: Thank you very much for coming down and having your routine interrupted by virtue of this. We appreciate it.

14.

JOHN DANIEL McCONNELL

Kaye-Smith had solicited a testimonial letter from Mr. John Daniel McConnell. He provided them with such a letter without any notarization or verification of his signature. Subsequently, on an unknown date, Ms. Carrie Matthew notarized this letter outside the presence of Mr. McConnell upon instructions from senior notary Ms. Noren. The letter was then filed with the FCC and all other parties on November 11th or 12th, 1982. As with all of the other testimonial letters that were affixed with illegal notarizations, Kaye-Smith did not reveal to Hoffart, or anyone else, that the notarial act had been performed outside the presence of the authors of the letters. As Ms. Noren has already testified, the letters were so notarized to make them legal. This revelation by Ms. Noren establishes intent to engage in misrepresentations to a federal agency, a felony. The acts were not accidental or inadvertent. Since at least four Kaye-Smith employees were involved with this particular McConnell illegal notarization, it is self-evident that conspiracy to commit a crime also surfaces. It also appears that Mr. McConnell was a willful party to the notarization of his signature outside of his presence.

Mr. John Daniel McConnell was duly sworn upon oath. He gave his home address and also his business address. It developed that he owns a public relations firm in Seattle.

TR:645   *Mr. Boros*: Now, in connection with your public relations activities, did a time come in the fall of 1982 when you were contacted by people from station KISW about supplying the station with a letter or a document setting forth your esteem or evaluation of the station?
Mr. McConnell: Yes, there did.
Mr. Boros: About when was that, if you can remember, sir?
Mr. McConnell: It was about midmonth in October, if I remember correctly.
Mr. Boros: Do you recall who called you or contacted you, or communicated to you from station KISW?
Mr. McConnell: I talked initially to Neil Mabery in the sales department, and also to Steve West.
Mr. Boros: When you say initially, was this in mid-October?
Mr. McConnell: Yes.

Mr. Boros: Do you recall what Mr. Mabery said to you about the letter or document he wanted from you and what you said to him?

Mr. McConnell: Yes. Certainly paraphrasing, but in general the conversation was that I was informed by Neil that there was a licensing hearing of some sort coming up for the station, and that he would like for me to, because of our past association, write a reference letter, if you will, for use in that hearing.

Mr. Boros: What did you say to him when he told you about the hearing?

Mr. McConnell: I said because of our past association I would be glad to do so.

Mr. Boros: Now, do you recall when Mr. West spoke to you about a reference sort of letter?

Mr. McConnell: I believe I talked to him either the same day or the day after Neil Mabery first contacted me.

Mr. Boros: What did Mr. West say to you about the letter?

Mr. McConnell: In much the same fashion, he said he needed a reference letter. He needed it notarized as well. And if I would provide that to him as soon as possible, it would be very helpful.

Mr. Boros: What did you say to Mr. West?

Mr. McConnell: I said I would endeavor to do so.

Mr. Boros: Now, sir, I show you a letter which consists of one page. In the upper right-hand corner above the name, The McConnell Company, appears the legend Kaye-Smith Exhibit 17, page 6, Will you look at that document, please, or that letter?[41]

Mr. McConnell: Yes, I have.

Mr. Boros: There's a signature there?

Mr. McConnell: Yes.

Mr. Boros: Is that your signature?

Mr. McConnell: It is.

Mr. Boros: And is that material which appears above your signature material which you authorized?

Mr. McConnell: That is correct.

Mr. Boros: Now, when you signed and affixed your signature to the letter, was there a notary public in the room?

Mr. McConnell: No, there was not.

---

[41]Appendix page 22. McConnell's original letter followed by the corrected exhibit on appendix page 23.

Mr. Boros: Thereafter, what did you do after signing the letter with the letter itself?

Mr. McConnell: Because there was no notary at hand and I had not been instructed as to where one was readily available, I thought timing was more important. So rather than leave the letter sitting on my desk, I put it in an envelope with a note on it to Steve West at the station saying that I knew it wasn't notarized, but perhaps the letter would help in the form in which I was sending it to him.

Mr. Boros: Did a time come when you heard from Mr. Steve West again about the letter which you first had sent, raising any questions about the letter and/or the notarization of it?

Mr. McConnell: Yes. It came late in the month, I believe it was the last week of October.

Mr. Boros: And what did Mr. West say to you?

Mr. McConnell: He said that because the letter that I had sent had not been notarized in my presence, that there might be some question as to the validity of the letter and my signature, and could I please provide for them another letter which I would then sign in the presence of a notary.

Mr. Boros: What did you say to Mr. West?

Mr. McConnell: I said I would be glad to do so.

Mr. McConnell has testified that Mr. West called him in regards to a new letter, properly notarized, in the last week of October. The original letter, the one bearing the phony verification, was dated October 29th, 1982. Giving Mr. McConnell the benefit of the doubt, because he might not have had an accurate recollection of events and dates, it still appears odd that Mr. West would have questioned the validity of Mr. McConnell's signature and also requested a new letter which, as will be proven, was not authored until November 16th. Kaye-Smith, however, had filed the letter with the phony verification upon Hoffart, the judge and the commission on the 11th or 12th of November. The question arises as to why the requested new letter was not authored until after Hoffart had written Mr. McConnell a letter questioning his appearance before Ms. Carrie Matthew. Dropping back to the sworn testimony by Ms. Matthew:

TR:559   *Mr. Boros*: Now, I am turning to page No. 6. There is a letter from the McConnell Company, and at the bottom there appears to be a signature of a Carrie Matthew. Is that your signature?

Ms. Matthew: Yes, it is.

Mr. Boros: How did that get on the page?

Ms. Matthew: I was instructed by a Meg Noren to sign and notarize this.

Going back to sworn testimony elicited from Ms. Noren, who instructed junior notary Ms. Matthew to illegally notarize the McConnell letter, and four others, Ms. Noren tells the court that it was Mr. West who wanted the letters notarized outside the presence of the authors of the letters:

TR:594 *Ms. Noren:* On the, when we were compiling all the letters and had them together and were going to send them out, we realized that there were some that were not notarized.

Judge Fitzpatrick: Do you mean send them to counsel?

Ms. Noren: Yes.

Judge Fitzpatrick: You realized that some of the letters were not notarized?

Ms. Noren: Yes.

Judge Fitzpatrick: Who realized that? All of you?

Ms. Noren: Steve and myself.

Judge Fitzpatrick: You went over the letters together?

Ms. Noren: Yes.

Judge Fitzpatrick: And you recognized that some of them did not contain notarizations?

Ms. Noren: I was in the process of making copies of them.

Judge Fitzpatrick: So then what did you do?

Ms. Noren: We had Carrie in our station notarize them.

Judge Fitzpatrick: Whose idea was that?

Ms. Noren: Well, at the time I was busy doing something else, so Steve said, "Well, Carrie is a notary so let her go ahead and do it."

It appears strange that Mr. West did not know that some of the letters were not notarized until they were sent to counsel, purportedly on the 9th or 10th of November. Mr. McConnell testified that he included a note with his October 29th letter advising Mr. West that the letter was not notarized. The reader is also reminded that Ms. Carrie Matthew affixed a phony notarial attestation as early as October 28th, when she purportedly notarized the McCullough testimonial letter.

TR:648 *Mr. Boros:* . . . would you look at that document which you have before you with the legend 6 (A) on it?

Mr. McConnell: Page 6 (A), and in parentheses it says corrected page 6, on the copy I have in front of me.

Mr. Boros: Now, there's a signature there?

Mr. McConnell: Yes.

Mr. Boros: Is that your signature?

Mr. McConnell: Yes, it is.

Mr. Boros: When did you put on that signature?

Mr. McConnell: In view of the date on here, it would have been on November 16th. And any statement I might have made as to timing, I believe I was confused by seeing the October date on the first letter and I thought that was the second letter.

Mr. Boros: Now, when did you affix . . .

Judge Fitzpatrick: Excuse me. I don't understand what you're saying.

Mr. McConnell: I had looked at the first exhibit here, thinking that it perhaps was the second letter that I had signed. And therefore I think I said I was initially, or secondarily, contacted at the end of November or the end of October. It would have been the middle of November at the time the second one was dated.

Judge Fitzpatrick: When you were asked by Mr. West for a second letter it was in the middle of November?

Mr. McConnell: That's correct.

Mr. Boros: Now, where did you affix your signature to the second letter, the letter which appears in page 6 (A)?

Mr. McConnell: At the KISW station.

Mr. Boros: Was anyone present when you affixed your signature?

Mr. McConnell: Yes. Steve West and a notary public in their office.

Mr. Boros: Did you sign in the presence of the notary public and Steve West?

Mr. McConnell: Yes, I did.

Judge Fitzpatrick: Was it Ms. Noren?

Mr. McConnell: Yes, that's correct.

Mr. Boros: Did you, at the time you signed the letter before Steve West and the notary public, impose any restrictions upon the use which could be made of the letter?

Mr. McConnell: I did not.

Mr. Boros: Do you intend . . .

Judge Fitzpatrick: Which letter are we talking about? The first one, the second one, or both?

Mr. Boros: The second one, because I said the one signed before . . .

Judge Fitzpatrick: Excuse me. You did?

Mr. Boros: Did you impose any restriction on the use which could be made of that letter?

Mr. McConnell: I did not.

Mr. Boros: What did you think would be the use which would be made of the letter at the time you signed it before Steve West and the notary public?

Mr. McConnell: I believe that it was going to be used in a hearing of some sort regarding licensing of the station, in the way of reference for past business practices by the station.

Mr. Boros: With reference to your letter as signed before Steve West and the notary public, is your letter and the statements set out therein true and correct?

Mr. McConnell: To my knowledge, yes.

Judge Fitzpatrick: Let me ask you a question. When you were first requested to send a letter, they had asked you to have it notarized?

Mr. McConnell: Correct.

Judge Fitzpatrick: Had you been told that it was to be submitted as sworn testimony in a proceeding before the FCC?

Mr. McConnell: They had not said that specifically, no. Only that it would be used in a proceeding of some sort.

Judge Fitzpatrick: Had you been told that you might possibly be subject to cross-examination concerning the content of your letter?

Mr. McConnell: No, I was not.

Judge Fitzpatrick: Now, when you wrote the second letter, were you told that it would be used as testimony in a proceeding before the FCC?

Mr. McConnell: I was told that it would be used in a proceeding, again not as testimony. Not those specific words, no.

Judge Fitzpatrick: Were you told with respect to the second letter that there was a possibility that you might be called to be cross-examined concerning contents of the letter?

Mr. McConnell: I was not.

This may be a good time to review the content of the supporting affidavit to Kaye-Smith exhibit 17 as executed by Mr. Steve West. Mr. McConnell is on the attachment list filed with this affidavit.[42]

The affidavit states, without equivocation, that it was explained to each affiant that his or her affidavit would be used as testimony in a proceeding before the Federal Communications Commission. Mr. McConnell states, in his sworn testimony that he was not so informed, either in the original request for a letter or the second request. The reader may also recall that the judge, at the pre-hearing, issued an order that all affiants were to be informed that they could be subject to cross-examination. Presumably counsel passed this information down to Mr. Smith and Mr. West. Yet here we have an affiant on the witness stand that testifies he was never informed that he would be subject to cross-examination. It will also be shown, *infra,* that another affiant that was on the attachment list relating to exhibit 16 also was not fully informed. That exhibit also had a similar affidavit executed by Mr. West. Thus we have repetition of a disregard of the judge's orders by Mr. West, and it is well settled that there is no need for a showing of willfullness when there is repetition involved.

You may recall what the judge found on this matter: "In some cases affiants were not informed, but this appears to be an oversight." And don't forget the review board's findings and conclusions: "hodgepodge of allegations and accusations . . . typical adverserial puff and much ado about nothing."

Representative Hanson should have been so lucky as to have judges with such wisdom sitting on the bench when he was charged with violations of Title 18, U.S.C. Section 1001, the statute against filing false statements with the U.S. Government.

TR:652   *Mr. Boros:* May I . . .
Judge Fitzpatrick: Let me ask one further question, and Mr. Boros, you can follow up to your heart's content. Did there come a time when you learned that the first letter that you wrote had been notarized by someone?
Mr. McConnell: Yes.
Judge Fitzpatrick: When did you learn that?
Mr. McConnell: At the same time I was asked to write the letter and to come to the station to sign it in presence of a notary.
Judge Fitzpatrick: This is with respect to the request for a second letter?
Mr. McConnell: Yes.

---

[42]Appendix pages 7 and 8. West's affidavit and attachment.

Judge Fitzpatrick: And they told you that they had notarized your first letter?

Mr. McConnell: Yes.

Judge Fitzpatrick: Had anybody asked your permission to do that?

Mr. McConnell: The station as such, I believe, yes, had asked my permission in the regard that they had asked that the letter be notarized and I had not done that for them.

Judge Fitzpatrick: Well, that's all that they asked you, to have it notarized?

Mr. McConnell: Correct.

Judge Fitzpatrick: But your sending an unnotarized letter to them didn't give them permission to do anything, did it?

Mr. McConnell: Perhaps implied, but no.

Mr. Boros: At the time you appeared before the notary and Steve West to sign the second letter, did you already then know that the first letter had been notarized outside your presence?

Mr. McConnell: I did.

Mr. Boros: Did you state any objection to . . .

Judge Fitzpatrick: Mr. Boros, I don't care whether he objects or doesn't object. He can't nunc pro tunc something that was done by consent of a later date. Please.

Mr. Boros: I'm going to make an offer of proof if I may, your Honor.

Judge Fitzpatrick: You may.

Mr. Boros: . . . that it was testified that he had no objection to his signature being notarized outside of his presence.

Judge Fitzpatrick: Maybe the rest of the world does, all right? And maybe this court does.

Mr. Boros: I'm just making an offer of proof.

Judge Fitzpatrick: It's been accepted as an offer of proof.

Mr. Boros: Now, when you were asked to appear here today, were you served with any summons or were you just asked to appear here today?

Mr. McConnell: I was just asked to appear by telephone call.

Mr. Boros: And you're appearing voluntarily?

Mr. McConnell: I am.

Mr. Boros: You're appearing as a citizen; is that the reason you're appearing?

Mr. McConnell: I am.

Mr. Boros: And you're not being paid for your appearance?

Mr. McConnell: I am not.

Judge Fitzpatrick: He wouldn't have to be a citizen to appear here. You could have a wetback.

Mr. Boros: Your Honor, you took away my last question.

TR:655   *Mr. Hoffart*: How were you approached by Mr. Mabery?

Mr. McConnell: Initially I was called on the telephone by Mr. Mabery.

Mr. Hoffart: Just exactly what did Mr. Mabery tell you as to the need for this letter?

Mr. McConnell: He said that there was a licensing hearing for renewal of the station's license, and that the station needed some local references of people or businesses that they have worked with, and would I write for him such a letter to be used in that hearing.

Mr. Hoffart: Were there any references as to who was challenging the license?

Mr. McConnell: Not specifically, no. I was not told that there was a challenge to the license.

Mr. Hoffart: Did you attach a note to the letter that you sent to Mr. West?

Mr. McConnell: To the first letter I sent, yes, I did.

Mr. Hoffart: Someplace there should be documentation that there was a note on this letter that you gave permission to have your letter notarized?

Judge Fitzpatrick: That's not the witness's testimony.

Mr. Hoffart: Was there a . . .

Mr. McConnell: There was a note on the first letter which said I knew the letter was not notarized because I had not found a notary, but that I hoped in its form the letter would be useful to the station.

Mr. Hoffart: Now, on the 16th, then, did you personally appear before a notary at KISW?

Mr. McConnell: That is correct.

Mr. Hoffart: Were you requested to produce identification?

Mr. McConnell: Yes, I was.

Mr. Hoffart: In what form was this identification?

Mr. McConnell: My drivers license.

Mr. Hoffart: Who asked for this driver's license?

Mr. McConnell: The notary, Ms. Noren.

The author, Hoffart, had cross-examined Ms. Noren about her notarization of the second McConnell letter on the 16th of November. The reader is again reminded that the events in this book were of quite recent nature, and as such it is hardly likely that a recollection of events is a factor here. Mr. McConnell was testifying on December 2nd, 1982 to a notarization of a letter dated the 16th, just about two weeks in the past. The fact that he did not know where to find a notary for his first letter supports a conclusion that he notarizes documents infrequently; therefore, this notarization, which required travel to KISW should have stood out in his mind, and probably did.

TR:622   *Mr. Hoffart*: 6 (A), Exhibit 17. Did you notarize for Dan McConnell?
Ms. Noren: Yes, I did.
Mr. Hoffart: Did you ask Mr. McConnell for any identification?
Ms. Noren: No, I didn't.
Mr. Hoffart: Did you know this man that was before you was Dan McConnell?
Ms. Noren: I was introduced to him as Dan McConnell, yes.
Mr. Hoffart: Who introduced you to him?
Ms. Noren: Neil Mabery.
Mr. Hoffart: Who's that?
Ms. Noren: He's an account executive for Dan's agency.
Mr. Hoffart: And you took their word that this man was Mr. McConnell, and you never checked?
Ms. Noren: Yes, I did.

We now have conflicting testimony in the official record. Ms. Noren swears upon her oath that she did not ask Mr. McConnell for identification. Mr. McConnell states she asked for identification and he produced his drivers license. Ms. Noren states that she was introduced to Mr. McConnell by a Mr. Neil Mabery before he affixed his signature. Mr. McConnell states only the notary, Ms. Noren and Mr. Steve West were present when he affixed his signature. Hoffart does not know who is resorting to untruths, Ms. Noren or Mr. McConnell. Perhaps some enterprising reporter will find this interesting. Usually when conflicting testimony is elicited from witnesses, it is from opposite sides of the case. In this case *all* of the conflicting statements are between Kaye-Smith personnel and Kaye-Smith witnesses or conflicting testimony between Kaye-Smith employees, or by the employee standing alone. There is also conflicting testimony by one or more of the authors of testimonial letters, as will be documented.

For the record, the Kaye-Smith employee roster shows a Mr. Neil Maberry as an account executive. The spelling of his name up to now is as it was recorded by the court reporter.

Mr. McConnell is one of the letters authors to whom Hoffart had written a letter asking him if he had personally appeared before Ms. Carrie Matthew. As with all the letters Hoffart sent, he had enclosed a copy of the exhibits as notarized by Ms. Matthew. Also enclosed was a self-addressed stamped envelope. Mr. McConnell had not responded to Hoffart.

TR:657   *Mr. Hoffart*: Would you look at this return receipt, certified?

Mr. McConnell: Yes, I see it.

Mr. Hoffart: And the return receipt is dated November 16, 1982?

Mr. McConnell: Yes.

Mr. Hoffart: Is that your signature on this return receipt?

Mr. McConnell: It is not.

Mr. Hoffart: Did you receive the letter on that date?

Mr. McConnell: I received the letter. I do not remember the date I received it.

Judge Fitzpatrick: It was received, acknowledged and received by somebody in your office on the 16th?

Mr. McConnell: Yes. On this receipt is the signature of one of my employees.

Mr. Hoffart: Then on the same date that this receipt was received at your office, you appeared at KISW with a new letter?

Mr. McConnell: That is correct.

Mr. Hoffart: Did you receive my letter before you received any calls from KISW?

Mr. McConnell: I don't remember in the order in which they were received. It was at about the same time.

Mr. Hoffart: But the call from KISW was the first you heard about any problem with this letter?

Mr. McConnell: That is correct.

Mr. Hoffart: My letter was not the first information you received?

Mr. McConnell: It was not. When I received your letter I knew of the problem.

Mr. Hoffart: Now, this letter, it says in here, "Please advise Hoffart by letter if you personally appeared before this notary, Carrie Matthew, and if so on what date and what location." And did you respond to Hoffart?

Mr. McConnell: I did not.

Mr. Hoffart: Did this letter contain a self-addressed stamped envelope?

Mr. McConnell: I don't remember.

Judge Fitzpatrick: Did you bring Mr. Hoffart's letter to the attention of anybody at KISW?

Mr. McConnell: Yes.

Judge Fitzpatrick: To whom?

Mr. McConnell: Mr. West.

Judge Fitzpatrick: What did you say to him and what did he say to you?

Mr. McConnell: I said that I had received a letter regarding this proceedings. I had not read it thoroughly. I had read through it to see that it was asking for some response regarding my first letter. I asked him if the letter I had notarized in the presence of their notary would suffice . . . in this matter, and was told by Mr. West, yes, it would.

Judge Fitzpatrick: Did you ask Mr. West whether or not you should communicate with Mr. Hoffart?

Mr. McConnell: Yes, I did.

Judge Fitzpatrick: What did he tell you?

Mr. McConnell: No, that was not necessary.

That ended the McConnell testimony. The judge had finished off what Hoffart was attempting to establish. The testimony just concluded shows that Mr. West advised a potential witness, and as it were, an actual witness, not to respond to Hoffart. Two similar incidents of interference with potential and actual witnesses will be documented. Hoffart had charged Kaye-Smith with witness-tampering. The charge was swept under the rug because witness tampering is unlawful and basically disqualifying.

15.

SEAN TAYLOR (SHAWN)

Mr. Sean Taylor's name is on the list of affiants that was affixed to the Eric Bogel affidavit in which he swore that all affiants were aware that their letter would be used in an FCC proceeding. The reader has already read some of the Bogel testimony as it relates to this Mr. Taylor. Now let's see the Taylor side of the picture.

Mr. Taylor was duly sworn upon oath and stated that he lives in Kirkland, Washington but has an office in Seattle. When asked his occupation he stated that he was an exploring executive for the Boy Scouts of America.

TR:662   *Mr. Boros:* Did a time come in the fall of this year when you, sir, were contacted by a representative or person from station KISW FM about giving a letter to station KISW FM for use by the station proceeding before the FCC?
Judge Fitzpatrick: Mr. Boros, I ask you to be a little less leading with the witness. Just ask was he contacted, what he was told.
Mr. Boros: Did a time come in the fall of this year when you were contacted by a representative of station KISW FM about an FCC proceeding?
Mr. Taylor: The topic came up. The conversation was initiated by me.
Mr. Boros: How did the topic arise?
Mr. Taylor: I was talking to KISW about their involvement with the Boy Scouts and I was talking about Beau Phillips and he said. "We're interested in building up our file of community service kinds of things, and this might be a good thing for us. Would you mind writing us a letter."
Mr. Boros: And what did you say to him?
Mr. Taylor: Sure.
Mr. Boros: Did Mr. Phillips give you any other information about the use he would make of the letter? And by Mr. Phillips you mean Beau Phillips, otherwise known as Eric Bogel? Or perhaps you don't know that.
Mr. Taylor: The person I was talking to at the time was a person I knew as Beau Phillips.
Mr. Boros: Right.

Mr. Taylor: And in that conversation I don't think he did give me any other information.

Mr. Boros: Now, did you thereafter do anything to present or provide Mr. Beau Phillips with a document for his use?

Mr. Taylor: Uh-huh. I drafted a letter.

Mr. Boros: You say you drafted a letter. Do you mean you authored it yourself?

Mr. Taylor: I wrote the letter. My secretary typed it and I delivered it to the station.

Mr. Boros: You delivered it personally to the station?

Mr. Taylor: Uh-huh.

Mr. Boros: And I direct your attention to a document before you which consists of two pages, and in the upper right-hand corner it has the legend Kaye-Smith Exhibit 16.

Mr. Taylor: Is there a page number?

Judge Fitzpatrick: Do you have pages 7 and 8?[43]

Mr. Taylor: That's correct.

Mr. Boros: Did a time come when you were asked to execute another letter?

Mr. Taylor: Yes.

Mr. Boros: When did that time come?

Mr. Taylor: I think the date on my second copy of this letter is November 23rd. But I can't . . .

Mr. Boros: Well, I direct your attention to the following two pages, pages 7 (A) and 8 (A) of Kaye-Smith Exhibit 16, and ask you to look at those pages and see if that refreshes your memory in any respect.[44]

Mr. Taylor: No, my memory was accurate to start with. It was the 23rd.

Mr. Boros: Now, what happened on or about the 23rd which caused you to write a second letter?

Mr. Taylor: I received a letter from Mr. Hoffart asking if my original letter had indeed been notarized in my presence.

Mr. Boros: What did you do when you received that letter from a Mr. Hoffart?

Mr. Taylor: I didn't do anything.

---

[43]Appendix pages 15 and 16. Page 16 is a phony notarial verification by Ms. Matthew.
[44]Appendix pages 17 and 18 Shawn Taylor's corrected letter.

Mr. Boros: Did a time come when someone called you about your original letter, other than Mr. Hoffart writing you?

Mr. Taylor: No. I brought that up in the course of a conversation that I had initiated with KISW on another matter.

Mr. Boros: When you say you brought that up, what did you bring up with KISW?

Judge Fitzpatrick: Can you identify with whom it was you were speaking?

Mr. Taylor: I think again on that occasion I was speaking with Beau Phillips. I may have been with Steve Montgomery but I believe it was Mr. Phillips.

Mr. Boros: What did you bring up with whomever you spoke to, when you spoke to them in the course of some other matter?

Mr. Taylor: I said, "Oh, by the way, I received a letter regarding my letter to you."

Mr. Boros: What was said to you in response by whomever you were speaking to at station KISW?

Mr. Taylor: I think he said, "What was that about?"

Mr. Boros: What did you say?

Mr. Taylor: I said that I had been requested to respond as to whether my original letter had been notarized in my presence or not. He said that there were some conflicts with the date of the notary stamp and the date of the letter, and would I mind sending them another copy of that letter notarized by someone that I would locate, in which the date on the letter and the date of the notary signature coincide.

Mr. Boros: And what did you say to that?

Mr. Taylor: Sure.

Now that is strange. The reader has already been made aware, through testimony by Mr. Bogel and by Ms. Matthew that there was no discrepancy between the date of the original Sean Taylor letter and the date of notarization. Both are dated November 5th, 1982. The reader may also note that the letter is signed Shawn Taylor, but the transcript heading shows Sean Taylor. Hoffart is following the transcript, verbatim. This discrepancy in names crops up elsewhere and is due to the fact that three different court reporters were used in this case. The judge had not anticipated the hearing to last more then two days, but the Kaye-Smith notarial imperfections fiasco turned the hearing into four days. But let's go back and review some of the Bogel testimony at this point.

TR:509   *Mr. Hoffart*: Now, in the new affidavit did Mr. Sean Taylor approach you or anybody at the station, to your knowledge, or did you approach Sean Taylor for the affidavit?

Mr. Bogel: For the corrected affidavit, is that what you're saying?

Mr. Hoffart: Yes.

Mr. Bogel: No. I called him back when it was pointed out to me by Steve West that there was a problem with the notary seal.

Judge Fitzpatrick: What was the problem?

Mr. Bogel: In this instance I was told that there were two problems, depending on which letters were going on. Some of them the letter was written on a different date from its notary seal, or as in this case the . . . yeah. To be quite honest with you, I don't see anything wrong with Sean Taylor's letter at all as far as this.

Judge Fitzpatrick: You don't see anything wrong with it. Then what did you tell Mr. Taylor when you called him? Why did you tell him it had to be done over again?

Mr. Bogel: Oh, I know. I think if I remember correctly, there were people we had to call and verify, in addition to getting a new letter. Some of the people we called, and I believe Sean was one. We had to find out from him if in fact he signed it in front of a notary, or whether he had given it to somebody to walk down the hall and sign.

Judge Fitzpatrick: What did you discover?

Mr. Bogel: Sean said that he had signed it in front of Carrie.

Judge Fitzpatrick: He said he had signed it in front of Carrie?

Mr. Bogel: Uh-huh.

Judge Fitzpatrick: Originally?

Mr. Bogel: If I remember correctly, yes.

Well, the Bogel testimony establishes that it was Mr. Bogel to whom Mr. Sean Taylor talked regarding a new letter. The reader should have no problem recognizing that the Bogel testimony stretches credibility. Mr. Taylor would hardly tell him he had signed the original letter before Ms. Carrie Matthew when that was not the case. Why go back to Mr. Taylor to ask him if he had appeared before a notary? Why not ask Carrie Matthew, the KISW notary? For that matter, Mr. West and Ms. Noren orchestrated this phony verification, so why have Mr. Bogel go back to Mr. Sean Taylor when they already knew the notarial verification was affixed outside of Mr. Taylor's presence? And who called whom about a second letter? Bogel says he called Sean Taylor back and told him there was a problem with the notary seal. Sean Taylor says he brought up the subject of having received a letter from Hoffart when he talked to KISW on another matter. And just why is Kaye-Smith using the one-week extension granted them in their filing of their Written Case, allegedly needed due to "steno problems," to secure additional testimonial letters to support their case?

The answer to the conflicting testimony that is prevalent throughout the case is that the witnesses did not hear each other testify. They were called to the stand as they appeared. Bogel, for example, testified on December 1 and Mr. Sean Taylor on December 2. If Mr. Taylor feels that this book sets him in a bad light and casts aspersions upon his character, he need look no further than Kaye-Smith Enterprises. His name appears in this book due to their affixing, illegally, a phony notarial verification to his testimonial letter. The act amounts to forgery. Forgery includes, by definition, any addition to any document without the knowledge of the author of the document, with an intent to deceive. Taylor has stated, under oath, that he first became aware that his letter had been notarized when he received a letter from Hoffart. Hoffart had included in that letter a copy of the original Taylor letter, as notarized by Ms. Carrie Matthew. Of course, the judge, in his wisdom, ruled that there was no intent to deceive anyone.

TR:666   *Judge Fitzpatrick*: When you first talked of your letter on November 5, 1982, did you have any reason to believe that a notarial seal was to be affixed to that letter?
Mr. Taylor: I had been asked to have it notarized, the original copy notarized.
Judge Fitzpatrick: But you didn't have it notarized?
Mr. Taylor: That's correct.
Judge Fitzpatrick: Did anybody tell you at any time that although you hadn't had it notarized, they were going to affix a notarial seal to it although you didn't sign it in the presence of a notary?
Mr. Taylor: No.
Judge Fitzpatrick: When did you first find out that that was done?
Mr. Taylor: When I received the letter from Mr. Hoffart.
Judge Fitzpatrick: Asking you whether you had signed it in the presence of a notary?
Mr. Taylor: The letter said, "Did you indeed write this letter, and did you have it signed in the presence of the notary."

Judge Fitzpatrick: Did that give you any concern?

Mr. Taylor: Not much.

Judge Fitzpatrick: All right. Did you ask anybody at the station whether or not they had affixed a notarial seal to your letter?

Mr. Taylor: No.

Mr. Boros: When you wrote the letter the first time, and when you signed it the first time, and when you signed a second time and before a notary, you used the same language in your letter, didn't you?

Mr. Taylor: It was a photocopy.

Mr. Boros: Was the letter true and correct at all times?

Mr. Taylor: Yes.

Judge Fitzpatrick: I think you've been assuming a fact not in evidence, Mr. Boros. You haven't questioned the witness concerning the execution of the second letter as to whether in fact he did do it before a notary. So I think you want to establish that fact before you assume it.

Mr. Boros: Directing your attention to page 8 (A), corrected page 8 of Kaye-Smith Exhibit 16, did a time come when you signed that letter?[45]

Mr. Taylor: Yes.

Mr. Boros: On that corrected page there appeared two signatures. Is any of that signature yours?

Mr. Taylor: Yes.

Mr. Boros: Now, when you affixed that signature, was anyone present when you put your signature down?

Mr. Taylor: Yes.

Mr. Boros: Who?

Mr. Taylor: The notary, whose signature is listed below.

Mr. Boros: Did you ask the notary to affix her signature?

Mr. Taylor: Yes.

Mr. Boros: Now, at the time you asked her to affix her signature, did you believe your letter to be true and correct?

Mr. Taylor: Yes.

Mr. Boros: Did you know what use, if any, would be made of your letter?

Mr. Taylor: I knew that it would be added to the file of letters relating to community service that all radio and TV stations keep.

---

[45]Appendix page 18. Corrected Taylor notarization.

Mr. Boros: Did you know whether it would be used in FCC hearing?

Mr. Taylor: Well, I knew that these files come up for periodic review, and since I had received Mr. Hoffart's letter I could conclude that, yeah.

Mr. Boros: Did you have any objection to your letter being used in that respect?

Mr. Taylor: Not at all.

Judge Fitzpatrick: With respect to both letters, were you at any time told that the letter was to be submitted to the Federal Communications Commission in a proceeding, and that there was a possibility of being called for cross-examination?

Mr. Taylor: I don't think it ever came up that there was a possibility I would be called for cross-examination. I think I was told that it could be used in the FCC review of that file.

Judge Fitzpatrick: Was it explained to you that your affidavit would be used as testimony in a proceeding before the Federal Communications Commission?

Mr. Taylor: I was aware of that, but I don't know that it had ever been explained to me.

Judge Fitzpatrick: How were you aware of it?

Mr. Taylor: Because in my business I deal with a number of radio and TV stations in town, and I was aware that they have a need to substantiate some community service time, and that those files then come up for regular review.

Judge Fitzpatrick: In your mind do you recognize the difference between writing a letter that's put in a file and submitting sworn testimony in a proceeding?

Mr. Taylor: Yes.

Judge Fitzpatrick: Did you know that your letter was to be submitted as sworn testimony in a proceeding?

Mr. Taylor: I don't know that I knew that. I don't think I knew that.

The author takes the reader back to the pre-hearing that was held in Washington, D.C. on August 6, 1982 wherein the ground rules for the hearing were established.

TR:106   *Judge Fitzpatrick:* Do you intend, Mr. Hoffart, to be adducing any evidence through any members of the public that Kaye-Smith is not meeting the needs of the community in its operation of the station in the last renewal period?

Mr. Hoffart: You mean bring in affidavits by other people in the Seattle area?

Judge Fitzpatrick: Well, it is in the form of an affidavit, but it is sworn direct testimony and in the affidavit, that is one thing that I should say, Mr. Boros, that in the affidavit as submitted, it should show in its face that these people know it is being given to the Commission, and that it is sworn testimony, you know, and that it is testimony in a docketed proceeding, and also they should be aware that they are going to be subject to cross-examination . . .

Well, the judge's ground rules were very explicit and unequivocal but there is no evidence, anywhere, that any of the affiants were told they might be subject to cross-examination. Furthermore, Mr. Taylor states, under oath, that he did not know his letter would be submitted to the FCC as sworn testimony. Let's, once again, go back to the affidavits submitted by both Mr. Bogel and Mr. West; those affidavits to which a list of affiants was attached. Appendix page 4 is the attachment list filed with the Bogel affidavit and a Mr. Shawn Taylor is listed on that page. The affidavit by Bogel states:

Eric S. Bogel, being duly sworn, deposes and says:
1. Each of the affidavits described on the attachment were obtained by me or those under my direction. It was explained to each affiant that his or her affidavit would be used as testimony in a proceeding before the Federal Communications Commission.

(s) Eric S. Bogel
Subscribed and sworn to before me this ___ day of November, 1982.
Carrie Matthew, Notary Public.

Author Hoffart will dispense with the remainder of the direct examination. Mr. Boros only established that Mr. Taylor was appearing as a citizen and was not being paid for his appearance, which had been requested by Mr. Beau Phillips.

Similarly, Hoffart will skip most of his cross-examination of Mr. Taylor. The direct testimony has established, in the opinion of the author, that KISW did not follow the judge's pre-hearing orders, that KISW employees willfully and repeatedly affixed phony verifications to testimonial letters, and that there was intent to deceive. Mr. Boros, as with all of the witnesses who wrote letters, attempted to establish that there was no difference between the original and corrected letters as to content and therefore there was no harm done. Hoffart has not questioned the content of the letters or the sincerity of the authors. The issue is not the content of the letters, but the fact that they were affixed, willfully and repeatedly, with phony notarial seals and signatures in order to make them admissable in a hearing before a federal agency.

The judge, in a decision that defies analysis, ruled that there did not appear to have been any intentional disregard to his orders or to requirements of proper notarization. In a footnote to this ruling the judge writes:

> These individuals were subject to cross-examination. No purpose would have been served by submitting improperly notarized testimony or not informing them that the letters were to be used as evidence since this fact could readily have been discovered during the hearing process. The affidavits of West and Eric S. Bogel, Station KISW program director, submitted as part of Kaye-Smith Exhibits 16 and 17 represented that they had explained to each of the affiants that his or her testimony would be used as evidence is this proceeding. In a few cases, these two individuals failed to inform the affiants of the fact that these testimonial letters were to be submitted as part of the Commission's proceeding. This appears to have been an oversight . . . at most it warrants no more than assessing a slight demerit.[46]

The judge says that the myriad of notarial misrepresentations and the supporting affidavits by West and Bogel served no useful purpose because the affiants could have testified directly. So why did Kaye-Smith affix the phony verifications and file affidavits that contained untruths? The answer is simply that they expected Hoffart to be as ignorant as they make themselves out to be, in patently self-serving testimony, and he would not detect the illegal and felonious acts. As to serving no useful purpose, that is already established. Ms. Noren has testified that the notarizations were placed on the letters to make them legal and admissable in court.

Quoting again from *WOKO, Inc.*, 329 U.S. 223 (1946):

> the willingness to deceive a regulatory body may be disclosed by immaterial and useless deceptions as well as by material and persuasive ones. We do not think it is an answer to say that the deception was unnecessary and served no useful purposes.[47]

But to get back to an excerpt from Hoffart's cross of Mr. Taylor:

TR:676   *Mr. Hoffart:* . . . if you get a copy of your letter back that you did not notarize that had a notary stamp on it, are you concerned about it?
Mr. Taylor: Concerned is probably more appropriate, yeah.

---

[46]98 FCC 2d at page 720, footnote 41.
[47]Citing *WIOO, Inc.*, FCC 83-367. (1983)

Mr. Hoffart: But you didn't do anything about it?

Mr. Taylor: No.

Mr. Hoffart: And you didn't reply to it? (with ref-to Hoffart's letter of inquiry).

Mr. Taylor: I did mention to KISW. I didn't reply to him.

Judge Fitzpatrick: Why not?

Mr. Taylor: I was in the process of forwarding other business with KISW, and when I mentioned it to Mr. Phillips he indicated that a response to Mr. Hoffart would not be in the station's favor, and I didn't respond.

Judge Fitzpatrick: Is that the words he used, the response to Mr. Hoffart would not be in the station's favor?

Mr. Taylor: I can't testify to what words he used.

Judge Fitzpatrick: Did he say if you were to respond to Hoffart and acknowledge that the notarization was not affixed in your presence, that it might be against the interest of the station? Is that what you're trying to convey to me, that thought?

Mr. Taylor: It was clear to me, yeah.

Judge Fitzpatrick: When you finished the conversation, it was clear to you that KISW didn't want you to communicate with Mr. Hoffart?

Mr. Taylor: That they didn't feel a response was necessary, I think would be more closely accurate.

Judge Fitzpatrick: Do you feel a response was necessary?

Mr. Taylor: No.

Judge Fitzpatrick: Do you have a desire to continue to do business with KISW?

Mr. Taylor: Yes.

Judge Fitzpatrick: Did that enter into your motivation?

Mr. Taylor: Yes.

Judge Fitzpatrick: You don't want to do anything to antagonize them, do you?

Mr. Taylor: No.

Judge Fitzpatrick: All right.

16.

DAVID WATKINS

If there is any doubt left in the minds of the readers that there was no intent to deceive anyone in this proceeding, the testimony elicited from this witness should remove any and all doubts that there has been a serious miscarriage of justice in this case. The reader has already read some of the testimony given by Mr. West and Ms. Noren regarding the two David Watkins letters. If the reader wants to refresh his or her memory, the letters are in appendix pages 13 and 14.

David Watkins was duly sworn upon oath by the judge and gave his name and address. He stated he was vice president of Marketing and Advertising for the Seattle Supersonics professional basketball team. The readers are reminded that this was in 1982. Mr. Watkins is no longer connected with this organization, to the best of the author's knowledge.

TR:682   *Mr. Boros*: Now, in the fall of 1982, did a time come when station KISW contacted you about a letter dealing with the Supersonics' relationship with the station?

Mr. Watkins: Yes, I was contacted by Mr. West and asked if I would write a letter.

Mr. Boros: What did Mr. West say to you and what did you say to Mr. West when he contacted you?

Mr. Watkins: As best I can recall, he asked me to write a letter for their files for FCC purposes.

Mr. Boros: What did you say to that?

Mr. Watkins: I said I'd be more than happy to, and I was in fact remiss that I hadn't written one before.

Mr. Boros: When Mr. West used the term "FCC purposes" or some such words which indicated FCC purposes to your mind, what did you think would be done with the letter?

Mr. Watkins: Well, like the previous witness, I am aware because of my involvement in this business of the necessity to have letters on file. And I don't recall if I was aware of an upcoming hearing or not, but I know of the nature of the letter because of my knowledge of the business and was happy to write it.

Mr. Boros: Did a time come when you wrote a letter to station KISW in response to the conversation you had had with Mr. West about obtaining such a letter for the station?

Mr. Watkins: Yes.

Judge Fitzpatrick: Was it explained to you that the document you were to be transmitting to the station would be used as testimony in a proceeding before the Federal Communications Commission?

Mr. Watkins: I don't believe so.

Judge Fitzpatrick: Was it explained to you that your letter was to take the form of an affidavit?

Mr. Watkins: I don't believe so.

Mr. Boros: Is it correct to say that you knew the letter you were writing would be used in connection with some FCC purposes?

Mr. Watkins: Yes, indeed.

Mr. Boros: Does it make any difference when you write a letter to be used for FCC purposes in your mind whether you swear to the letter or you just sign your signature?

Mr. Watkins: Well, in this particular case with these particular people, it makes absolutely no difference.

Mr. Boros: A time did come when you did write such a letter, is that correct?

Mr. Watkins: Yes.

Mr. Boros: Do you know about what time that occurred?

Mr. Watkins: I'm cheating. The date here is October 22nd, pretty much as I remember.

Mr. Boros: That corresponds with your recollection, does it?

Mr. Watkins: Yes.

Mr. Boros: When you wrote the letter, did you write it yourself or author it yourself?

Mr. Watkins: Yes, I did. I typed it myself and my secretary retyped it.

Mr. Boros: And what you said in the letter, is it true and correct?

Mr. Watkins: Yes, indeed.

Mr. Boros: Now, with respect to the letter, that letter which you wrote the first time which your secretary retyped, is that letter the same as the letter which appears on page 5 of Kaye-Smith Exhibit 17?[48]

Mr. Watkins: Yes, it is.

Mr. Boros: Is that your signature there?

Mr. Watkins: Yes.

---

[48]Appendix page 13. Original David Watkins letter notarized by Mr. Anthony Tucker.

Mr. Boros: In the right-hand corner, lower right-hand corner, parallel to your signature there's another signature. Whose signature is that?

Mr. Watkins: That is Anthony Tucker, who is a vice president of our company, and a notary.

Mr. Boros: Was Anthony Tucker present when you signed your signature?

Mr. Watkins: Yes, he was.

Mr. Boros: After you signed your signature, did Mr. Tucker affix his signature?

Mr. Watkins: Yes, he did.

Mr. Boros: Then what did you do with the letter?

Mr. Watkins: Gave it to my secretary to mail.

Mr. Boros: Did a time come when you heard further about this letter?

Mr. Watkins: Yes. A couple of weeks thereafter I received a call from KISW telling me that the notary should have been dated. There should have been a date with the notary, and would I rewrite the letter, and I said fine, I would be happy to, and I had my secretary retype the letter. But our notary was not there, and he was in fact out of town for several days.[49]

The author brought this sworn testimony by Mr. Watkins to the attention of the reader when Ms. Noren was on the stand. She had stated, also under oath, that Mr. Watkins told her that his notary was ill. This is another case where the witness did not know what a previous witness had testified to. Ms. Noren had been the first witness on the 2nd day of December, and Watkins had not been there. Significantly, Hoffart had not questioned the Watkins's notarial attestation. It lacked the date of notarization but that, by itself, would not raise any questions in the mind of the author as to the validity of the notarial act. Hoffart had not written Mr. Watkins a letter so you can imagine the surprise when Kaye-Smith filed a corrected letter, now notarized by Ms. Noren.

TR:686   *Mr. Boros*: So what did you do?

Mr. Watkins: I was in and out of the office that day. My secretary retyped the letter. She contacted or talked to somebody at KISW, and I'm not positive whom it was, and told him then that we had a problem getting the notary done ourselves. And they asked that we forward the letter over to them, that they would notarize it there,

---

[49]Appendix page 14. Corrected Watkins letter bearing a phony Watkins signature and phony notarization.

and I told her that was fine. I was not in the office at the time. I told her if she couldn't wait for me to get back for her to sign it, which she frequently does with my correspondence, sign my name, and she did. And she sent the letter over, and I talked to Meg at KISW, I believe that afternoon. And she informed me that she was notarizing it, and I said, "fine", I hope this one works.

Here we have another conflicting statement in sworn testimony Mr. Watkins states, under oath, that KISW asked that the letter be sent over to them when they were advised that the notary was not available. Ms. Noren, however, also in sworn testimony, stated that she had been in receipt of an unnotarized letter from him. Let's review the Noren testimony, verbatim:

TR:605   *Ms. Noren*: The letter came from Dave Watkins. I did not see him sign it, but I affixed my notary signature and seal to it after speaking with him on the telephone.
Mr. Boros: Well, how did it happen that you spoke to him on the telephone? Did he call you or did you call him?
Ms. Noren: I called him.
Mr. Boros: What did you say to him?
Ms. Noren: I told him I had been handed the letter from him but it was not notarized, and he said that his notary was out ill that day. And I asked him, would it be with his approval if I notarized it for legal purposes, and he said yes.
Judge Fitzpatrick: Now this conversation took place on November 17th?
Ms. Noren: Yes.
Judge Fitzpatrick: This was after all of the difficulties had already come to your attention?
Ms. Noren: Yes.

As this case moves along, it raises more questions than it answers. One of the unanswered questions is why Mr. Watkins agreed to have his second letter notarized when he was fully aware that he had not signed it. Since he was apparently aware, or should have been aware, that KISW was going to use his letter in a legal proceeding, the question arises whether this action by Watkins amounts to co-conspiracy to file fraudulently notarized documents with all parties in the hearing. Perhaps there is more than meets the eye here. An inquisitive investigative reporter may find the answers. It would be idle for the author to ask Mr. Watkins, his former secretary, Mr. Anthony Tucker, or any of the KISW employees. As Mr. Taylor had testified before, they probably, like Taylor, do not want to antagonize Kaye-Smith.

TR:686   *Judge Fitzpatrick*: Did you tell the notary at the station that it was not your signature, that you had not affixed it to the November 17th letter?
Mr. Watkins: I don't recall. I don't know if my secretary did or not.
Mr. Boros: Who initiated the phone conversation that you had with the station on this date of November 17th? Was it you or was it the station?
Mr. Watkins: I think it was the station that called. I believe it was Steve Montgomery. I'm not positive.
Mr. Boros: Could it have been Meg Noren?
Mr. Watkins: It could have. I believe it was Steve that called that day. I talked to a lot of them several times during the course of a week or so.
Mr. Boros: Do you speak to Meg Noren on occasion?
Mr. Watkins: Yes.
Mr. Boros: Do you know her voice?
Mr. Watkins: Oh, yes.
Mr. Boros: She knows your voice?
Mr. Watkins: Yes, indeed. I hope so.
Judge Fitzpatrick: When you authorized your secretary to sign your signature, and when you authorized the notary at the station to notarize the signature affixed to the letter by your secretary, did you know that it was going to be submitted to the Federal Communications Commission?
Mr. Watkins: I assumed it was going to the FCC. In what form I had no idea.
Judge Fitzpatrick: And you were not concerned that a document was being sent to a government agency which did not contain your signature, and which was notarized by somebody saying that it in fact was your signature?
Mr. Watkins: No, because the parties that were involved I trusted completely.
Judge Fitzpatrick: Well, how about the parties who were going to rely upon the document when they received it as to whether or not it was your signature and it was authenticated by a notary public?
Mr. Watkins: I'm not a lawyer. I know of no difficulties with this, other than the notary the first time hadn't dated it. And I didn't know that was a problem until they

brought it to my attention, so I didn't feel I was in a position to make additions. They have my support at the station, and the people involved I trust explicitly, so I had no problem. If I had known it was going to be in a court situation, then maybe I would have been concerned.

Judge Fitzpatrick: You did know it was going to be a court situation.

Mr. Watkins: I didn't know it was going to be and I had to be here today.

Judge Fitzpatrick: You didn't know the letter was being submitted as sworn testimony?

Mr. Watkins: Sworn testimony, no, I don't believe so.

Mr. Boros: With respect to the first letter which you actually signed in the presence of Mr. Tucker and the second letter, insofar as the content of the letter is concerned, was there any difference?

Mr. Watkins: No, I believe she just retyped it from the first one.

Mr. Boros: Did you give instructions about what she should do, she being your secretary?

Mr. Watkins: I told her either to retype it or to photocopy it and redate it. I'm not sure which she did. I think she retyped it.

Judge Fitzpatrick: Let me ask a question. After your November 17th letter, it was signed by your secretary and forwarded to the station. Did you receive a call from somebody at the station, did you say?

Mr. Watkins: I talked to, I believe it was Meg Noren at the station.

Judge Fitzpatrick: Who?

Mr. Watkins: Meg Noren at the station, regarding her notarizing it, which I said was fine.

Judge Fitzpatrick: Did she ask you if it was your signature?

Mr. Watkins: I don't think so.

Judge Fitzpatrick: She just asked you if she could notarize it?

Mr. Watkins: Yes.

Judge Fitzpatrick: And you said it was fine?

Mr. Watkins: Yes.

Mr. Boros: Do you recall whether she suggested notarizing it or whether you suggested it, or how that developed?

Mr. Watkins: I don't know. I was horribly rushed that day, and my only concern was accommodating them in any way I possibly could.

The author will skip his cross-examination of Mr. Watkins since it is superfluous. It is well-established that a second round of phony verifications were filed by KISW, and that Ms. Noren and Mr. West were directly involved and knew, beyond any doubt, that they were engaging in misrepresentations with intent to deceive all parties, particularly Hoffart. The reader may recall that counsel told Mr. West, "you can't do that" when it came to their attention that the letters were affixed with phony verifications; and you may remember that Ms. Noren testified that she told Mr. West that she had notarized the Watkins corrected letter outside his presence and he had again said it was "fine." The perjury by Mr. West, however, has to take the prize. Under cross-examination by Hoffart he had stated, without equivocation, that Mr. Watkins had appeared before his notary/employee at KISW and he witnessed the notarial act. Compounding these felonious acts was the fact that the corrected letter was not signed by Mr. Watkins, but by his secretary and still Ms. Noren stated in her notarial attestation:

Subscribed and sworn before me this 17th day of November, 1982. (s) Marget E. Noren, Notary Public.

And what did the three wise men on the review board rule on the charges by Hoffart that there was perjury? They said:

the charge that West, Bogel and Noren gave perjured testimony is over-blown on the part of Hoffart. Perjury generally connotes a knowingly false statement made under oath. Mere mistakes in recollection or isolated incidents of forgetfullness do not rise to this level. Our examination of the specific statements made by the three individuals above, reveals nothing more serious than that the statements are either at times equivocal or show at most an incorrect recollection on the part of the witness . . . it is much ado about nothing, and a traditional adversarial attempt to puff those matters into deliberate attempts to deceive.[50]

It appears to Hoffart that the review board is engaged in a deliberate attempt to deceive the public. A grand jury needs to review this case.

---

[50]98 FCC 2d at page 681, Review Board Decision, 6-8-84.

17.

JULIE GAIL McCULLOUGH

Julie Gail McCullough was one of the persons from whom Kaye-Smith solicited a testimonial letter supporting their renewal application. Mr. Bogel listed her on his affidavit attachment list, but as was established in his testimony earlier in this book, he had very little to do with the actual solicitation.

Ms. McCullough was duly sworn upon oath on December 2nd, 1982. She stated she was employed by Greenpeace, an international environmental organization.

TR:750   *Mr. Boros*: Did a time come in the fall of 1982 when a representative of KISW FM approached you or some other people, to your knowledge, in Greenpeace about obtaining a testimonial letter from Greenpeace about prior relations between Greenpeace and KISW?
Ms. McCullough: Yes.
Mr. Boros: Do you recall about when that happened?
Ms. McCullough: Let's see, I'd say it was about a month ago, somewhere in late October, perhaps early November.
Mr. Boros: Were you personally the person who was contacted, or was it someone else?
Ms. McCullough: No, it was me directly who was contacted.
Mr. Boros: Do you recall who contacted you?
Ms. McCullough: Paul Sullivan.
Mr. Boros: Do you recall what he said to you and what you said to him at the time of this contact?
Ms. McCullough: I can't remember exactly the words, but basically he said that the license for the station was up for renewal, and that he was wondering if I would write some kind of brief letter explaining the relationship that Greenpeace has had in the past with KISW. And I said I was more than happy to do so. Also, I thought it was important to add in this letter our relationship specifically with Paul, who has been acting in an advisory capacity on administrative and promotional matters for us, and he's always done this during the business hours of the station, and I thought that was worth mentioning in the letter.

Mr. Boros: Did he tell you what use would be made of this letter, or what use was contemplated of being made of the letter?

Ms. McCullough: He wasn't terribly specific on it, but it was my understanding that it would be filed along with the application for station, for the station's license renewal.

Mr. Boros: Now I direct your attention, Ms. McCullough, to a document which is before you, I believe. If it is before you, it should say in the upper right-hand corner by way of legend, Kaye-Smith Exhibit 16, page 6. Do you have a document which is so marked before you?[51]

Ms. McCullough: Yes.

Mr. Boros: That document purports to be a letter from Julie McCullough to Paul Sullivan, and it has a signature there. Is that your signature?

Ms. McCullough: Yes.

Mr. Boros: And this letter which appears above the signature, or the text of the letter, is that something that you wrote or did someone else write it?

Ms. McCullough: No, I wrote and typed it myself.

Mr. Boros: After you did that you affixed your signature, is that correct?

Ms. McCullough: Yes.

Mr. Boros: Now, at the time you affixed your signature, did you have any instructions or requests from Mr. Sullivan as to what you would do after you prepared the letter in terms of delivery to him?

Ms. McCullough: I'm not sure I understand what your question is.

Mr. Boros: And he told you send the letter to him or to deliver it to him, or mail it to him?

Ms. McCullough: Yes. He asked me to mail the letter to him.

Mr. Boros: Did he ask you to have it notarized, or did he not ask you, or did he say nothing about it?

Ms. McCullough: No, I was not asked to notarize the letter.

Mr. Boros: Now, did a time come when Mr. Sullivan called you again and raised the question of having another letter prepared?

---

[51]Appendix page 9. McCullough original letter bearing a phony notarization affixed by Ms. Matthew.

Judge Fitzpatrick: Before we get into that, may I ask the witness a question? Did Mr. Sullivan at any time tell you that the document that he requested you to give would be used as testimony in a proceeding before the Federal Communications Commission?

Ms. McCullough: I don't remember specifically Paul telling me that it would be used as testimony. But he did tell me that there was a chance that it would be handed in with the application.

Judge Fitzpatrick: Did he tell you that there was a possibility that you would be called for cross-examination?

Ms. McCullough: You mean during this first conversation that we had?

Judge Fitzpatrick: That's correct.

Ms. McCullough: No.

Mr. Boros: In a subsequent conversation, did Mr. Sullivan mention to you that you might be called as a witness for cross-examination in a proceeding before the FCC?

Ms. McCullough: Subsequent conversation? You mean after this initial discussion?

Mr. Boros: Yes.

Ms. McCullough: Yes, but it was quite recent that I heard that.

Judge Fitzpatrick: It was after you sent your first letter?

Ms. McCullough: Yes, it was.

Mr. Boros: When Mr. Sullivan told you more recently . . . quite recently, to use your word quite . . . that you might be called as a witness, what did he say to you?

Ms. McCullough: He said that there was going to be a hearing going on, and if it was possible for me to get away during my business day that the station . . . that he and the station would appreciate my appearing to give this testimony about these letters.

Mr. Boros: What did you say?

Ms. McCullough: I said sure, I'd be glad to.

Judge Fitzpatrick: Was this conversation this week?

Ms. McCullough: Yes.

Mr. Boros: You're not appearing pursuant to subpoena, are you?

Ms. McCullough: No, I received no subpoena.

Mr. Boros: It is fair to say the only reason you're appearing is in order to do your civic duty to the government?

Ms. McCullough: Sure.

As with the other witnesses, it appears that this witness had not been informed that Kaye-Smith was under orders from the judge to bring into court the affiants whose letters had been affixed with phony notarial verifications. The witness has stated that she was appearing only in performance of her civic duty. If she had not been informed by Kaye-Smith that she was ordered to appear, she may have been mislead and deceived into thinking that her appearance was voluntary on her part. That was not the case. The judge's orders in this regard have surfaced earlier in this book.

TR:754   *Mr. Boros*: With respect to the time which came to pass when you were asked for a second letter, could you recall when that occurred?

Ms. McCullough: I think it occurred about two weeks after the first letter. It would be when I was . . . the day that I was requested for the second letter I also wrote the letter moments after I had the conversation.

Mr. Boros: Well I direct your attention to page 6 (A) This is otherwise called, in parentheses, corrected page 6 of Kaye-Smith Exhibit 16. I think you'll find that immediately after the first letter. Do you have that before you?[52]

Ms. McCullough: Yes.

Mr. Boros: Now, that bears the date of the 16th. Is that the date on which you wrote the second letter?

Ms. McCullough: Yes.

Mr. Boros: Now, when you were asked to write a second letter, who asked you to write a second letter?

Ms. McCullough: I wasn't specifically asked to write a second letter. What happened was, I had received some correspondence from Mr. Hoffart and in the letter that I had received from him it asked some questions about this first letter you're calling page 6. And he, in this letter, asked me if it had been notarized in my presence, and it was . . . the letter was full of details saying that this tickler along with the second letter . . . or the first letter I received from him . . . would be filed with the Judge and that my reply would be filed with the Judge, and so on. And rather than replying to his letter, saying no, it wasn't notarized in my presence, what I did was I wrote a whole new letter and had a notary there to notarize it after I finished writing, signing that letter, I just thought that

---

[52]Appendix page 12. Corrected McCullough letter filed by Kaye-Smith counsel November 24th, 1982.

would be the simplest way to do it and the most direct way to handle the situation.

Mr. Boros: Was that your own decision?

Ms. McCullough: Oh, yes. Yes. And then what I did was, I wrote this letter and I had notarized, this page 6 (A), I had that notarized in my presence, and I believe I had the copy of it notarized too. And once I got that taken care of I called Mr. Sullivan and let him know what I had done, and he said, "Thank you" and that was it.

Mr. Boros: Ms. McCullough, at the time you signed the first letter knowing that it might be submitted to the FCC, did it make any difference to you, in terms of the fact that it was going to be submitted to the FCC, whether or not you swore to it?

Ms. McCullough: I'm not sure I understand what your question is.

Mr. Boros: Would you have written a different letter if you knew that you would have your signature notarized than the letter you originally wrote?

Ms. McCullough: No.

Judge Fitzpatrick: When you received the letter from Mr. Hoffart, do you recall what date you received this letter?

Ms. McCullough: It was in the end of October. I would say it was somewhere around the 20th of October. That was a guess. I don't remember the exact date.

Judge Fitzpatrick: I recognize that. Did you make an effort to determine whether or not a notarization had been placed on the letter that you sent to the station?

Ms. McCullough: You mean the first letter?

Judge Fitzpatrick: That's correct.

Ms. McCullough: No, because he had sent me a copy of it.

Judge Fitzpatrick: Oh, he had sent you a copy. I'm sorry, you did say that.

Ms. McCullough: Which showed a notarization, and it was not notarized in my presence ... and I just decided to go ahead and write a whole new letter and have it notarized right there.

Judge Fitzpatrick: Did you inquire of Mr. Sullivan or anybody at the station as to how it came about that they added this notarization to your letter?

Ms. McCullough: I did ask Paul. I just explained to Paul what the letter that I had received from Mr. Hoffart said, and then I explained to him what the question was, you know, was this notarized in your presence. And I told him that, and he just acknowledged, and of course we both knew that it wasn't notarized in my presence. And I suggested, he didn't ask me, I suggested that I write a new letter, and that's what I went ahead and did.

Now this testimony raises some questions in the author's mind. Ms. McCullough seems to be saying that she suggested to Paul Sullivan that she write a new letter. Earlier she had indicated that she wrote the second letter moments after she had the conversation. Since she had no conversations with Hoffart, who requested her to write a second letter? She stated that she did not call Paul Sullivan until after she had written the second letter and after she had it notarized. Her testimony does not add up. What would your reaction be, reader, if a copy of a document you had authored, but had not notarized when you delivered or sent it to KISW, showed up in your mail, now notarized? Would you not immediately call Mr. Sullivan and ask what is going on? And would this not be the reaction of all of the authors of solicited testimonial letters who were similarly served with copies of their letters, now notarized, from Hoffart? This is an example of apparently conflicting testimony from a witness. Perhaps some inquiring reporter will check out her story with Greenpeace, Mr. Paul Sullivan or the second notary, Ms. Diana Blane, whose notarial attestation appears on Page 6 (A), of Kaye-Smith Exhibit 16.

The author cross-examined Ms. McCullough to find out why she had not responded to his inquiry of whether she had or had not appeared before Ms. Carrie Matthew in connection with the notarization of her letter.

TR:759 *Mr. Hoffart*: Ms. McCullough, you received my letter . . . I have shown it to counsel . . . see if this is the letter you received. This letter is dated November 13th, signed Vincent L. Hoffart.

Ms. McCullough: Yes, I believe it is.

Mr. Hoffart: Did you receive it certified?

Ms. McCullough: Yes.

Mr. Hoffart: Would this be the date you received that, on the 15th?

Ms. McCullough: Well, to the best of my recollection.

Mr. Hoffart: Well, the post office put that date on the 15th. I'd like to read part of this letter to you, now.

"Please advise if you personally appeared before Ms. Matthew and deposed that the content of the letter, copy attached, is true and correct. You might note that this letter was notarized on October 28th and it was dated

144

October 22nd, 1982. A copy of this letter and your response will be filed with the Judge."
Is that correct, to your recollection?
Ms. McCullough: Yes, to my recollection.
Mr. Hoffart: Did you respond?
Ms. McCullough: Yes.
Mr. Hoffart: You sent me a letter?
Ms. McCullough: Yes, I did. Didn't you get it? I mean . . .
Judge Fitzpatrick: Don't hold conversation.
Mr. Hoffart: You sent me a letter with a new notary?
Ms. McCullough: Yes.
Mr. Hoffart: You didn't answer Mr. Hoffart's question, though, did you?
Ms. McCullough: What was the question?
Judge Fitzpatrick: The question in the letter was to whether or not you had signed that document in front of the notary. You never answered him, did you?
Ms. McCullough: I don't remember answering him, no.
Judge Fitzpatrick: Was there any reason why you didn't tell him what the facts were?
Ms. McCullough: No, there wasn't really a reason.
Judge Fitzpatrick: Did anybody suggest that you not answer him?
Ms. McCullough: No, no. May I make . . .
Judge Fitzpatrick: Surely, please.
Ms. McCullough: I just thought that it would be most simple and just expedite things if I just sent a new notarized letter, because I saw he was quite right. The letter had not been notarized in my presence. But I didn't mean to be dishonest about it.
Judge Fitzpatrick: No one was suggesting, certainly not myself, that you would be dishonest any way.
Mr. Hoffart: Is this a copy of the new notarized letter you sent back, dated November 16th?
Ms. McCullough: I sent you a personal letter, I believe.
Mr. Hoffart: Along with this?
Ms. McCullough: Yes.
Mr. Hoffart: Now, I'd like to read you this letter, sent to Mr. Vincent L. Hoffart, November 16, 1982.
"Dear Mr. Hoffart: Here is a notarized letter with proper dates as you requested." Now, did I request a letter with proper dates on it?
Ms. McCullough: No.
Mr. Hoffart: And it goes further:

145

"this was signed this evening in the presence of Diane Blane, a notary public, and myself. Please do not hesitate to contact me if I may be of further assistance . . . "

Now, my letter to you was very specific. I wanted to know if you appeared before a notary.

Mr. Boros: I object, your Honor, to the statement. I think it's appropriate to ask a question, but not to make statements to a witness.

Judge Fitzpatrick: Well, I'll overrule it. All he's saying is "my letter is specific in what my request was." We know what the request was, so he has a right to characterize. Now, what's the question?

Mr. Hoffart: My question is, is this letter responsive, your reply responsive, to my letter to you?

Mr. Boros: Object.

Judge Fitzpatrick: The letter speaks for itself. You can ask her if she believed when she wrote it that it was responsive.

Mr. Hoffart: Did you believe it was responsive to my answer that I requested?

Ms. McCullough: Yes.

Mr. Hoffart: Does that letter specifically state that I wanted to know whether you appeared before a notary?

Mr. Boros: Object, your Honor. You've already stated the letters will speak for themselves.

Judge Fitzpatrick: Overruled. The letter speaks for itself and he's making reference to it. Now, the letter did ask you a question. You never answered him, did you?

Ms. McCullough: That's right.

Judge Fitzpatrick: Is there any reason why you didn't answer him?

Ms. McCullough: The reason that I didn't answer him is because I thought in my judgment that it was smartest to just provide new letters for you that were notarized in my presence. It was my interpretation of the question that there was a need to have these dates matching, and that there was a need for this letter to have any validity that it been notarized in my presence. So perhaps I was overstepping things or getting a jump ahead of things.

Judge Fitzpatrick: Did you realize that Mr. Hoffart, rather then trying to validate the letters, was attacking them by questioning you concerning their validity?

Ms. McCullough: I didn't really feel that he was attacking.

Judge Fitzpatrick: Did you at any time realize that he was opposing the station's renewal license?

Ms. McCullough: After I had finished writing this letter I had, and after this second letter I had written, I did call Paul and say, "who is this gentleman that sent me this letter?"

Judge Fitzpatrick: But at the time that you wrote the letter, you didn't know who he was?

Ms. McCullough: Oh no.

Mr. Boros had some redirect which did not touch upon the phony verification of her original letter. After that she was excused.

The reader can make up his or her mind as to what happened here. Notice should be taken of the testimony in which she stated that she suggested to Paul that she just write a new letter, properly notarized. Earlier she testified that she called Paul and told him what she had done, and he said thank you, and that was it. The author finds her testimony somewhat conflicting. Perhaps Ms. Diana Blane, the notary who verified the McCullough corrected letter can shed some light on this matter, or maybe Mr. Paul Sullivan, under oath before a grand jury.

18.

CHARLES E. BLACKSMITH

Mr. West's notarized statement listed on the attachment one Charles E. Blacksmith as an individual approached by him for a testimonial letter. Mr. Blacksmith wrote such a letter lacking notarization. This letter, and the corrected version filed about two weeks later, are reproduced in the appendix.[53] The reader will note that the first Blacksmith letter was notarized by Ms. Carrie Matthew and filed with the FCC and all other parties as true and correct in all respects. Before we take up the Blacksmith testimony, let's review some conflicting testimony given by Mr. West and by Ms. Carrie Matthew regarding who asked her to affix a phony notarial verification to his testimonial letter.

TR:307   *Judge Fitzpatrick:* Do you know how it came about that Carrie Matthew had notarized Mr. Blacksmith's signature?

Mr. West: Yes, Mr. Blacksmith didn't have a notary and he asked if we would to it.

Judge Fitzpatrick: Who?

Mr. West: Me.

Judge Fitzpatrick: You dated it October . . . just explain to me what happened.

Mr. West: In the case of Mr. Blacksmith and a few others, They didn't have a notary that they could use. And we were in a timeframe where we were in a hurry. They asked if we would notarize it.

Judge Fitzpatrick: Now, you got Mr. Blacksmith's letter and it wasn't notarized and you talked to Mr. Blacksmith about it?

Mr. West: Yes.

Judge Fitzpatrick: Before . . .

Mr. West: Yes.

Judge Fitzpatrick: Mr. Blacksmith asked you to have somebody notarize it?

Mr. West: Yes.

Judge Fitzpatrick: Then you asked Mr. Matthew to come in and affix notarization?

Mr. West: Yes.

Judge Fitzpatrick: Did she tell you that that's not the way you do it?

---

[53]Appendix pages 24 and 25.

148

Mr. West: No.

How do you, the reader, evaluate this testimony by the KISW station manager, repeated here for emphasis? Was there intent to file a fraudulently notarized testimonial letter with an agency of the federal government or was this an inadvertent oversight or accidental? Remember that the judge himself developed this testimony which he later ruled, along with all other similar acts, warrants only a slight demerit because of the ignorance of Kaye-Smith employees. Mr. West had testified earlier that an affidavit, in his view, was a testimonial letter on somebody's letterhead. While this testimony is inherently unbelievable, Mr. West's self-serving testimony is only surpassed by the arrant conduct of those sitting in judgment of this case.

Ms. Carrie Matthew, the KISW notary who had affixed her notary seal and signature to this Blacksmith letter, had followed Mr. West on the witness stand. Her testimony is in conflict with that just given by the station manager.

TR:557   *Mr. Boros*: Now, with respect to page 24 of Kaye-Smith Exhibit 16, could you turn there, please. Do you have that before you?[54]

Ms. Matthew: Yes.

Mr. Boros: At the bottom of the page above the words "notary public" appears a signature. Is that your signature?

Ms. Matthew: Yes, it is.

Mr. Boros: How did your signature happen to come to be put on that page?

Ms. Matthew: I was instructed by Meg Noren.

Mr. Boros: To do what?

Ms. Matthew: To notarize it.

Mr. Boros: Was Charles E. Blacksmith before you at the time?

Ms. Matthew: No, he wasn't.

A review of the testimony shows that Mr. West stated, under oath, that he asked Ms. Matthew to come into his office and asked her to notarize the Blacksmith letter outside the presence of Mr. Blacksmith. Ms. Matthew, however, also a Kaye-Smith employee, stated under oath that it was Meg Noren who instructed her to notarize the letter. It really does not make any difference as to who is testifying falsely. Suffice to say that false testimony is given by Kaye-Smith employees. Perjury in a hearing is disqualifying. Perhaps this is why the judge did not mention

---

[54]Appendix page 24. Blacksmith original letter with a phony notarization affixed by Ms. Carrie Matthew.

this in his findings of facts. It should be remembered that he also stone-walled the untrue testimony given by Mr. West regarding the second David Watkins letter notarization. Let's see if Mr. Blacksmith can shed some light as to what happened.

Mr. Charles E. Blacksmith was duly sworn and stated that he resides in Renton, Washington and further stated that he was a record merchandiser employed by Roundup Music, a division of Fred Meyer Company.

TR:771   *Mr. Boros*: In connection with your work for the Fred Meyer Company, do you from time to time have contact with Station KISW?

Mr. Blacksmith: Yes, sir. I do.

Mr. Boros: Did there come a time in the fall of this year, 1982, when representatives of Station KISW contacted you with respect to securing a letter or a testimonial from you about station KISW which you could use as reference in any matter?

Mr. Blacksmith: Yes, sir.

Mr. Boros: When was that?

Mr. Blacksmith: I have copies of the letters here. It was on or about October the 27th.

Mr. Boros: Who contacted you, sir?

Mr. Blacksmith: I believe it was Sue Phillips, our sales representative.

Mr. Boros: When you say our sales representative, was he someone in your organization?

Mr. Blacksmith: No, no. Sue Phillips is a salesperson for KISW.

Mr. Boros: What did he say to you?

Mr. Blacksmith: It's a she, by the way. Sue.

Mr. Boros: What did she say to you?

Mr. Blacksmith: She simply indicated that they would like to secure a letter on behalf of our company talking about KISW's involvement in community activities and speaking a little bit to the integrity of Mr. Steve West, whom I've known for a long time.

Mr. Boros: What did you say?

Mr. Blacksmith: I said it would be fine. I'd be happy to do it.

Mr. Boros: Did there come a time when you wrote a letter?

Mr. Blacksmith: Yes, sir.

Mr. Boros: I direct your attention to a document or piece of paper before you which has in the upper right-hand corner the legend Kaye-Smith Enterprises Exhibit 16, and in the notes it also says page 24 in the upper right-hand corner. Do you have that before you?

Mr. Blacksmith: Yes, I do.

Mr. Boros: Now, that letter has typewritten Charles E. Blacksmith, and above it a signature. Is that your signature?

Mr. Blacksmith: That is my signature.

Mr. Boros: And above it there is text. Who wrote that text?

Mr. Blacksmith: I did.

Mr. Boros: Were you the author of it?

Mr. Blacksmith: Yes, sir.

Mr. Boros: And after you wrote it, did you affix your signature?

Mr. Blacksmith: I did.

Mr. Boros: What did you do after you affixed your signature to the letter?

Mr. Blacksmith: Well, I attempted to get it notarized because that was the instructions I had. And I went next door to my Savings and Loan that normally does that, and the person that would be available to notarize it was missing and I was going out of town. So I sent the letter back to Steve. I directed it to Steve West without the notarization on it.

This testimony states, without equivocation, that Mr. Blacksmith signed the document and then went next door to the Savings and Loan to have his signature notarized. Since the letter had already been signed, had the bank notary affixed his or her notarial attestation, it would have been irregular unless Mr. Blacksmith produced identification and re-signed the letter in the presence of the notary.

TR:774   *Mr. Boros*: Did you send him any note along with the letter, or did you make a phone call at the time?

Mr. Blacksmith: I called and I said that if it was necessary to have it notarized, could they do it at the station. They certainly could do it with my permission because I didn't have the time.

Judge Fitzpatrick: Who did you say this to?

Mr. Blacksmith: To Steve West.

151

Mr. Boros: Did a time come when Steve West got back to you and said there was some problem with your first letter?
Mr. Blacksmith: Yes.

Mr. Boros went into the details of obtaining the "corrected letter" and, attempting to mitigate the phony vertifications, again went into his spiel of eliciting testimony that no difference existed between the text of the first letter and the corrected letter. The reader, being perhaps more intellectual than the Kaye-Smith manager and employees, based upon the picture painted by Mr. Boros, will recognize that the issue here is not the content of the letters but the fact that Kaye-Smith tried to pass the documents off upon a federal agency as being legally notarized, when this was not the case. It was the manager, Mr. West, who was called by Mr. Blacksmith, proving that there were no lower echelon Kaye-Smith individuals responsible for this illegal act.

TR:775   *Judge Fitzpatrick*: Did Ms. Phillips, when she requested the letter, explain to you that your letter as notarized would be used as testimony in a proceeding before the Federal Communications Commission?
Mr. Blacksmith: She did indicate to me that there was a hearing of some sort coming about and that's basically what the letter was for. I didn't really know the details of it.
Judge Fitzpatrick: Did she indicate to you that your letter with proper notarization was being submitted as your sworn testimony in the proceeding?
Mr. Blacksmith: Yes, you Honor.
Judge Fitzpatrick: And even though you were so notified, you told Mr. West that somebody could put a notarization on it who didn't see you affix your signature to the document?
Mr. Blacksmith: I did.
Judge Fitzpatrick: Did you consider that to be appropriate at the time?
Mr. Blacksmith: I did at the time, yes.
Judge Fitzpatrick: Do you now?
Mr. Blacksmith: Well, evidently not. I guess I wouldn't be here otherwise.

This is one affiant who was told that his letter had to be notarized and gave Kaye-Smith permission to notarize it outside of his presence. If Mr. West's affidavit that avers all of the affiants on his attachment list to exhibit 16 is true, then Mr. Blacksmith would have known that his

152

letter would be used as sworn testimony in a proceeding before the FCC. That being the case, Mr. Blacksmith would be a co-conspirator to the filing of a falsely verified document with a federal agency. Furthermore, as his opening testimony shows, he was acting on behalf of his employer, Fred Meyer Company. The question that arises is whether or not his employer is responsible for his illegal act under the concept of *respondeat superior*. Mr. Blacksmith used Roundup Music Distributors letterhead stationary when he wrote his letter, and that letterhead also states that this Roundup Music is a Division of Fred Meyer, Inc. Mr. Blacksmith was apparently acting on behalf of his employer, with the actual or apparent authority to do so. The fact that Kaye-Smith obtained a correctly notarized letter and filed it with the FCC does not mitigate the fact that the original letter was affixed with a phony notarial act which was expressly authorized by Mr. Blacksmith.

Mr. Blacksmith was one of the seven so-called affiants that were sent letters of inquiry by Hoffart on the 13th of November, 1982. Mr. Blacksmith did not respond, even though a self-addressed stamped envelope had been enclosed. It has already been documented that both Mr. Dan McConnell and Mr. Shawn Taylor had been told by Kaye-Smith employees not to respond to Hoffart's letters. Hoffart's cross-examination of Mr. Blacksmith also revealed that he was told not to respond to Hoffart.

TR:777   *Mr. Hoffart*: Now, did you note in the bottom, did you receive a self addressed stamped envelope?
Mr. Blacksmith: Yes, I did.
Mr. Hoffart: Did you respond to Hoffart?
Mr. Blacksmith: No.
Mr. Hoffart: Did you contact KISW, or were you in contact with KISW immediately after getting this letter?
Mr. Blacksmith: As I recall, I called Sue and told her that I had received the letter and wanted to know, since I had already redid the letter, had it properly notarized, if I needed to respond. And she indicated that she didn't think it was necessary.
Mr. Hoffart: You called KISW?
Mr. Blacksmith: I did.
Mr. Hoffart: They didn't call you?
Mr. Blacksmith: No, they didn't call me.
Mr. Boros: At the time you received Hoffart's letter, had you already re-executed before a notary your first letter?
Mr. Blacksmith: Yes.

The question arises as to how Mr. Blacksmith knew that he needed to file a correctly notarized letter. While he states he was not called by KISW, he may have been referring only to the receipt of Hoffart's letter. Mr. Blacksmith was the last testimonial letter witness called to the stand. All five were authors of letters in which Ms. Carrie Matthew affixed a phony notarial verification upon suggestions from the manager, Mr. Steve West. Hoffart, however, has stated that he wrote seven letters of inquiry. Letters had been written to one Bob Curran, U.S. army retired, military co-ordinator for Seafair and also to Mr. John Taylor, promotion director for Bumbershoot. Ms. Margit Noren, KISW senior notary, notarized both of these letters.

Hoffart wrote these letters because: 1. He knew Ms. Noren was a KISW employee; 2. The Bob Curran letter was not dated as to when it was written; and 3. The John Taylor letter was not dated as to when Ms. Noren notarized his signature.

The judge ruled that Mr. Curran and Mr. John Taylor need not appear based upon the testimony given by Ms. Noren, under oath, that Mr. Curran had come into KISW and she notarized his signature with Mr. Curren before her. Similarly, she had testified that Mr. John Taylor had appeared before her when she notarized his signature on an unknown date. The reader will recognize that the judge did not allow the record to be fully established in this matter. We have only the self-serving word of Ms. Noren that she testified truthfully.

Hoffart had mentioned to the judge, when he ruled that testimony by Mr. Curran and Mr. John Taylor would be cumulative, and as such not necessary, that he had written letters to both of these individuals and they had not responded. Hoffart's statements to the judge were clear indications that he wanted to cross-examine both of these individuals. It should be clear to anyone that such one-sided adjudication prejudiced Hoffart's case. The judge was already aware, at this point in time, that Ms. Noren had perjured herself in notarizing the David Watkins corrected letter and allowing it to be filed with the FCC. Anything that Ms. Noren was connected with became suspect. To rule that her testimony regarding Mr. Curran and Mr. John Taylor is truthful in the light of what has happened defies analysis. Let's take a short journey back into some of the testimony as it relates to these two affiants. Mr. Curran first.

19.

BOB L. CURRAN

Mr. Curran's letter appears in the appendix.[55] No corrected letter was filed by Kaye-Smith since Ms. Noren states, under oath, that Mr. Curran had appeared before her at KISW, presumably on October 26th, 1982; the date she shows that she notarized his letter. The letter, the reader will note, is undated. Let's review the Noren testimony that the judge found conclusive.

TR:591   *Judge Fitzpatrick*: Tell us how you went about getting that letter from Mr. Curran.

Ms. Noren: I called him on the telephone at his work and explained the situation, that we were going to have a hearing which I think he was already aware of, and that I needed a letter stating how we were, how he had been involved with us during Seafair and different community events during the license period in question, and that the letter needed to be notarized, and that I needed it by a certain date.

Judge Fitzpatrick: Then what happened concerning Major Curran's letter?

Ms. Noren: A couple of days later he came into the station and I notarized his letter for him and he signed it in front of me.

Judge Fitzpatrick: But he affixed the signature in your presence?

Ms. Noren: Yes.

This is the testimony, then, that the judge found to be of sufficient credibility that no need existed for Mr. Curran to appear and be cross-examined by Hoffart. However, let's go back a little further to testimony by Mr. West which has not been reported herein up to this time.

The judge had been questioning Mr. West regarding his knowledge relating to the phony verifications. Mr. West made the following sworn statement regarding the Curran letter:

TR:316   *Mr. West*: Some of these people mailed us letters and some of them brought them in. I know that Bob Curran from Seafair brought it in because I know him.

Here Mr. West gave a sworn statement that he knows Mr. Curran. This testimony was given on November 30, 1982. The very next day,

---

[55]Appendix page 21.

while under cross-examination by Hoffart, the testimony went like this, also sworn to upon oath:

TR:432   *Mr. Hoffart*: Now, page 28 of Exhibit 16, this is another one of yours. You have this covered in your affidavit, right?

Mr. West: Right.

Mr. Hoffart: This is a Major Curran. Can you tell me where the date is on this thing?

Mr. West: On the letter? There isn't one.

Mr. Hoffart: Did you personally ask Mr. Curran for this letter of commendation?

Mr. West: No, I did not.

Mr. Hoffart: Who did this?

Mr. West: Meg Noren. I don't even know Mr. Curran.

A funny thing happened to Mr. West. The day previous to this testimony Mr. West was acquainted with Mr. Curran and the next morning he is contradicting his own sworn testimony. This testimony, plus the fact that Mr. Curran did not respond to Hoffart's letter of inquiry, raises substantial questions regarding the Noren testimony. It appears that a response to Hoffart's inquiry would have been in favor of KISW if Mr. Curran had appeared before Ms. Noren.

The author casts no aspersions upon Mr. Curran. As the testimony exists today in the official records and transcript, Mr. Curran appeared before Ms. Noren on the 26th of November. Ms. Noren says so. Perhaps an investigative reporter will ask Mr. Curran about this. It would be idle for the author to approach him. He has already declined to respond to one inquiry. Perhaps he is another one of the affiants who was told not to respond to Hoffart. Perhaps a grand jury will have better luck in finding the answers.

20.

JOHN R. TAYLOR

Kaye-Smith filed an original and a corrected testimonial letter solicited from Mr. John Taylor, promotion director for Bumbershoot, a Seattle Arts Festival event. Both letters are reproduced in the appendix.[56] As with all solicited letters, the author does not question the sincerity of Mr Taylor as to the content of his letters. Mr. Taylor's name appears in this book because there is some doubt in the author's mind as to whether or not Mr. Taylor had appeared before Ms. Noren at KISW when she allegedly witnessed his signature on an unknown date. In addition, a fair reading of some of her earlier testimony suggests that Ms. Noren did affix her notarial seal and signature to one or more of the testimonial letters outside of the presence of the affiants. Since only two letters were notarized by Ms. Noren in the original filings, that by Mr. Curran and that by Mr. John Taylor, one or both of these letters may have been affixed with phony notarial verifications by Ms. Noren.

The judge's ruling that any testimony by Mr. Curran or Mr. John Taylor would be cumulative robbed Hoffart of his right to question both of these authors of letters. The judge himself had ruled, at the pre-hearing, that all affiants were to be advised that they would be subject to cross-examination, and then he changes his mind based solely upon testimony from a witness who is hostile to Hoffart.

One or both of these witnesses may have taken issue with the Ms. Noren testimony, and if so, she would have been proven to have given false testimony. This would have been nothing new. She had already testified that she was not an experienced notary and also that the routine of notarizing performance affidavits had not been changed when she became a notary. Both of these sworn statements are untrue, as the record evidence proves.

Noren testified that the John Taylor testimonial letter had to be redone because she had not dated her notarial act on his original letter. She stated that she obtained a second letter, now dated November 22nd, 1982 which she notarized the next day when he brought the letter to KISW and signed it in front of Ms. Noren. This November 23rd, 1982 notarized letter, notarized in Seattle, was sent to Hoffart the next day, November 24th, along with the other corrected letters, from New York. Significantly, one of the reasons why Kaye-Smith's Mr. West ordered some of the letters redone was because the date of the letter and the date of the notarization were not the same. Here, however, we have a corrected letter notarized one day after it was authored.

---

[56]Appendix pages 19 and 20. Taylor's two letters.

The author had written Mr. Taylor a letter inquiring if he had appeared before Ms. Noren on an unknown date and if his original letter signature had been verified by Ms. Noren. Mr. Taylor was unresponsive. Here again it would appear that an affirmative answer would have been in the station's favor and there would have been no need for a corrected letter filing. By a preponderance of evidence test, therefore, Mr. Taylor did not appear before Ms. Noren to have his first letter notarized and as such the Noren testimony becomes suspect. Again the author hopes that the news media will seek some answers. The possibility of a congressional investigation is always present also. The public may demand some answers from the FCC in this matter. They may demand some answers from the judge and those who upheld his findings and conclusions that the case warranted only a slight demerit.

The author now recites some of the testimony from the hearing that pertains to Mr. John R. Taylor and Mr. Bob Curran:

TR:780 *Judge Fitzpatrick*: ... in my view we've developed the record, as far as I know, concerning this notarization problem, unless ... do you intend to explore it any further, Mr. Hoffart?

Mr. Hoffart: As far as I am concerned, we've established a record, but there are two more to come in, Mr. Curran and John Taylor. But as far as I am concerned ...

Judge Fitzpatrick: Mr. Curran? Well, let's talk about that, then. What pages are Mr. Curran and Mr. John Taylor? Can you tell me where I can find him? It's the Major in the ...

Mr. Boros: United States Army, retired.

Judge Fitzpatrick: What page is he?

Mr. Boros: My recollection is he appeared. He is on page 28 of Kaye-Smith Exhibit 16, and he, I believe ...

Judge Fitzpatrick: Yes, Ms. Noren testified that Mr. Curran came in to the station and appeared before her and affixed his signature before her. So with that testimony, I don't see the need to Mr. Curran to come in.

Mr. Hoffart: Your Honor, if I may state that I sent Mr. Curran a self-addressed, stamped envelope and I received no reply.

Judge Fitzpatrick: All right. The record will so show.

Mr. Boros: We have no objection to the record so showing.

Judge Fitzpatrick: The other one is John Taylor?

Mr. Young: I believe that's the same situation.

Judge Fitzpatrick: I believe so, too, but can you tell me what page I'll find that one?
Mr. Young: Surely, that would be Exhibit 16, page 13.
Judge Fitzpatrick: Let me get that. I'd like to put these finishing touches before we go any further. John Taylor, I believe, Ms. Noren testified that the only problem with Mr. Taylor was that he did appear before her the first time but she didn't date it, and that therefore they went through all the trouble of doing it again and dating it, and it was done in her presence. I wouldn't require his appearance in the light of that sworn testimony.
Mr. Hoffart: I do not. I just wish to state that I did sent him a letter similar to the others with a self-addressed stamped envelope, and I received no reply.
Judge Fitzpatrick: All right. With the completion of all that testimony, are you reoffering Exhibit 16 . . . ?

While Hoffart stated that he did not object to Mr. Taylor not appearing, this comment was based upon the judge's remark that the record had been established. Hoffart was of the opinion that the record showed an abuse of processes the likes of which probably never surfaced in a proceeding before the Federal Communications Commission. The author had reminded the judge that both Mr. Taylor and Mr. Curran had not responded to his letters of inquiry. The judge should have put the finishing touches, as he put it, to exhibit 16 by having both Mr. Taylor and Mr. Curran appear so that Hoffart could ask them whether or not the Noren testimony is true. As the record now stands, only the testimony of a Kaye-Smith biased witness supports the fact that two authors of testimonial letters appeared before notary Ms. Noren, and that biased testimony is by Ms. Noren herself.

Hoffart had, in his exceptions to the judge's Initial Decision, listed this as one-sided adjudication which prejudiced Hoffart's case. Of course the case was already replete with perjury, and apparently the judge felt that one more untruth would only be cumulative; however, as it turned out, with a ruling favorable to Kaye-Smith, an additional proven perjury charge might have been too much for even Judge Fitzpatrick to swallow. The review board refused to hold that the judge's cumulative testimony ruling prejudiced Hoffart's case. As the reader already knows, they found that the author's allegations were a hodgepodge of accusations, typical adversarial puff and much ado about nothing. What to you think, reader? Did the judge's ruling that Mr. Taylor and Mr. Curran's testimony was not needed satisfy the rules of jurisprudence; rules which say that testimony by a witness may be rebutted by the opposing side? If, as an aftermath of this book, either

Mr. Curran or Mr. John Taylor comes forward and contradicts the Noren testimony, Hoffart may well petition the FCC to reopen the record of this case.

21.

C. CLARK GRIFFIN

It has been proven, beyond any doubt, that Ms. Noren affixed a phony verification to the second David Watkins letter on November 17th, 1982 and that this act came after all of the difficulties had come to her attention. A review of her sworn testimony will refresh the reader's memory.

TR:605   *Ms. Noren*: The letter came from Dave Watkins. I did not see him sign it, but I affixed my notary signature and seal to it after speaking to him on the telephone.

Mr. Boros: Well, how did it happen that you spoke to him on the telephone? Did he call you or did you call him?

Ms. Noren: I called him.

Mr. Boros: What did you say to him?

Ms. Noren: I told him that I had been handed the letter from him but it was not notarized, and he said that his notary was out ill that day. And I asked him, would it be with his approval if I notarized it for legal purposes and he said yes.

Judge Fitzpatrick: Now, this conversation took place on November 17th?

Ms. Noren: Yes.

Judge Fitzpatrick: This was after all of the difficulties had already come to your attention?

Ms. Noren: Yes.

The author has already reproduced this document in the appendix as page 14. The reader is again invited to review the notarial attestation affixed to that letter by Ms. Noren. It states:

> Subscribed and sworn before me this 17th day of November, 1982. (s) Margit Noren, Notary Public.

This phony notarization by Ms. Noren, coming after she had become aware that phony verifications had already been filed with the FCC, does not stand alone. She also notarized a corrected letter Kaye-Smith filed that was obtained from a Mr. C. Clark Griffin. The original and corrected Griffin testimonial letters are in the appendix.[57]

With reference to the original C. Clark Griffin letter, the reader should note that it was notarized before a Ms. Christine Woolson on the 29th of October, 1982. The letter itself is dated October 21, 1982. As

---

[57]Appendix pages 26 and 27.

with the other authors, Hoffart does not question the sincerity of Mr. Griffin as to the content of his letter. What Hoffart questions, however, is the validity of the notarization by Ms. Woolson. This is due to the fact that Kaye-Smith filed a corrected version, now notarized by Ms. Noren, even though the author had not sent a letter to Mr. Griffin and had not questioned the fact that the notarial attestation came a week after the letter was dated. Since there is nothing amiss with this difference in dates, the question arises as to why a corrected letter was solicited. The author reasons that the Christine Woolson notarization is a phony. Some support for the authors conclusions can be gleaned from testimony given by Mr. West.

TR:322   *Judge Fitzpatrick*: On page 8 of Exhibit 17, and I am talking about the original page 8 and not the corrected page 8, which purports to be a letter of a C. Clark Griffin, do you know the circumstances surrounding that notarization . . . I can't read her writing and . . . do you know who she is?[58]
Mr. West: No.
Judge Fitzpatrick: Do you know why a corrected page with a new notarization is being submitted?
Mr. West: We went back to the people that didn't have a corresponding date from top to bottom. Those are the people that we went back to, and some of them resubmitted letters, and others waited, and they walked down the hall to their own business and we didn't do that, but the ones that wrote new letters . . .
Judge Fitzpatrick: Do you know this individual that appears to be Christine . . .
Mr. West: There is a Chris . . . I don't know. I know a girl that worked . . .
Judge Fitzpatrick: I don't want you to speculate.
Mr. West: I don't know that person.

There is no evidence in the record that proves Mr. West is untruthful. There is, however, circumstantial evidence that bears review. First, the employment roster filed by Kaye-Smith in their Direct Written Case exhibit no. 7 lists a Ms. Christine Woolson as traffic manager at KISW. She is listed as having been hired on April 21, 1975 and left on June 25th, 1979. Her tenure at KISW, therefore, was over four years. The author knows that Mr. West moved to Seattle from Spokane, Washington around 1973 to take the position of program director at KJR. KJR was the sister AM station to KISW and to the best of the author's

---

[58]Appendix page 26. Original Griffin letter notarized by a Ms. Christine Woolson.

recollection, the KJR AM studios and the KISW FM studios were in the same building at the time Ms. Woolson was hired. It appears, therefore, that both Mr. West and Ms. Woolson were working in the same building in 1975 and for the same employer. This being the case, it goes beyond the zone of reasonableness that Mr. West did not know Ms. Woolson and vice versa. Mr. West's testimony, *supra*, finds him changing his mind after he first states he knows a girl named Chris and then reverses himself and states he does not know the notary who verified the C. Clark Griffin signature one week after the letter was authored.

The testimony by Mr. Smith shows that he ordered Kaye-Smith employees to "drop everything" and get the next thing counsel asks for, "even though we are in a very busy time of the year." Since Ms. Woolson was a former employee of KISW, with some four years of experience, it is possible that she was called back to assist in the operations of the station while the key employees were engaged in compiling the Direct Written Case, or perhaps she may even have assisted in the research and collating of the filing. Assuming that this is a possibility, she may have been asked to notarize the C. Clark Griffin original letter by Mr. West or by Ms. Noren, just as Ms. Matthew had been instructed to violate her oath of office as a commissioned Washington state notary public.

This could be another area where an investigative reporter may ask questions. Ms. Woolson was a notary public in 1982 and therefore her address would be a matter of record with the Secretary of State and/or the Department of Licensing. It would be interesting to know if the author is wide of the target in his hypothetical analysis of what may have transpired in the notarization of the original C. Clark Griffin testimonial letter. Let's move on to the corrected letter filed by KISW, now notarized, allegedly, before Ms. Noren on November 23rd in Seattle, Washington and sent to Hoffart as a corrected exhibit from New York the following day.

TR:612   *Mr. Boros:* Now, with respect to page 8 (A), if I could ask you to turn to page 8 (A), there's a letter addressed to Paul Sullivan, and there's a signature there and at the bottom what appears to be your signature. Could you state how the signature which appears to be a signature of a C. Clark Griffin came to be on that page, and how your signature came to be on that page?[59]

Ms. Noren: The letter was delivered to me by Paul Sullivan, who received it from Mr. Griffin.

---

[59]Appendix page 27. Corrected Griffin letter now notarized by Ms. Margit Noren, KISW senior notary.

Mr. Boros: How do you know he received it from Mr. Griffin?

Ms. Noren: Because he told me that he had just come from Mr. Griffin's office.

Mr. Boros: That's what Mr. Sullivan said to you?

Ms. Noren: Yes.

Mr. Boros: And when he delivered the letter to you, did it have Mr. Griffin's signature on it?

Ms. Noren: Yes, it did.

Mr. Boros: What did you do after you received this letter from Mr. Sullivan which had Mr. Griffin's signature on it?

Ms. Noren: I called Mr. Griffin and told him that the letter needed notarization, and he said for me to go ahead and notarize it.

Mr. Boros: Where did you call Mr. Griffin? Do you know where you called him, at what number?

Ms. Noren: I called him at his office and the number was taken off of Paul Sullivan's Rolodex card.

Mr. Boros: We have no further questions of Ms. Noren, your Honor.

The author cross-examined Ms. Noren regarding this notarization of a corrected letter outside the presence of the affiant.

TR:622   *Mr. Hoffart*: How about 8 (A), now. That's Exhibit 17. Mr. Griffin. It shows that on November 23, 1982, you notarized his signature. Did Mr. Griffin show up at your station?

Ms. Noren: No, he did not.

Mr. Hoffart: How did you meet Mr. Griffin?

Ms. Noren: I called him on the telephone.

Mr. Hoffart: Another telephone identification?

Ms. Noren: Yes.

Mr. Hoffart: Did you know whether you were talking to Mr. Griffin?

Ms. Noren: Yes.

Mr. Hoffart: Did you personally know Mr. Griffin?

Ms. Noren: No.

Mr. Hoffart: How did you know you were talking to Mr. Griffin?

Ms. Noren: I asked for Mr. Griffin, and when he got on the phone I asked if this was Clark Griffin. He said yes.

This testimony established that Ms. Noren had notarized the corrected Griffin testimonial letter without benefit of having Mr. Griffin present or ever having known him personally. She relied upon a telephone identification. This was on November 23rd, one week after she had similarly notarized a corrected letter solicited from Mr. David Watkins outside the presence of Mr. Watkins, and in actual fact without a valid signature from Mr. Watkins. The commission found that there is no evidence in the record that Ms. Noren knew that it was improper to notarize the corrected letters outside the presence of the affiants because the record does not specifically show that counsel talked to Ms. Noren about this matter.

Hoffart disagrees with the commission's patently biased analysis of the testimony in this regard. It goes beyond the zone of reasonableness that Ms. Noren did not know it was improper to notarize documents outside the presence of the affiants, especially in connection with the Watkins and Griffin corrected letters; and especially since the entire "corrections" fiasco was based upon the discovery by Hoffart, on November 12th, of what appeared to be phony verifications on seven testimonial letters out of a total of twenty-four filed. The author now picks up testimony from the transcript which supports his contention that Ms. Noren did know that what she was doing was illegal.

TR:570   *Judge Fitzpatrick*: Now, let me ask you this: When did you first learn that what you did was, at least as it relates to Exhibits 16 and 17 in having notarized signatures of people who didn't appear before you and affix their signatures . . . and I'm talking about Shawn Taylor, McCullough, Balint, Blacksmith and McConnell. When did you first find out that what you did was improper?

Ms. Matthew: After they had been sent to our authorities, and they told us that it was wrong and that they had to be notarized in front of them.

Judge Fitzpatrick: Who told you this? Were you told by the attorneys? Who told you?

Ms. Matthew: No, Meg Noren did.

Judge Fitzpatrick: Tell me what she told you.

Ms. Matthew: She told me that we were wrong, and that we should have had either them notarize it in front of whoever signed it, or I should have had them come in and notarize it in front of them.

Ironically, it was Ms. Noren, acting in concert with Mr. Steve West, the KISW manager, who instructed Ms. Matthew to notarize the five testimonial letters outside the presence of all five of the authors, and without their knowledge in some cases, and also without their consent, in some cases. Then she chides Ms. Matthew for doing what she did. How hypocritical can she get, in this apparent shift of blame? This conversation between Ms. Matthew and Ms. Noren must have preceded the phony notarization of the Watkins corrected letter on the 17th by Ms. Noren. The record shows that Ms. Noren notarized nine affidavits in which Ms. Matthew was the affiant on the 16th of November. These affidavits were filed by Kaye-Smith to establish that the missing dates to nine affidavits were all November 9th, 1982. There can be no doubt, therefore, that the phony verifications fiasco was discussed by the 16th, and yet Ms. Noren affixed her notarial attestation to the Watkins letter on the 17th and to the C. Clark Griffin corrected letter on the 23rd.

If the reader has lost track of how many notarial imperfections were filed in this case, which in actual fact were statutory violations of the criminal code, join the club. The author has also lost count. Take, for example, when counsel filed affidavits from Ms. Matthew to supply the missing dates to nine notarial acts, excluding the five phony verifications, Hoffart received eighteen documents from counsel, all sent to him on the 23rd. Nine of these documents were copies of the Matthew attestations that were originally filed, lacking the date of notarization. Nine were affidavits by Ms. Matthew attesting to the fact that the nine missing dates were all November 9th, and these nine were all notarized by Ms. Noren. Confusing, isn't it?

The question of why counsel filed documents in the first instance that would not pass muster before the judge has not been addressed or answered anywhere in the record. Clearly counsel was employed by Kaye-Smith and as such Kaye-Smith is responsible for their acts in this case. The author can only conclude that the judge included counsel as being among the Kaye-Smith employees who were found to be innocent of any wrongdoings because the improprieties in notarizations were the result of ignorance. The general public may well use this precedent, albeit an administrative decision, the next time they find themselves before a judge. Feigned ignorance is now a valid defense. Judge Fitzpatrick says so.

22.

NINA L. EVERS

Kaye-Smith solicited a letter of commendation from a Nina L. Evers, district director of the Muscular Dystrophy Association. Ms. Evers wrote such a letter dated November 8, 1982. This letter is reproduced in the appendix.[60] The author does not question the sincerity of Ms. Evers and her name appears in this book courtesy of the individual who solicited this letter and filed it with the FCC, namely, KISW employees.

First, with respect to the date of the letter, the November 8th date shows that Kaye-Smith solicited this letter after the original due date of the Kaye-Smith Direct Case, which was November 5th. Hoffart had been called by Mr. Stuart Young, co-counsel for Kaye-Smith, and advised that they wanted an extra week to complete their filing and that the delay was due to "steno problems," as he put it. The author reluctantly agreed to a one-week delay. However, the same day that Hoffart advised the judge that he had no objections to the delay, the author received a letter from the Washington, D.C. office of Kaye-Smith's counsel in which Mr. Gastfreund advised the judge that the extra week was needed to get documents from the Seattle area and from the FCC. This is not what Hoffart had been told by Mr. Young. The author then immediately filed an objection to the extension of time with the judge, citing the conflicting reasons given for the need of the delay. The judge's secretary called Hoffart and stated that the judge had already granted the extension and any objections were too late. At this point in time the judge should have found Kaye-Smith basically disqualified for failure to meet the mutually agreed upon exchange date.

It is clear from the Nina Evers letter that Kaye-Smith and their counsel wanted the extra week to obtain additional testimonial letters to bolster their case. Other letters filed by Kaye-Smith that were solicited during this extension of time were the Shawn Taylor letter, which was solicited on the original due date of November 5th, a letter solicited from the english instructor at Lynnwood Senior High School, dated November 9th, 1982 and notarized that same day, and a letter solicited from the Puget Sound Radio Broadcasters Association and authored and signed by a Mr. Todd M. Bitts, dated November 3rd, and notarized that date. This November 3rd letter probably could not have reached counsel in New York in time for a turnaround to be received by Hoffart on the 5th due date.

---

[60]Appendix page 31. This letter is notarized on the 10th of November. She was not an affiant on the 9th.

Hoffart avers that rather than steno problems, Kaye-Smith wanted the extra time to bolster their case with additional testimonial letters. Incidently, no documents from the FCC were filed or needed, as the Washington, D.C. office of Kaye-Smith counsel had represented.

Now, for the second reason why the Nina L. Evers letter belongs in this book: Ms. Evers is listed on the Eric Bogel affidavit attachment list, appendix page 4, as the second name from the top, following that of Mayor Royer of Seattle. Testimony elicited from Ms. Matthew and Ms. Noren and Mr. West and Bogel establishes that the Bogel and West affidavits were signed before Ms. Matthew on the 9th of November. A check with the Nina Evers letter, however, will show that it was not notarized until the 10th of November. It becomes self-evident that Ms. Evers was not and could not have been an affiant on the 9th, as Bogel avers through his attachment list. By a preponderance of evidence test, then, the only logical explanation is that Mr. Bogel could not have had the attachment list before him on the 9th and most probably it was authored by counsel in New York on the 10th or later. Mr. Bogel, then, pre-executed his affidavit and had no direct knowledge of who was on the attachment list.

23.

CHARLES ROYER, MAYOR

Kaye-Smith made a great ado about the fact that the mayor of Seattle, Mr. Charles Royer, sent Kaye-Smith a testimonial letter in support of their renewal. This letter was solicited from the mayor by Mr. Eric Bogel, KISW program director. The mayor's letter is reproduced in the appendix.[61]

The quotes taken from this letter include his statement that he, the mayor, was very impressed with the station's civic consciousness and high professional standards and also that he had participated in two campaigns for food for the Northwest Second Harvest which showed a strong, effective commitment to broadcasting in the public interest.

The author does not doubt the sincerity of the content of the mayor's letter. No doubt the mayor would write a letter of commendation to any station that requested one. However, let's take a look at the Eric Bogel testimony in regards to the solicitation of the letter from the mayor and also to a subsequent misrepresentation by counsel before the U.S. Court of Appeals, D.C. Circuit, in a Petition to Intervene Brief filed in support of the FCC's decision to grant renewal to Kaye-Smith; a decision which the author charged was arbitrary, capricious, an abuse of discretion, and also contrary to congressional intent when they enacted the Communications Act of 1934.

TR:488 *Mr. Boros*: Well, directing your attention to the letter from Mr. Charles Royer, Mayor of Seattle, what did he say to you and what did you say to him about appearing in this case?

Judge Fitzpatrick: If anything.

Mr. Boros: If anything.

Mr. Bogel: There was no gesture on his part to say that he would be willing to appear. There was nothing to the contrary. There was no offer made.

Mr. Boros: Well, what did you say to him and what did he say to you:

Mr. Bogel: I explained to him that what I said prior, that our license is up for renewal and we need to go back to major community leaders or services that we've been involved with. And being that we'd been involved with the Mayor on two food bank drives, he said he'd be more than happy to get a letter to us.

61Appendix page 32. Letter solicited from Mayor Royer.

Mr. Boros: Did you mention to him that a hearing would be held before the FCC in Seattle?

Mr. Bogel: I mentioned to him that it would be used in court.

Mr. Boros: What did he say to that?

Mr. Bogel: He didn't seem to say anything. He said, "I'll get you the letter as soon as I can."

The mayor's endorsement of the community efforts by KISW is not minimized by the author. The reader, however, should keep an open mind regarding the mayor's statements attesting to the station's civic consciousness and high professional standards and their strong, effective commitment to broadcasting in the public interest. It must be recognized that the mayor, as the official spokesman of the Seattle residents, was expressing the views of those people without, perhaps, looking deeper into the actual programming by KISW. The author will come back to these statements by the mayor when complaints received from area citizens regarding the KISW programming will be featured in this book.

Now for the second reason for featuring the Mayor's letter in this book: subsequent to the commissions affirmation of the review board's upholding of the judge's initial decision to renew the KISW license, Hoffart filed a notice of appeal with the United States Court of Appeals, D.C. Circuit, which has jurisdiction in such matters. Kaye-Smith counsel filed a Brief in support of the commission, who was the designated appellee. In this Brief, which will not be reproduced, counsel made the following statement to the court:

> The various adjudicatory authorities charged with resolving the contest between Kaye-Smith and Hoffart, on an agency level, consistently have held KISW's past performance to be meritorious. (citations omitted) That conclusion derived not only from Station operation but also from local evaluation thereof. Thus Station KISW has received numerous letters from community leaders, throughout the license period, commending the Station for its public service programming. (citation omitted). As the Mayor of Seattle stated during hearing, Kaye-Smith has demonstrated a " . . . strong, effective commitment to broadcasting in the public interest." (citations omitted). Accordingly, a substantial preference was awarded to Kaye-Smith for its past broadcast record.

The author submits that a fair reading of the above represents to the court that the mayor appeared at the hearing. The statement: "As the Mayor of Seattle stated during hearing," cannot be construed any other way. The mayor, of course, did not make any such statements at the hearing. The mayor's involvement was limited to the filing of a solicited letter of commendation.

Hoffart alleges that the above statement in the brief before the court of appeals is a blatant abuse of processes and a misrepresentation by counsel. Counsel Boros knew when he affixed his signature to the brief that this statement is untrue.

Media reporters may wish to interview the mayor in this regard and specifically ask if he knew that this was a court situation and that he was subject to cross-examination. Mr. Bogel has stated, under oath, that he told the mayor that his statement would be used in an FCC proceeding and that a court situation was involved.

24.

CRAIG SIEGENTHALER

The author had filed a subpoena with the judge demanding the appearance for cross-examination of Mr. Craig Siegenthaler, the KISW chief engineer. The judge ruled that no subpoena was necessary since Mr. Siegenthaler was an upper echelon KISW employee and Kaye-Smith had the obligation of producing him. Hoffart wanted to ask some questions involving the technical operations of the station during the renewal period.

The reader may recall that the author, through inspection of the KISW public file at the studio, and through discovery, obtained over one hundred documents which were subsequently studied and which triggered some cross-examination questions.

First, inspection of the file showed that Engineer Siegenthaler made the requisite equipment performance measurements as required by the rules on September 29th, 1980. Mr. Smith, in his application for renewal dated September 26th, represented to the commission in that application that the measurements had been made, when in actual fact that was not the case. Mr. Siengenthaler did not know who checked off the box on the application blank which had his signature and which indicated that the measurements had been made. Misrepresentations in the application for renewal were proven, but were swept under the rug. The conclusions made no mention of this untrue statement in the KISW 1980 application. Just who made the entry is unknown since the commission is not interested, apparently, in such misrepresentations.

The actual date of the performance measurements was obtained from a block diagram of the performance measurements set-up, as required by the rules. This block diagram also showed that KISW had installed a new microwave transmitter, a 12 watt Time and Frequency Technology model 7700 without obtaining prior authority from the commission. The installation of unauthorized radio apparatus and use thereof is a statutory violation of Title 47, U.S.C. Section 301. In addition, the rules require that a construction permit be first obtained if a microwave transmitter is changed to a different manufacture or if a higher power transmitter is installed. KISW violated both of these rules during the renewal period. In actual fact KISW applied for a renewal of their old 7 watt Moseley microwave on September 26th, 1980 which was at a time when the TFT model was in actual use. The FCC records show that KISW filed for a modification of the microwave on February 20, 1980, but that application was not granted due to the fact that it was incomplete. The section requiring a make and model number of the new equipment was left blank by KISW. No amendment to correct this omission was filed by Kaye-Smith until June 18, 1982, some three weeks after they were advised that Hoffart's application had been accepted and that a comparative hearing would be required. Thus the commission's records show that KISW operated an illegal microwave transmitter from at least February 20, 1980 until a license was issued on June 25, 1982. During this interval Mr. Smith had signed an application for renewal of a microwave transmitter that was not in use.

Section 301 of the Communications Act of 1934, as amended, states, without equivocation, that it is unlawful to operate radio apparatus without authority or permit thereto from the commission. Furthermore, there is no need for a showing of willfullness when an illegal act is repeated, and repeated means simply more than once. Here we have undisputed documentation that a microwave transmitter was used illegally for over two years. Quoting now from the transcript:

TR:713   *Mr. Hoffart*: At the time in 1980, did you have a license to have a TFT model 7700 as a microwave?

Mr. Boros: Object, unless you define "you". Do you mean station KISW (FM)?

Mr. Hoffart: Yes. KISW. Was there a license in existence for that?

Mr. Siegenthaler: No, and I shall explain this. Previous to this, KISW was experiencing microwave interference. At times the microwave interference was bad enough to make the main channel practically unlistenable. My concern was keeping the audio quality up, and sound as clean as possible.

I referred this problem to the manager. We discussed it, and the new TFT, this particular transmitter link, was purchased and it was specifically installed to solve the interference problem. The TFT microwave has superior adjacent frequency interference characteristics than does the microwave link that was used previous to this.

At the time I put this transmitter in, I thought that all that was required was a proof of performance similar to the deregulation that is now current with the main transmitter or auxiliary transmitter. If you do not change the power, all that is required is a proof of performance to make the system legal or in compliance.

This is not what the rules stated in 1980. The rules and the application blank specifically require a manufacturer to be listed on the application and the type number plus the maximum rated power output. The February 20th, 1980 application left this information off the document.

Mr. Siegenthaler's testimony does not reveal why this information was not filed, but what is more egregious is that an application on a short form, patently not allowed when changes are made, was dated and signed on September 26th, specifying that KISW was using a Moseley PCL-303 C model with an operating power of 7 watts. Equally egregious is the fact that KISW continued to operate the TFT without authorization for over two years. An application is not an authorization. Upon Hoffart's insistence a stipulation to that effect was entered into the record by Kaye-Smith counsel.

The judge ruled that this unauthorized operation of radio apparatus, a statutory violation, was an oversight. No demerits were warranted. Ignorance of the law is now an excuse. Judge Fitzpatrick has so ruled.

The author hopes that the reader will bear with him in what may appear to be a departure from the notarial imperfections, the main topic of this book. Hoffart needs to bring the statutory and rules violations into focus since these violations are relevant factors in a comparative hearing. The preceding unauthorized installation and repeated use of the microwave should have resulted in a substantial demerit against KISW. Perhaps some other broadcasters were not so fortunate and had to ante up a fine. If so, perhaps they should ask for a rebate since like cases require like treatment, or they should request an explanation as to why disparate action is warranted.[62]

Hoffart now goes into yet another technical violation which may be of special interest to all of the other licensees in the Seattle area.

Hoffart became aware that KISW was operating a translator on Queen Anne Hill in Seattle with a directional antenna. Hoffart was also aware that the license issued for this FM 10 watt rebroadcast installation called for the use of a non-directional antenna, a Gibson 3 element vertical dipole. This Gibson antenna was specified by Kaye-Smith at the time they filed for a construction permit. The permit issued specifically authorized only a Gibson antenna.

KISW, however, without any further application or modification of their construction permit, installed a TACO Y-51 five element directional antenna orientated 204 degrees from true north so as to cover dead spots, namely, Alki Point, which is a favorite nitetime parking spot and which is shadowed from Cougar Mountain, the location of the KISW main transmitter.

KISW filed an application for this installation, duly showing that they had substituted a TACO Y-51 Yagi for the authorized 3 element Gibson antenna. The commission issued KISW a license which specifically al-

---

[62]*Melody Music, Inc.*, 120 U.S. Appeals, D.C. circuit (1964).

lowed only the use of the Gibson antenna. A copy of this license is reproduced. [63]

This license, issued on May 22, 1979, specifically states, in the fine print, the following:

This license shall not vest in the license any right . . . in the use of the frequencies designated in the license beyond the terms thereof, nor in any other manner than authorized herein.[64]

Thus KISW was put on notice that the license was not valid because the license specified an antenna other than the one installed by KISW and used for well over four years. As with the microwave transmitter, Mr. Smith again signed a short-form renewal application for this translator, known as K283AA, on September 26, 1980 without advising the commission that the license did not agree with the installation. The rules, circa 1978, specifically state that no change may be made in a translator that involves a change in the transmitting antenna system, including the direction of radiation or directive antenna pattern. The author asked Mr. Siegenthaler some questions about this illegal installation:

TR:725   *Mr. Hoffart*: Do you recall what type of an antenna the construction permit called for?
Mr. Siegenthaler: It gives them three-element colinear array.
Mr. Hoffart: Is that what you installed?
Mr. Siegenthaler: No, it was not.
Mr. Hoffart: Are you aware of the rules that . . . again I'd have to look for them, your Honor. Are you aware of any rule that requires you to have prior permission before changing an antenna on a transmitter to an antenna that's other than that in a construction permit?
Mr. Siegenthaler: When we finished the construction of The translator or K283AA, we installed a different antenna. The antenna performance characteristics were all tabulated and it was entered in the application for a license.
Mr. Hoffart: But you made application afterwards? You didn't have permission to install a Y51 antenna on the translator from the Federal Communications Commission?

---

[63]Appendix page 40. Invalid translator license.
[64]Appendix page 40, last paragraph.

Mr. Siegenthaler: We had authority to operate it when we got the license. I mean . . . oh, do you mean specifically that antenna?
Mr. Hoffart: Yes.
Mr. Siegenthaler: The license itself received from the FCC did not state the original antenna. I mean, it stated the original antenna. It did not show . . .

The questioning by the judge went along the lines that KISW had informed the commission that they installed an antenna other than the one authorized. Apparently the judge found this mitigating since he made no adverse conclusions based on this flagrant violation of terms of the construction permit. The use of this unauthorized apparatus is a violation of Title 47, U.S.C. Section 301, which prohibits the installation and use of radio apparatus without a permit or authority from the commission. No valid license was ever issued by the FCC.

Mr. Siegenthaler admitted on the witness stand that he was aware that the license did not comport with the installation. Significantly, the invalid license expired on December 1, 1981 and KISW had filed for a renewal in September of 1981, again specifying the antenna not authorized by the construction permit. The author has been unable to locate any documents granting KISW an extension of their invalid license beyond December 1, 1981, yet KISW apparently continued to use this translator for well over a year, with no authorization of any kind.

In this matter there can be no question of intent. It required a specific act to install an antenna not authorized. It required a specific act to operate the translator with the unauthorized apparatus. The fact that the license issued allowed only the use of a GIBSON antenna and KISW installed and used a TACO directional antenna, willfully and repeatedly, should have basically disqualified KISW for violations of the Communications Act of 1934, as amended.

The judge needs to explain why statutory violations by a licensee, proven beyond any doubt, are not disqualifying.

The rules at the time of the application for the translator construction permit required public notice in an area newspaper of wide circulation and also announcements on KISW. These public notices are required to alert concerned citizens and other broadcasters as to what a licensee is contemplating. Anyone who would look at the application would expect that a non-directional Gibson antenna would be installed.

The application for a license, however, does not require any public notice. With a change of antennas it becomes apparent that only those who sought a copy of the license application would know that KISW installed unauthorized apparatus. Hoffart submits that the illegal installation was not common knowledge to the other Seattle area broadcasters and that the unauthorized use of the directional antenna enhanced the KISW ratings for over four years. This clandestine operation gave KISW a competitive advantage since they were the only broadcaster who had its main transmitter located on Cougar Mountain to have coverage in West Seattle and Alki Point.

The author will dwell more on this illegal installation later in this book when he reviews the commission's order upholding the review board. Hoffart will charge the full commission with preferential treatment and untruths in their Order No. 85-192 regarding the grant of the translator application. The author will support his allegations with a letter from former chief of mass media, Mr. Laurence E. Harris.

Through discovery Hoffart obtained copies of the KISW operational logs for the six months period ending in October, 1980. These logs showed that KISW failed to follow the rules and regulations in regards to Emergency Broadcast actions. The author tabulated the loggings and asked Mr. Siegenthaler to verify the accuracy of the tabulations. A stipulation was entered into the record stating that the tabulations were correct. The logs supported Hoffart's charge that there were serious rules violations by KISW during the renewal period in this vital public interest area approximately 50 percent of the time. These violations standing alone, should have resulted in a substantial demerit or a fine. As might be expected, the rules violations were swept under the rug. The commission, however, in their Order upholding the review board, noted the fact that there was an apparent violation of the rules in this matter, and also in regards to the unauthorized installations. The author will print the commission's order in full toward the end of this book. It's a complete whitewash.

In the matter of EBS violations, the commission had set precedents. KSWR, Rifle, Colorado, had been assessed a forfeiture of 200 dollars for EBS logging violations. Then in December of 1985, after KISW was given a clean bill of health for their EBS violations, *Capitol Media* of Cheyenne, Wyoming was assessed a forfeiture of 4000 dollars for, *inter alia*, violations of EBS rules and regulations. Capitol Media may well ask for a remission of the forfeiture based upon the case precedent set by the commission in this Kaye-Smith case. It becomes obvious that like cases do not require like treatment, particularly when the same treatment given others might be enough to disqualify a renewal applicant in a comparative hearing. When it comes to assessing fines against influential broadcasters, there appears to be a complete vacuum in the commission's records.[65]

Mr. Siegenthaler had actually testified before some of the other witnesses, but the author has taken leave to review his testimony out of

[65]Appendix pages 60 and 61. Capitol Media forfeiture.

sequence in order to present all of the notarial imperfections in a manner which establishes continuity.

Mr. Smith is now recalled to the witness stand to present rebuttal testimony. At one point his testimony was interrupted when Mr. Blacksmith showed up to testify, but generally the testimony went as next presented. Hoffart leaves out matters which are redundant or of no significance.

25.

LESTER M. SMITH—Rebuttal

TR:767   *Judge Fitzpatrick:* Mr. Smith, if you'll come forward we'll give you a fresh swearing, all right? Your's has worn off, I'm afraid.

Mr. Boros: Mr. Smith, would you state what involvement you had during the license period of station KISW FM? That's the period beginning February 1, 1978 and ending on the 31st.

Judge Fitzpatrick: Don't say anything. What's the form of this testimony? Are you on your rebuttal phase of your case or what? What are we doing now?

Mr. Boros: That's true.

Judge Fitzpatrick: You had mentioned one time that you were calling Mr. Smith to testify concerning the execution of these affidavits and his knowledge or lack of knowledge concerning the notarization problem. I thought that's why he was being called at this time.

Mr. Boros: You're quite right, your Honor. I have combined three different areas. I'm calling him now by way of preliminary statement to talk about the affidavits.

Judge Fitzpatrick: This would be an appropriate place to do that.

Mr. Boros: Mr. Smith, when did you first learn that there were questions raised about the execution and validity of various pieces of paper from members of the citizenry in Seattle which were being exchanged by Kaye-Smith Enterprises in this renewal proceeding?

Mr. Smith: In detail, in this courtroom on Monday.

Mr. Boros: And prior to that detail, did you at any earlier period of time learn that there were some questions about these papers?

Mr. Smith: There was conversations, and I don't remember exactly when, with Steve West, the manager, as the problem. And I said, "You work it out with counsel," I said, "this is your ball." And originally were were talking about letters, not affidavits. And I said, "If counsel is not getting through to you, you get back to these fellows and get this thing straightened out." I said this is one thing that we decided, through all the years that I've been in business, that we were going to let the station manager and counsel work hand in hand with one another.

Mr. Boros: Do you recall when you made this statement or these statements to Mr. West in terms of the month and perhaps the week?

Mr. Smith: I don't understand the question.

Mr. Boros: When did you get to Mr. West and tell him to work out problems with counsel?

Mr. Smith: Well, when the matter first came up was that I assigned the duties of working up these letters with the station manager. I said at that time, "You will work directly with counsel rather than with me." And I didn't give them any instructions other than the fact to drop everything they're doing and get the whole staff together and get letters. Not affidavits, letters. That was my instructions.

Mr. Boros: Now, a time came, didn't it, when you heard that . . .

Judge Fitzpatrick: Excuse me. You said you told Mr. West to get letters, not affidavits?

Mr. Smith: I didn't say affidavit, but the word affidavit was never used.

Judge Fitzpatrick: It wasn't used by you?

Mr. Smith: Right.

Judge Fitzpatrick: Now, you were passing this to Mr. West. Who asked you to get the documentation?

Mr. Smith: I said letters.

Judge Fitzpatrick: Who said?

Mr. Smith: Counsel.

Judge Fitzpatrick: They never said affidavits?

Mr. Smith: No.

Judge Fitzpatrick: All right.

Mr. Boros: Did a time come after you initially gave instructions to your staff, Mr. Smith, about getting papers from people in the Seattle community, that you heard there was some problem with the papers which had been obtained?

Mr. Smith: Yes.

Mr. Boros: When was that?

Mr. Smith: I couldn't give you the exact date. It was probably sometime about the 15th of November.

Mr. Boros: What did you do when you received that information?

Mr. Smith: Told him to work it out with counsel.

Judge Fitzpatrick: Well, can we establish when he heard of the problem?

Mr. Smith: The problem . . . I'll answer your question. That there was a problem, basically, that some of the letters weren't in quite the right form or whatever. But I didn't even realize at the time. The word to me was rather short. There was a problem. I said, "Work out your problem."

Mr. Boros: When did you first learn of the details of the problem?

Mr. Smith: In this courtroom, Monday.

Judge Fitzpatrick: For the record's sake, it was Tuesday. We started Tuesday.

Mr. Smith: Tuesday, that's right. I'm sorry.

Judge Fitzpatrick: It seems like a month to you, doesn't it? I understand.

Mr. Smith: November 30th, correct.

TR:790   *Mr. Hoffart*: Mr. Smith, when you first found out there were problems with these affidavits, did you in turn personally start working on this problem?

Mr. Smith: No, sir.

Mr. Hoffart: Did you turn this over to your general manager at KISW?

Mr. Smith: And counsel.

Mr. Hoffart: Did you personally turn it over to counsel?

Mr. Smith: Counsel initiated it to begin with.

Mr. Hoffart: You yourself have never involved yourself in any of that work?

Mr. Smith: No, sir.

Mr. Hoffart: Do you have ultimate responsibility for the operations of this station?

Mr. Smith: Yes, sir.

Mr. Hoffart: I believe that's all I'll ask him.

The author believes he established active indifference by Mr. Smith to becoming involved in this matter of the original five proven phony notarizations. You, the reader, may recall Mr. Smith's testimony in regards to these same illegal acts committed by his employees:

TR:203   *Judge Fitzpatrick*: . . . You were responsible for certain exhibits . . . ?

Mr. Smith: Right.

Judge Fitzpatrick: You have to stand here and be responsible for them, isn't that right?

Mr. Smith: Right.

Judge Fitzpatrick: Others weren't responsible for the exhibits, were they?

Mr. Smith: Right.

Judge Fitzpatrick: But you are the number one man here in Seattle?

Mr. Smith: No question about it.

Judge Fitzpatrick: And at no time did Mr. West and Mr. Bogel or anybody tell you, "Hey, we have a problem here; we have got some letters and we want to put them in as part of our direct case, but they're not notarized and so we are going to have somebody else notarize them?

Mr. Smith: Counsel is the one that brought it to our attention.

Judge Fitzpatrick: Counsel brought it to your attention?

Mr. Smith: Yes.

Judge Fitzpatrick: Explain that to me?

Mr. Smith: He called on the phone and I said "if you have a problem, call the radio station."

This rather flippant testimony by Mr. Smith speaks volumes. This is proof of active indifference by the executive director of Kaye-Smith Enterprises. Such conduct has been found disqualifying in other cases.

> ... the Commission must insist upon effective exercise by the licensee of actual control over station operation and management ... it is only by holding the licensee accountable for the operations and management of the station that there can be any assurance that operation and management will be responsible. The degree of responsibility imposed and the standard of conduct required are the same for all licensees, irrespective of their form or relative size of their operation.[66]

It should be clear to the reader that the commission in 1985 is merely paying lip service to this 1968 ruling. It does not apply to Kaye-Smith Enterprises.

While Mr. Smith states he is the number one man in Seattle, the number one man and woman are Mr. and Mrs. Danny Kaye by virtue of owning 80 percent of Kaye-Smith Enterprises through their 100 percent ownership of Dena Pictures.

Smith's testimony shows that he took an ostrich-like stance in this matter. He turned the matter of the phony verifications over to the very person who orchestrated them in the first instance, Mr. Stephen West. This failure by Mr. Smith to assume active control resulted in two more phony verified letters filed upon Hoffart and the commission, and also

---

[66]*Continental Broadcasting Co v. FCC.*, 15 FCC 2d at 120, 131 (1968).

resulted in the perjury by Mr. West in regards to the notarization of the David Watkins corrected letter.

Smith's testimony also re-establishes the fact that he did not review most of the documents filed by counsel on behalf of Kaye-Smith before they were filed with the commission and Hoffart. He had a paramount obligation to do so. Had he done so—assuming he didn't do so—he should have realized that some fourteen documents showed no date of notarization, and thirteen of these were notarized by his employees with at least five phony notarizations.

New precedents are being set in this case. A broadcast licensee is not responsible for the acts of his employees or his counsel. The reader may remember that counsel advised Mr. Smith it was okay to pre-execute his exhibit 15 affidavit when they were aware that exhibit was incomplete.

The judge was still undecided on the question of who first discovered the illegal acts, Hoffart or counsel for Kaye-Smith. Just why the judge wanted this in the record is mystifying. It is irrelevant and immaterial who knew about the phony notarizations first. Hoffart, for one, discovered the phonies at first glance into the Direct Case. The undated notarial acts stood out like a sore thumb, and just why counsel did not notice them, assuming that they did not, is equally mystifying. If, as the next testimony shows, counsel became aware of the misrepresentations on the same day service was made to Hoffart, why did they not call Hoffart and the judge on that day, the 12th of November? The preponderance of evidence shows that Hoffart's letters to seven of the so-called affiants mailed on the 13th and received by some on Monday the 15th, are what opened this can of worms. Sure, Stephen West and his cohorts in this felonious conduct knew that the documents to be filed were falsely verified as early as October 28th, the date Ms. Matthew purportedly affixed her notarial seal and signature to McCullough's letter.

So why is the judge asking if it is all right to have Counsel Stuart Young speak from the floor as an officer of the court on this subject? The answer is simply that he was faced with a dilemma. Here all of the testimony demanded that an influential broadcaster be denied renewal. It is obvious that any such decision would not find favor with the commission or the "Fifth Estate," as the broadcasters like to be called. So the judge was looking for ways and means of mitigating the illegal acts, and one way would be to establish in the record that it was Kaye-Smith counsel who first brought this matter to the attention of the court.

The FCC card file shows that Hoffart advised the judge, the commission and the public that phony verifications had been filed in this case through his rebuttal to the Kaye-Smith Direct Written Case and that filing reached all parties prior to the 23rd of November, the date that Kaye-Smith first filed corrections to supply missing dates, and the 24th, the date Kaye-Smith filed corrections to the phony verified testimonial letters.

It just does not wash, judge. Hoffart was the first to bring the felonious conduct by Kaye-Smith employees to your attention, and you know it. As proof, Hoffart invites anyone to review the Docket in this case, FCC file No. 82–265, Card Number 14, page 28. It reads: "Rebuttal to Direct Exhibits of Kaye-Smith filed by Vincent L. Hoffart for Hoffart Broadcasting," dated 11-22-82. On the 24th, then, without leave to file, Kaye-Smith counsel filed their "corrected" testimonial letters, two of which were again affixed with verifications outside the presence of the affiants by a KISW notary/employee, and in actual fact one of those letters was not signed by the affiant, but by his secretary affixing his name. Of course there was no intent to make misrepresentations to anyone . . . the judge, in his wisdom, says so.

26.

STUART YOUNG, ESQ.

TR:791   *Judge Fitzpatrick*: Now, Mr. Hoffart, would you have any objections? My understanding is that it was Mr. Young who first brought the problem to the attention of the licensee. Do you have any objection to Mr. Young, as counsel, just making a statement as to the date it was that he first brought this matter to their attention?

Mr. Hoffart: I have no objection.

Judge Fitzpatrick: Mr. Young?

Mr. Young: Should I speak from here?

Judge Fitzpatrick: We're not calling you as a witness, just to make a statement as counsel in an office of court.

Mr. Young: The day after we placed our exhibits in the Federal Express on the evening of the 11th for the 12th exchange date. And on the 12th itself I called, had a moment to take a second look, and discovered, perceived that there might be a problem, and then asked questions.

Judge Fitzpatrick: So that was on the 12th? All right. That's all I wanted it to know. Now, Mr. Boros, Mr. Hoffart has no other questions in this area.

Mr. Hoffart: I was going to ask Mr. Young one question. Did you state that these Direct Case Exhibits went out on the 11th?

Mr. Boros: That's what he did state. He just stated it went out on the 11th, I guess.

Mr. Hoffart: And in reference to two of the exhibits here that were signed by Noren on the 10th in Seattle, these arrived in New York in time to put them in this, get it out on the 11th?

Mr. Young: Yes.

Mr. Hoffart: All right. I have no further questions.

Mr. Young: We use Federal Express a great deal.

Judge Fitzpatrick: This hearing could be an advertisement for Federal Express, I think.

Mr. Boros: It sure could.

Now this testimony, albeit not from the witness chair under oath, establishes that the direct case exhibits were sent to New York by Federal Express on the 10th of November. This supports testimony given by Mr. Smith.

TR:200   *Judge Fitzpatrick:* Let me ask him a couple questions. Did you have any knowledge as to whether there was any difficulty in getting direct testimony in meeting the schedule that we have?

Mr. Smith: Well, Federal Express has been a life saver, getting stuff clear cross the country by U.S. mail is for the birds.

Judge Fitzpatrick: Did it come to your attention that some of the public witnesses whose testimony is to be submitted did not have their signatures notarized?

Mr. Smith: Yes, earlier counsel said everything had to be notarized and had everybody scurrying around after these people and getting them notarized . . .

Well, Mr. Smith, what did you just testify to in the preceding chapter, under a new oath because your old one had worn off?

TR:770   *Mr. Smith:* I didn't say affidavit, but the word affidavit was never used.

Judge Fitzpatrick: It wasn't used by you?

Mr. Smith: Right.

Judge Fitzpatrick: Now, you were passing this to Mr. West. Who asked you to get the documentation?

Mr. Smith: I said letters.

Judge Fitzpatrick: Who said?

Mr. Smith: Counsel.

Judge Fitzpatrick: They never said affidavits?

Mr. Smith: No.

Judge Fitzpatrick: All right.

By a preponderance of evidence test Mr. Smith was aware that all of the public witness testimony had to be notarized. He so stated under oath on November 30th and then changes his mind on December 2nd, in his rebuttal testimony.

Let's review some of the Ms. Noren sworn testimony in regards to the use of Federal Express. The author has a purpose in mind, as will be shown shortly.

TR:597   *Judge Fitzpatrick:* (with reference to the fact that Ms. Noren had asked Ms. Matthew to notarize five testimonial letters outside the presence of the authors of the letters.) Why didn't you do it?

Ms. Noren: Because I was in the process of getting other papers together and getting other letters at that time, and we were . . . Federal Express was on its way to pick up our package, and I was getting it together for them.

The author had cross-examined Ms. Noren in this matter of using Federal Express. Now, with reference to an affidavit from Mr. Steve West, which she had notarized on November 10th, the questioning went like this:

TR:620   *Mr. Hoffart*: The date on this is the 10th of November. Do you remember what time of day this was?
Ms. Noren: No, I don't.
Mr. Hoffart: What happened to this notarized letter after you notarized it? Whom did you give it to?
Ms. Noren: I sent it to counsel.
Mr. Hoffart: You sent it to counsel?
Ms. Noren: Yes.
Mr. Hoffart: How did you do that?
Ms. Noren: Federal Express
Mr. Hoffart: Did you call Federal Express to pick it up?
Ms. Noren: I don't recall.
Mr. Hoffart: How did it get to Federal Express?
Ms. Noren: They picked it up. Either myself or someone who I asked to called them.
Mr. Hoffart: You sent it?
Ms. Noren: I packaged it up and got it ready to send to Federal Express.
Mr. Hoffart: Somebody called Federal Express, they showed up, and you gave them that package?
Ms. Noren: Right.
Mr. Hoffart: And you don't remember what time of day?
Ms. Noren: No, I don't.
Mr. Hoffart: Do you remember who called Federal Express?
Ms. Noren: No. I don't.

The official transcript has three references to the fact that the documents were sent to New York by Federal Express. Mr. Smith has stated that Federal Express was a life-saver. Getting stuff across the country by U.S. Mail is for the birds. Mr. Stuart Young has testified that the exchange was by Federal Express and Ms. Noren also states the same.

Now, the author has stated that he has a purpose in mind in bringing all this sworn testimony together for review. The procedures required that all parties file what is called Proposed Findings of Facts and Conclusions of Law in which each party analyses the testimony in the case and submits it to the judge prior to the Initial Decision. This is akin to a closing argument in a jury case, wherein each attorney gives his views before the jury retires for deliberations.

Kaye-Smith, in their filing, stated the following as part of their filing, (more of the Proposed Findings of Facts later in this book):

for inclusion in its direct case, Kaye-Smith sought testimonials from Seattle area residents as to Station KISW's performance during the license period. Kaye-Smith counsel telephoned Lester M. Smith, Executive Director of Kaye-Smith, concerning such testimonials. Smith understood counsel to refer to unverified letters of endorsement rather than affidavits.

... area residents responded by furnishing letters; some arrived at station KISW by mail; some were hand-delivered. Upon receipt, each letter was channeled to Margaret Noren, administrative assistant to Mr. West, and a notary in the State of Washington. Noren retained the statements, pending mailing to counsel in New York.

... Prior to such mailing, West and Noren noticed that five letters ...

... the testimonials in Station KISW's possession were mailed to counsel, who exchanged them by mail, on Thursday, November 11, 1982, as part of Kaye-Smith's written case. On Monday, November 15th, counsel spoke to West. That conversation revealed to counsel that Matthew had affixed her notarial seal and supplied her signature to the Balint, Blacksmith, McConnell, McCullough and Taylor letters, without having those persons before her at the time ... [67]

The reader should immediately recognize what the author's purpose is. The Kaye-Smith Proposed Findings of Facts make no mention of the use of Federal Express. In fact, three references are made to the fact that the exchange was by mail. The question that the author poses to the reader is this: Was the exchange of the phony verified documents and other documents by Federal Express or by mail, or is Federal Express a mail service? We also need to go back and take another look at Mr. Stuart Young's testimony. He stated that he called on the 12th, when he "preceived" that there were problems, and then asked questions. In the proposed findings of facts Kaye-Smith counsel states that West was called on the 15th. West, however, states that it was Noren that was called or got a letter from Stu Young:

TR:309   *Mr. West*: We got a letter or phone call from Stu Young the following Friday because I wasn't at work and he talked to Meg Noren and I then talked to him first thing Monday morning and he instructed me to go back out.

The official transcript also shows testimony in regards to this call by Mr. Stuart on the 12th elicited from Ms. Noren by Mr. Boros:

TR:600   *Mr. Boros*: Did counsel directly call you about these letters and raise questions about them?

---

[67]Although due by February 11th, 1983, the transmittal letter was dated February 14th. It was late-filed without leave and with impunity.

Ms. Noren: No. They called Steve West.

By the preponderance of evidence from the sworn testimony, it appears that only testimony from counsel Stuart Young states that any phone call was made to anyone at KISW on the 12th of November, the day Mr. Young purportedly "perceived" that there were problems with the Direct Case exhibits as had already been filed with the FCC.

27.

PROPOSED FINDINGS OF FACTS AND CONCLUSIONS OF LAW

The date of February 11th, 1983 was set as the date the Proposed Findings of Fact and Conclusions of Law were due, and the date of March 4th, 1983 was set for Reply Findings. The author met the deadlines. Kaye-Smith did not. They filed their Findings and Conclusions on the 14th and also failed to meet the due date of their Reply Findings. They should have been denied renewal due to failure to timely prosecute. No adverse findings and conclusion were reached by the judge in this matter. No doubt that if Hoffart had failed to meet due dates without leave to do so he would have lost his case at that point.

Hoffart's Findings of Facts and Conclusions paralleled the charges made in this book. The reader has already been exposed to the sworn testimony and it would be redundant to repeat it here. Hoffart charged Kaye-Smith with filing fraudulently notarized documents with a federal agency in violation of *Title 18, U.S.C. section 1001*, the statute against knowingly and willfully making misrepresentations in a federal matter. Additionally, Hoffart brought out the fact that there were two statutory violations of *Title 47, U.S.C, Section 301* which prohibits the installation and use of radio apparatus without authority or permit thereto.

In sum, Hoffart's fifty-page filing brought out all of the relevant factors adduced at the hearing. You, the reader, already know that the judge found there was no intent to file anything that violated the laws and that the review board called all of the book up to this point, and more to come, a hodgepodge of accusations, typical adversarial puff and much ado about nothing.

Kaye-Smith's Proposed Findings and Conclusions were as follows as it related to the hodgepodge of allegations and accusations:

NOTARIAL IMPERFECTIONS IN KAYE-SMITH EXHIBITS ARE THE PRODUCT OF INNOCENT ERROR BY KISW EMPLOYEES.

Par. 12. The record establishes that the sworn Kaye-Smith exhibit exchanged in November of 1982 were notarially imperfect. The imperfections were a function of certain acts, omissions and commissions of two employees of Station KISW who are notaries in the State of Washington. The individuals in question are of relatively tender age, were untrained and uninformed as to duties of a notary and each was without any prior experience as a notary serving the public generally.

13. Their acts were neither willful nor knowing. To the degree KISW supervisory personnel were aware of the situation, such personnel

were innocent of knowledge that the in-house notaries were acting in error.

14. No Kaye-Smith principal either knew of the details of the notarial acts or commissions or knew of any substantive problems therewith. The acts occurred on the station level . . . without the involvement of knowledge of any Kaye-Smith principal. Kaye-Smith did not benefit from the notarial imperfections. It had no motive for countenancing such imperfections. The evidence is monolithic that the acts are the product of innocent error by KISW employees. No *mala fides* were involved. Under the circumstances, Kaye-Smith's qualifications, including the comparative qualifications, are unblemished by the notarial imperfections. In context, the acts in question are non-culpable.[68]

The reader will immediately recognize that the relevant factors have been omitted by Kaye-Smith counsel. The most significant of those relevant factors is the fact that Mr. Smith told counsel, purportedly on the 15th of November, "If you got problems, call the radio station." Smith had been put on notice that there were problems, and refused to become involved. This "active indifference" resulted in two more illegal acts of filing false information with the FCC. Just how counsel can find that there is no culpability involved by the licensee because he allegedly did not know what was going on is beyond analysis.

The record virtually reeks with evidence that there was intent to deceive. Ms. Noren testified that it was Mr. West who suggested that Ms. Matthew notarize the initial five testimonial letters outside the presence of the authors of the letters, without their knowledge in some cases, and without their consent in some cases. That there was no intent to file misrepresentations, as the judge ruled in his Initial Decision, is not supported by the record.

A relevant factor that was omitted by Kaye-Smith counsel is that a second round of misrepresentations was filed by Kaye-Smith and that this second round had the blessings of the station manager, Mr. West. When Noren advised him of the fact that she had notarized the David Watkins corrected letter without Mr. Watkins being before her, he said "that is fine." And of course the reader will remember that Mr. West stated, under oath and without any equivocation, that Mr. Watkins had appeared before him and Ms. Noren at KISW and that this was proven untrue by both Ms. Noren and Watkins's testimony. Hoffart, and only Hoffart, brought this second round of willfull felonious conduct to the attention of all other parties.

Kaye-Smith counsel says there was no motive for countenancing such imperfections. Ms. Noren has contradicted that finding when she stated,

---

[68]Kaye-Smith's Findings of Facts and Conclusions, from pages 73 and 74 of that filing with the FCC.

under oath, that the phony verifications were filed to make the documents legal and acceptable as legally notarized testimonial letters. Counsel's findings must therefore fall.

The reader may remember Hoffart's quotes from the WOKO case that had been before the U.S. Supreme Court. The Court had stated, in part:

> ... one who is not candid and trustworthy in all circumstances cannot be accorded the privilege of a Commission license ... the willingness to deceive a regulatory body may be disclosed by immaterial and useless deceptions as well as by material and persuasive ones. We do not think it is an answer to say that the deception was unnecessary and served no purpose. ... the fact of concealment may be more significant than the facts concealed.[69]

The Broadcast Bureau, or Mass Media Bureau as they are now known, had no representatives at the hearing. The public, therefore, was not represented at the hearing. The bureau did not file any Findings of Facts and Conclusions. The rules are explicit. Any party that does not file Findings and Conclusions is out of the contest. The question arises, is the bureau a party? It appears so since the rules also require service to all parties and service to the bureau is a requirement. Regardless, the bureau filed a reply to both Hoffart's and the Kaye-Smith Findings and Conclusions and Reply Findings. They recommended to the judge that the KISW license should be renewed based upon the transcript record and the conclusions they reached that the KISW programming was so meritorious that renewal was warranted. They agreed with Kaye-Smith that the conduct by them was innocent error.

The author now quotes just one of many precedents in which the commission, has held that a meritorious programming finding has to be equated with all other relevant factors developed in a case:

> ... where programming, technical and other operational violations of the magnitude described are shown to exist, they cannot be overlooked or excused on the grounds that another aspect of the stations performance has been in the public interest. The statutory and regulatory provisions that have been breached are all components of the public interest, and their importance cannot be dismissed in the regulatory scheme.[70]

It is clear that the commission has changed course by not articulating why the Kaye-Smith myriad of transgressions, both regulatory and statutory, do not apply to a station owned by Mr. and Mrs. Danny Kaye and Mr. Lester M. Smith. The public should ask why not, and demand a

---

[69]U.S. Supreme Court, cited as 329 (1946).
[70]*Vinita Broadcasting v. FCC*, 30 FCC 2d at 458, 466.

grand jury investigation. Hoffarts charges of preferential treatment to Kaye-Smith by the commission are fully justified and proven.

28.

THE INITIAL DECISION

Judge Fitzpatrick issued his Initial Decision on November 18, 1983 and it was released on November 25th, 1983, almost a full year after the ending of the hearing.[71] For those readers who may wish to read all of the Initial Decision there is one library in each state that is a repository for these FCC reports. A list of the libraries is available from the superintendent of documents. In addition, a number of the large broadcast licensees subscribe to the issues. The author has been a subscriber since June of 1978 and derived most of his expertise in FCC proceedings and precedents from reading cases that have been before the commission.

The commission has recently proposed that it would be better just to release summaries of their decisions. Perhaps they do not feel that *pro se* applicants and non-lawyers like the author should have access to the content of their Findings and Conclusions because they can be embarrasing, as in this case.

With respect to the Initial Decision, under appearances, it is shown that Mr. Daniel Sarno appeared on behalf of the chief of the Broadcast Bureau. This is a misrepresentation. A fair reading indicates to the public, in this public publication, that a Mr. Daniel Sarno appeared at the hearing. At this point in time Mr. Sarno had already been taken off the case, and had so notified Hoffart prior to the hearing. The misrepresentations in this case are not exclusive to Kaye-Smith but are also engaged in by the commission.

The Findings of Fact in this decision devotes nine pages to the programming by KISW during the renewal period. This is followed by a list of community leaders whose testimony established that KISW has rendered exceptional service to the Seattle area through their programming and involvement in community affairs. This was followed by findings that KISW made efforts to comply with FCC rules and regulations during the renewal period. Kaye-Smith's other media interests, which included stations in Spokane, Washington and Portland, Oregon, were listed.

The judge then superficially went through the notarial imperfections by Kaye-Smith. Suffice to say most of the relevant testimony was not touched upon by the judge. For example, nothing was said about the Steve West perjury as it relates to the David Watkins second letter notarization. The judge omitted all references to the fact that Mr. West had been told by Ms. Noren that she had affixed her notary seal and signature to the corrected David Watkins letter and that he had okayed

---

[71]98 FCC 2d at page 688.

194

the submission of this falsely notarized corrected letter to the commission. Overlooked was the fact that Smith told counsel to "call the radio station" if they had problems. Overlooked were all of the conflicting testimonies given by Kaye-Smith employees and some of the affiants who wrote letters. Overlooked were the facts that Ms. Noren warranted that commercials were aired when she had no direct knowledge of whether or not her sworn statements were true, and that she had done so for four years.

The judge found Hoffart financially qualified and also gave the author preference in mass media ownership under the Policy Statement on Comparative Renewals and also gave Hoffart credit for Integration of Ownership into management. The judge did not have much choice in these matters. Kaye-Smith had five high-powered stations concentrated in the northwest and Hoffart had no media interests. Smith proposed thirty hours per week in day-to-day operations of KISW, refusing to state how much time he would spend at his other four stations or on his other known business interests.

In sum, no demerits were issued against Hoffart and none were warranted. So that there can be no questions as to what the judge ruled relating to the "notarial imperfections" and the rules violations, the author prints his conclusions verbatim. Quoting from the Judge's conclusions:

It is now necessary to consider the "notarial imperfections" issue specified against Kaye-Smith. As detailed in the findings, the Presiding Judge made clear that the direct written testimony of witnesses was to be appropriately notarized and that the witnesses were to be informed that they were subject to being called for cross-examination. However, the findings establish that the written testimony of 5 witnesses had not been notarized. Steven L. West (West) general manager of FM Station KISW, instructed Margaret Noren, West's administrative assistant, to have the written testimony of these 5 individuals notarized and forwarded to communications counsel.[40] Noren instructed Carrie Matthew, a station employee, to do the notarizing, which she did by affixing her signature and seal to the 5 signatures. Matthew had not previously notarized anyone's signature and was unfamiliar with the appropriate notary practices. She mistakenly believed that she was not acting improperly when she notarized the documents outside the presence of the affiants. West similarly believed that what was being done was not improper. The record establishes that the "notarial imperfections" were the result of error by the station employees intrusted with the assignment of obtaining the written testimony of community leaders. There does not appear to have been any intentional disregard of the Presiding Judge's instruction or of the requirements of proper notarization. It is concluded that the failure represents an innocent error and that there was no intention to mislead the Commission.[41] The Presiding Judge agrees with the Bureau that the improprieties in notarization were the result of ignorance, rather than design. While this unfortunate incident should never have happened, it is ruled that there was no intention on the part of the licensee to mislead this Commission or abuse its processes. At most it warrants no more than assessing a slight comparative demerit. (citing from WIOO, Inc, FCC case 83-367 released September 16, 1983.)[72]

40—The written testimony was in the form of communications on the letterhead of local organizations attesting to the cooperation and programming of Station KISW.

41—These individuals were subject to cross-examination. No purpose would have been served by submitting improperly notarized testimony or not informing them that the letters were to be used as evidence since this fact could readily have been discovered during the hearing process. The affidavits of West and Eric S. Vogel (sic), station KISW Program Director, submitted as part of Kaye-Smith Exhibits 16 and 17 represented that they had explained to each of the affiants that his or her testimony would be used as evidence in this proceeding. In a few cases, these 2 individuals failed to inform the affiants of the fact that these testimonial letters were to be submitted as part of the Commission's proceeding. This appears to have been an oversight.

The judge's ultimate conclusion was that the KISW programing during the renewal period was of a meritorious nature and that this finding outweighed the slight demerit given KISW for all of the transgressions the author has documented in this book. The meritorious programming finding also outweighed Hoffart's clear preference in Mass Media Diversification and his clear preference in Integration of Ownership into Management. Hoffart had proposed 100 percent integration against thirty hours per week for the 20 percent owner Mr. Lester M. Smith. The Kaye's proposed no time, and they never have been involved in stations operations although they were 80 percent owners.

The precedents set in this case virtually guarantee any and all broadcasters the grant of a license in perpetuity, something not intended by Congress when they enacted the Communications Act of 1934, as amended.

The author now takes the reader back to the pre-hearing and some of the testimony:

TR:17   *Mr. Hoffart:* Now, I may be getting out of line, your Honor . . . if I file an affidavit and I depose falsely, what happens?
Judge Fitzpatrick: You can go to jail.
Mr. Hoffart: Does that apply to Kaye-Smith?

---

[72]98 FCC 2d at page 720, paragraph 5.

Judge Fitzpatrick: Does that apply to Kaye-Smith? If they file any affidavits that are false, they can go to jail, too, if the prosecutors decide. The commission doesn't send people to jail. The U.S. Code Title 18, section 1001 provides that any statement knowingly made to the United States Government or its officials or agents, can be prosecuted as a felony.

Mr. Hoffart: My case rests on that, pretty much.

This pre-hearing was on August 6, 1982, some ninty days prior to the notarial imperfections fiasco. So a funny thing happened on this case. The judge makes decisions on statutory violations when the proper forum is the U. S. attorney general. A grand jury should have been convened to ascertain if an indictment was warranted on the filing of false information with an agency of the federal government. The U.S. Court of Appeals, in a decision involving Berlin Communications, a double billing case, issued an injunction to the FCC in which they stated that the commission has the responsibility to report statutory violations that come to their attention during a hearing to the U.S. Justice Department for presentation to a grand jury. What ever happened to this injunction?

In a footnote to that case the court of appeals held:

We note that section 401 (c) of the Communications Act grants the Commission authority to direct that the United States Attorney prosecute all violations of the Act. Certainly this provision assumes even greater importance when the violations in issue contravene Federal Criminal Laws as well.[73]

Since the U.S. Court of Appeals declined to apply this injunction in this case, perhaps that court should explain why statutory violations by Kaye-Smith need not be reported by the commission to any U.S. Attorney. Can it be that the court makes its decisions based upon who is involved and not upon the record evidence? The congressional committee on judiciary matters should investigate this matter and require the three U.S. Court of Appeals, D.C. Circuit, judges to explain their judgment upholding the commission.

---

[73]*Berlin Communications v. FCC*, 200 U.S. Appeals, D.C. Circuit 5, 626, F 2d at 869 (1979).

29.

EXCEPTIONS TO THE INITIAL DECISION

The procedures allow any party to file exceptions to an Initial Decision. In this case both Hoffart and Kaye-Smith filed exceptions. Kaye-Smith, for one, stated that the record did not support the assessing of even a slight demerit against them since only low echelon Kaye-Smith personnel were involved in the submission of falsely verified testimonial letters. Since Mr. West, Bogel and Noren were all upper echelon employees, the reader can readily see that counsel is again resorting to untruths. This was a willfull misrepresentation by counsel to the review board. Mr. Boros knew that this low echelon characterization was false.

Hoffart brought out most of the points he has related in this book. He also filed for enlargement of issues to include the false testimony and whatever other conflicting statements he could get into his exceptions filing. The review board agreed with the bureau that Hoffart could not file for enlargements after the decision. Hoffart disagrees. The enlargements came at a time when Kaye-Smith had filed a supplemental renewal application, three years having gone past since the 1980 renewal and a new filing "window" was open. As might be expected, Hoffart's arguments were not persuasive.

The review board's decision is a matter of public record.[74] In the heading of appearances it is shown that the chief of Mass Media is now represented by Mr. Charles E. Dziedzic and Robert A. Zauner. Mr. Sarno is not mentioned.

After both parties filed exceptions to the Initial Decision, the review board scheduled Oral Argument for February 24, 1984. Hoffart gave notice of appearance. Kaye-Smith late-filed their notice of appearance and stated that they would appear on the 27th. Hoffart then filed another notice stating that he would not appear in Washington, D.C. for the oral argument due to the late-filed notice of appearance by Kaye-Smith counsel and the fact that they would appear on the wrong date.

The oral argument went ahead as scheduled on the 24th. Mass media personnel did not appear, nor did Hoffart. The author will not go into the details of the argument since it has already been shown what the review board thought of Hoffart's presentations—a hodgepodge of accusations and allegations, typical adversarial puff and much ado about nothing.

With Hoffart not attending the Oral Argument, and the Mass Media Bureau also absent, the review board allowed Mr. Boros fifty-seven minutes of argument. In other words, while the argument order speci-

---

[74]98 FCC 2d at page 675, released June 8, 1984.

fied twenty minutes time to be allowed each party, the time not used by Hoffart and the Mass Media was given to Kaye-Smith. Hoffart had charged that this fifty-seven minutes of argument prejudiced his case. The FCC review board ruled this this is tough luck. Hoffart, they said, was on notice that oral argument was being held on the 24th, and he lost his rights by failing to appear.

One matter that was raised in the Oral Argument bears reporting at this time. Other quotes will follow, *infra.*

TR:1038   *Board Member Jacobs*: The judge made extensive findings when he concluded to the meritorious past programming of your client. He focused on the news and public affairs percentages. The 6.6 percent vs. the 6.0 percent proposal. Can you also tell us what the total non-entertainment percentage was? What percentage of the programming during the composite week was?

Mr. Boros: I think it was in three catagories. The three categories being news, public affairs and other. We had a total of 6.6 percent.

Mr. Jacobs: That included the whole?

Mr. Boros: That included the whole. The rest was entertainment, although as the record shows, much of the entertainment, programming, and we hope it remained entertaining, was from time to time, also used to convey information, news and other pieces of intelligence which were helpful to the listeners of the community.

Mr. Jacobs: Well, in your reply to exceptions, you refer to the Victor Broadcasting, the recent Victor Broadcasting case as supporting your client's meritorious programming. I notice that their 20 percent overall non-entertainment, 8.25 percent of it was news and public affairs. The Commission found this to be very meritorious. In this case we have only your client's programming. We don't have any comparison with other stations. Of course Mr. Hoffart has raised the question whether there was even a failure of proof because we have nothing to compare your client with. It would seem that comparison with Victor would certainly show your client to have less of a meritorious program than he. Do we need to have the data for other stations?

Mr. Boros: No, because all that is necessary is that we be beyond mediocre and we are far beyond mediocre. The Mayor of Seattle testified to the exemplary programming. Person after person, perhaps not in political life, but in civic and social and communal life, testified to the responsiveness of this station to local needs. Now percentages can be helpful and they also can be a little misleading. It reminds me that Disraeli used to say that there are three types of lies. Lies, damned lies and statistics. Now we certainly think the statistics here are not damned lies and favorable to us.

Chairman Marino: Mr. Geller would disagree with you, wouldn't he?

Mr. Boros: You don't mean Henry? you mean . . .

Chairman Marino: No I mean Mr. Henry Geller who wanted to make it all fan on numbers, didn't he? In fact, the Commission had an outstanding rulemaking who seemed to adopt some magic numbers.

Mr. Boros: I think you are right, and I guess of course, in Mr. Geller's diftering with Mr. Disraeli, it was in a round to defend his position.

Chairman Marino: Go ahead.

Mr. Boros: But . . .

Mr. Blumenthal: Neither is Mr. Geller. He was relieved of his command.

Chairman Marino: And the Commission did not adopt his proposal in the court of . . .

Mr. Blumenthal: I think it was shortly after he made that proposal that Mr. Geller had other employment.

The author's reason for reviewing this oral argument testimony is to establish that Mr. Jacobs raised the question of whether there was proof in the form of comparison with other stations that the KISW non-entertainment was above average. The KISW figures, from their renewal application, showed that they aired 6.61 percent non-entertainment at a time when the commission's rules required a minimum of 6 percent. By some magic the 6.61 percent was translated into above average, that is, meritorious, by the judge.

The author took this cue and ordered the renewal applications of similarly situated commercial FM stations in the Seattle area and filed them with the review board. He filed the data received from the FCC and also six complaints by area citizens that alleged the KISW was engaged in airing obscene and indecent utterings at times when children could be expected to be in the audience. This was filed in a petition for reconsideration.

200

30.

PETITION FOR RECONSIDERATION

The author filed a Petition for Reconsideration with the review board. All such petitions have to cite new items, that is, facts that have come to the attention of the petitioner since the last decision. It took Hoffart considerable time to obtain a transcript of the Oral Argument and more time to obtain the renewal applications of other Seattle stations. One of the problems was that the industry continually changes call letters; hence, if a file number is unknown, one may get data on a Texas station, for example, as actually happened to the author.

While the case was before the review board, Hoffart was alerted through a media article that KISW had a talk-show guest by the name of Billy Idol on the air live. The article stated that Mr. Idol had engaged in obscene and indecent language on March 27th, 1984. Yes, we are up to 1984 now, from a case that started in December of 1980.

The author surmised that one or more Seattle area citizens would have filed a complaint with the FCC regarding the Billy Idol talk show if indeed obscene and indecent language had been aired. Hoffart ordered a search of the KISW files in Washington, D.C. by a copy company who specializes in research and copying of the public files for a fee.

The copy company representative called Hoffart and advised him that the enforcement division refused access to the KISW files. Hoffart then filed for the records under the Freedom of Informations Act. (5 U.S.C. 552). The FOIA officer responded that the records were open to the public and as such they would not entertain the FOIA request. They did, however, state where the records were located and whom the copy company representative should contact. Hoffart then passed this information on to the copy company with orders to search the files for complaints.

The author was correct in his thinking that someone may have filed a complaint regarding the Billy Idol airing. He received one letter of complaint and the response the FCC sent to the complainant. In addition he received five other complaints. Some of these complaints indicated that KISW was in receipt of copies or similar complaints by the same complainant. These should have been in the KISW public file in Seattle. They were not. Similarly, Hoffart had inspected the KISW public file in Washington, D.C. on August 5th, 1982, the day before the pre-hearing conference. There were no complaints in the file in the public file room at 1919 M street. More about these complaints in the next chapter.

With respect to the subject at hand, the non-entertainment statistics on file by other Seattle Area FM stations, the following information was taken from their 1980 applications:

KBLE-FM programmed 84.2% non-entertainment.
KZOK-FM programmed 7.3% non-entertainment.
KIXI-FM programmed 12.0% non-entertainment.
KING-FM programmed 7.3% non-entertainment.
KSEA programmed 8.5% non-entertainment.
KRPM-FM programmed 10.23% non-entertainment.

The average non-entertainment time by five of the above six stations is nine percent. In all fairness the author did not include KBLE-FM, the religious station since this would cause an inbalance that would not result in a fair comparison with other similarly situated commercial stations. The 9 percent average, then, is a fair figure. It shows that, rather than being above mediocre as Mr. Boros averred to the review board in oral argument, KISW was, in actual fact, about 25 percent below the average of five other FM stations and more than that if the religious station is included.

The review board ruled that Hoffart's presentation was too late. He should have brought these statistics into the picture at the hearing since they were available to him at that time. Hoffart would have done so, had there been a meritorious programming issue requested by KISW. They had not requested that their programming be appraised as meritorious, so, in actual fact, with no issue specified, the case was decided on a non-issue. A precedent exists:

The Commission, as a matter of course, does not designate meritorious programming issues in renewal proceedings. It is incumbent upon renewal applicants to request such a designation.[75]

Action Radio was given a short term renewal in that case for news staging, that is, airing fictitious weather temperatures. Compare with Kaye-Smith. The author will devote a chapter to news staging and also fictitious commercials that have recently surfaced in Portland, Oregon where allegedly KXL and KKCW, now owned by Mr. Lester M. Smith in full, participated in hoax broadcasts.

Even though proof beyond any doubt was filed with the review board that KISW was about 25 percent below the average of other FM Stations in Seattle in terms of non-entertainment, the review board refused to accept this offer of proof. It is well established that no programming

---

[75]*Action Radio, Inc., v. FCC*, 38 FCC 2d, at 489. Review Board (1972).

credit can be given to any station which programs average.[76] The reader and the public can assess the review board's finding and reach their own conclusions. Does KISW deserve a meritorious programming rating? If in doubt, read the next chapter.

> (note: The author's information is that KXL-FM changed its call letters to KKCW. It now appears that there has been a switch back to KXL-FM. This is the Portland, Oregon station owned by Mr. Lester M. Smith.)

---

[76]Policy Statement on Comparative Broadcast Hearings, 1 FCC 2d, adopted July 28, 1965, page 398, "average performance will be disregarded since average future performance is expected."

31.

PORNOGRAPHY PROGRAMMING COMPLAINTS

While Mr. Boros repeatedly brings into the picture the solicited testimonial letters, including those illegally notarized, he did not reveal the existence of complaints against KISW programming by area listeners. These complaints, being unsolicited and uncomplimentary, should have been revealed as a matter of candor.

With six complaint letters located in the FCC files, all after the renewal period, it seems strange that no complaints were in the KISW public file for the renewal period of February 1, 1978 thru January, 1981. If any Seattle area residents can recall sending KISW complaints during this time period, the author would like to hear from you. The rules require that complaints must be placed in the public file unless otherwise requested by the complainant. Complaint letters may have been destroyed or otherwise removed from the file in anticipation of Hoffart's inspection.

Now, with respect to the letters located in the FCC Enforcement Division's files in June of 1984, the author will type out the letters and also include those that are legible in the appendix. Hoffart elects to delete the names of the complainants as a matter of courtesy. These individuals should be commended for their efforts to clean up KISW's programming.

If any readers wish to confirm the existence of these letters, the author obtained them from the FCC Enforcement Division, Room 6202, 2025 M St. N.W. Washington, D.C. 20554. (202) 632-3922. The actual copying was done by Hoffart's copy company agent, for a fee.

The six complaint letters received are presented in chronological order. First, a letter dated 2-7-1981:

Federal Communications Commission
Washington, D.C.

Sirs:
I have a complaint to give to your office and perhaps your Commission can give me the help I need . . . I have lived here for some 20 years. I am a professional within the State of Washington.

My request is this; Is it possible your Commission may stop/prohibit the filthy/hog slop obscene programs which are being given to us over the television/radio reports these days. Do not inform me that all I need to do to stop such programs is to turn the dial to 'OFF' and I shall no longer view the obscene programs.

I am aware of the above fact, but the so-called 'SHOWS' continue whether I watch such or whether I do not. Children still see and 'eat' the filthy shows and if such is wrong for me to see, the same is true for any child. Also, is it feasible that the radio station in Seattle, (Washington) which is KISW, may be prohibited from cursing and "enjoying" the obscene language which is done each day. I am certain of this because I hear it each day until I can not bear up under such curses as is provided via radio, usually in the A.M. on Sunday from 6–9 AM. Cannot such cursing be STOPPED in some manner; are we forced to hear such filthy words over the air.

Some years ago I had a part in stopping a 'show' via radio due to the fact the people were using obscene/swearing language day after day; that program soon was taken off the air. I am sure there are yet folk who are decent and I am positive I am one of such people.

Hoping your Commission may give me the help I need; we love good clean 'shows' given via the media but I shall fight HOG SLOP, OB-SCENE/CURSING being aired via any manner whatsoever. May we have this STOPPED NOW/AT ONCE.

Thanking you kindly (s) (Deleted by Hoffart)

The author reprints the letter as he has received it from the FCC files.[77] As stated, the name and address of the complainant has been deleted. This letter was not addressed to KISW so it would not appear in their files unless the FCC sent them a copy or made some effort to halt the obscene language about which this complainant writes.

Letter number two is dated 11-18-81 and is not reproduced in the appendix due to poor copy from the FCC. With difficulty the author finds it reading as follows:

To: Federal Communications Commission
3256 Federal Building
915 2nd Avenue, Seattle, WA, 98174

Dear Sirs:
I have a serious complaint about radio station KISW. On the morning of November 2, 3rd or 4th they had a take-off of the old show "Leave it to Beaver." It's the kind of thing that they take and make fun of the program doing their own story but using the characters from the old show. (Beaver, Wally, Mr. and Mrs. Cleaver and Wallys friend Eddie Hankel.)

On this particular morning the version was worse than usual. It was very immoral and in very bad taste, and particularly bad in content. It was Mrs. Cleaver talking to Beaver, after Eddie, her son's friend came over. She told Beaver that her and Eddie were going upstairs to the bedroom and that they were going to play a game, but Beaver was not to disturb them or come into the room at all, nor was he allowed to let anyone else come upstairs for any reason. After sounds of going up the stairs there

---

[77] Appendix pages 41 and 42.

were comments made that were obviously not talking about a game. Also sounds of groaning and moaning (obscene) during this time. My son, 16 years old, who had it turned on the radio and was listening to it in his bedroom realized it was not good and turned it down because he didn't want me to hear it. Talking to him afterward, he said he 'couldn't believe that they would have that on the radio.'

The series goes on, and Mr. Cleaver comes home and comes upstairs and gets after Eddie and Eddie says 'I didn't mean it' and Mr. Cleaver says 'Well you could at least move over.'

The series is usually on about 6:15 or 6:20 AM and its not on it every day so it may be hard to catch it without listening to it every day until you hear it. They have different episodes each time.

I am very much surprised and disgusted that this kind of trash is allowed on radio, and would like it looked into and taken off the air.

I question whether the station should be given a license when it comes up for renewal.

Please let me know what is done about this.

(s) (Deleted)

A letter complaining about obscene language broadcasts on KISW dated January 9th, 1982 is date-stamped as having been received by the Seattle office of the FCC on January 12th, 1982. This letter is also date-stamped January 15th when it was apparently received by the FCC in Washington.

To Whom it May Concern:
This is to protest the obscene language used on the radio station KISW. My radio was tuned to this station by someone else in my home so I left it on to this talk show.

The D.J. had a pimp come on and talk and his language was filthy, including mother-fucker, ass, shit and bullshit.

Has the FCC become so low that they now allow this thing? It was my experience up to now that they either bleeped it out or cut them off the air. I know there is a seven second delay.

Please look into this matter.

The time was between 7:30 AM and 8:00 AM, Saturday, January 9th, 1982.

(s) (Deleted)

P.S. I called the station and am sending them a letter also. Talk shows are very good, but not this kind of talk.[78]

This complainant states that she wrote KISW a letter. This letter should have been in the station's public file. The author inspected every document in that file in late August of 1982. There was no such letter of

---

[78]Appendix pages 43 and 44.

complaint in that file. The preponderance of evidence is that KISW personnel cleaned out the file of any and all such obscene programming complaints that the Seattle citizenry may have sent to them. KISW was aware that Hoffart would inspect that file. The pre-hearing transcript established the date when the author was to be in Seattle to give and take oral deposition and review the public file.

This complainant received a response from the FCC. The copy obtained by Hoffart does not show who authored this response. Excerpts from the FCC's letter read as follows:

> . . . the information in your letter is not sufficient to indicate whether the KISW talk show you have objected to would be considered violative of the criminal statute discussed in our enclosures. If you wish to send this office additional detailed information concerning the program, for example, accurate quotations of statements broadcast, it will be given full consideration. But there is no law prohibiting broadcast discussion of any given subject, and the FCC cannot direct stations in the selection of talk show participation. Comments in writing to stations about specific programs can be effective in influencing broadcasters' programming practices.[79]

In this case the complainant had already sent a letter of complaint to KISW. The fact that it was not in the file suggests that the complaint was destroyed.

Shortly after the hearing in Seattle a complaint letter addressed to Mr. Steve West, general manager KISW-FM, was authored by a complainant. This letter is dated February 18, 1983.

> Dear Mr. West:
> I am writing to complain about something I heard on KISW-FM Thursday, 17 February that I feel was offensive and in very poor taste.
> At approximately 2:24 PM that day, a record ended and the sound of a crying infant was heard. The announcer said something to the effect "What the hell is this? Hey, close the door, will ya!"The crying ended with the slam of a door followed by the announcer saying "that's our rock baby we picked up a month or two ago. He was alright then, now he's a pain in the ass." I believe this sort of 'bush league' radio would be more expected from a small, far away radio station where professionalism's sorely lacking and not from a highly rated station in this country's 15th largest radio market, which professes to play Seattle's best new Rock.
>
> It's common knowledge that deregulation has freed radio to be more 'blue' which is usually tolerable since it reflects what's spoken in society. But I believe that reference to an infant as a 'pain in the ass' is inherently harmful and mean and intolerable on any media under any circumstances. As a result, I will no longer listen to KISW-FM and I'll advise others I meet and know to do the same. A copy of this letter has been sent to the

---

[79]Appendix page 45.

Complaints and Compliance, FCC Broadcast Bureau and the Regional Director of the FCC office in Seattle.

Regretfully (s)[80]

Complaint letter number five that was located in the FCC files in Washington, D.C. is dated May 24, 1983. It is date-stamped as having been received by the FCC mail branch on May 31, 1983.

FCC: Mass Media Bureau
Washington, D.C. 20554

Sirs:
Enclosed find a letter which I sent to radio station KISW, Seattle, Wa. I would appreciate any help that you can offer in eliminating obscene and perverse dialog from Radio Station KISW which primarily services adolescents and teenage audiences.

Thank you (s) (Deleted)[81]

The copy of the letter sent to KISW on this same day of May 24th, 1983 was enclosed. It reads as follows:

KISW, 712 Aurora North
Seattle, WA.

Sirs:
At approximately 7:10AM, Thursday, May 19, 1983, while listening to your radio station KISW, I heard what I considered to be obscene and pervasive dialog. The dialog was of a man who was sad because she wouldn't do it with him but would do it with him and with him and with him, etc. The man also went into talk about a braless woman.

I would appreciate in the future if your disc jockeys would monitor what they consider to be appropriate dialog for their teenage and adult audiences.

Thank you for your cooperation.

Sincerely, (s) (Deleted)[82]

Copy: FCC, Mass Media Bureau, Washington D.C. 20554.

The author has stated that he was alerted through the print media that rock star Billy Idol had allegedly engaged in obscene and indecent language during a talk show on March 27th, 1984. He obtained a copy of a complaint letter that was filed by a concerned citizen living in the Seattle area. It was this newspaper article that lead Hoffart to the five complaints already printed.

---

[80]Appendix page 46.
[81]Appendix page 47.
[82]Appendix page 48.

Dear FCC:
On March 27th, 1984 at 3:10 PM a local rock station in the Seattle area had a rock star who goes by the name of Billy Idol on the air waves live. The station was KISW. Billy Idol started telling about how he liked to eat Pussey, then he went on to tell about masterbation. He went on to make sound effects. The whole time the radio announcer's laughed their butts off. Then he got some phone calls on the air and told one girl to go masterbate. He also said fuck several times. Also, the radio announcer told him that this is America and he could say anything they wanted to over the radio. What I want to know is, is that true? If it's not true who the hell is going to do something about it?

Sincerely (s) (Deleted)[83]

The complainant received a response from the FCC. The response indicates that there was other correspondence with this concerned citizen, but the author has not located any other letters. In any event, excerpts from the FCC response read as follows:

May 21, 1984

Dear ...
As we stated in our previous response to you in this matter, Court decisions distinguishing between material protected by the First Amendment and that which is obscene or indecent (the use of which can be subjected to government regulation) are clearly stated, and the Commission is necessarily guided by decisions of the Supreme Court in making determinations regarding specific material. In regards to sexually-oriented programming, unless it can be demonstrated that a connection exists between a specific presentation and the Court's standards for identifying obscenity or indecency (the threshold requirement of evidence in establishing a *prima facie* case) that material would be protected under the First Amendment to the Constitution. Based on the information you provided, we are unable to make the required connection and, thus, Commission action on your unsupported allegations would be unwarranted.

Sincerely, Edythe Wise, Chief
Complaints and Investigations Branch
Enforcement Division Mass Media Bureau[84]

All six of the complaint letters were filed by the author with the FCC Review Board. The board held that six such complaints in a thirty-eight month period does not change their opinion that KISW is being programmed meritoriously.

In this connection KISW did not deny the broadcast was made, but stated that Mr. Idol was cut off when he refused to modify his language. A mitigating factor was that KISW broadcasted an apology allegedly obtained from Mr. Idol. Mr. Boros, Kaye-Smith counsel, stated, in

---

[83]Appendix page 49. The Billy Idol complaint letter.
[84]Appendix page 50.

response to the author's filings in this regard, that KISW took swift action in this matter. In actual fact the alleged airing was on a Tuesday and the apology was not aired until Friday and over the weekend. Furthermore, while Mr. Idol was apparently cut off, how long does it take to reach a microphone switch? It is clear from the complaint letter that the obscene language was of a significantly long duration that responsible action could have prevented any listener from being told to go and masterbate, presumably in response to a telephone complaint.

The author disagrees with Ms. Wise. There is a statute on the books that prohibits obscene and indecent utterings on the airwaves.

Whoever utters any obscene, indecent, or profane language by means of radio communication shall be fined not more than $10,000 or imprisoned not more than two years, or both. (Title 18 U.S.C. 1464)

While the First Amendment guarentees freedom of speech, the courts have recognized the uniqueness of radio broadcasts and have held that such airings require special treatment due to the fact that radio broadcasts can enter into a home without warning: as such they are distinguished from print or other methods of communication which require an act on the part of an individual to participate willingly in the reception of pornography. The Supreme Court has specifically stated that such programming, at a time when children can reasonably be expected to be in the audience, can be classed as obscene and/or indecent, and as such unlawful.

In this case the author submits that the commission had an obligation to turn the complaint letter over to the U.S. Justice Department for presentation to a grand jury under the statute prohibiting obscene and/ or indecent utterings by means of radio communication, Title 18, U.S.C. section 1464.

Hoffart, upon receipt of a copy of the Billy Idol complaint, filed a request with the review board for post-hearing discovery. The author asked that Kaye-Smith be ordered to give Hoffart a copy of the Billy Idol airing and the apology. The review board denied the discovery request.

It is clear that the commission shirks their statutory obligation when it comes to pornography complaints. They have an obligation to turn such matters over to the U.S. Justice Department. Instead, they act as judge and jury in matters where they have no jurisdiction. The act does not give the FCC authority to adjudicate statutory violations.

If any reader takes issue with the commission in regards to obscene and or indecent utterings, don't expect more than a *pro forma* letter from them advising you that the First Amendment gives broadcasters and telecasters *carte blanche* in programming, including what your children should hear on the air. The fact that the programming may be

210

filthy no longer concerns the commission, nor will they refer such statutory violations to the U.S. Justice Department for adjudication before a competent tribunal. They consider pornography to be in the public interest, convenience or necessity, or so it seems.

The commission, in this case, also appears to find that non-fact programming is in the public interest, convenience and necessity. The next chapter supports this contention.

32.

NON-FACT PROGRAMMING

The author, in his inspection of the KISW public file in Seattle, found a memo addressed to the public file that was written by Mr. Beau Phillips, KISW program director, and which was notarized by Ms. Noren. This memo[85] was intended to "clear up" any confusion regarding the announcement of Daylight Saving Time earlier this year.

The author prints this memo. The reader should take particular note that it is dated July 20th, 1982, some four months after the non-fact programming. Hoffart will show a nexus between this date and the date Kaye-Smith received a letter of admonishment from the FCC for this untrue event airing. The memo reads:

To: Public file, from Beau Phillips, RE: Daylight Saving.

This memo is intended to clear up any confusion regarding the announcement of Daylight Saving Time on KISW earlier this year. While the first actual day of Daylight Saving was April 23rd, we learned of current legislation that would've turned the clocks forward March 27th. The House of Representatives had already passed a bill that would allow one extra month of daylight in an energy conservation effort. This bill is now before the Senate.

KISW's broadcast of Daylight Savings Time beginning on March 27th arose out of uncertainty surrounding the bill. Our news department was doing a story on energy conservation and the Daylight Savings Bill issue came up. We received word from what we considered at the time to be a credible source that the early D.S.T. date would be implemented this year starting in March. As it happens, Daylight Savings Time is set to start on month ahead of schedule in 1983.

We first broadcast the incorrect clock setting information on Friday, March 26th of this year. It was not until 4PM the following day that the error was caught and immediately corrected. We ran live disclaimers throughout the remainder of the weekend explaining the mistake and restating the correct start date. Inevitably there were some people who never heard those disclaimers. I received 2 complaint letters (which I regrettably did not save) and explained to them what I've said above. KISW does not make a habit of broadcasting mis-information. We apologize to those who called and wrote and to our listening audience as well. It was an honest mistake that arose while investigating a news item we felt would be of interest. This is simply an instance of sketchy communication and human error on my part. There was no intent to deceive listeners or knowingly broadcast false information.

Sincerely, Beau Phillips, Program Director.

---

[85]Appendix page 33.

Marget E. Noren
comm expires 6-15-83.

The existence of this memo in the KISW public file raised some questions as to why there were no complaints in the Washington, D.C. KISW public file. Hoffart ordered a search of the files by a copy company and received a complaint letter from a Seattle area listener and also some other documents relating to this non-fact reporting. First, the complaint letter.

Mr. Stephen F. Sewell. (FCC)
I wrote this letter to Mr. Beau Phillips of radio station KISW (FM 100) in Seattle, WA. after being careless enough to allow myself deceived into believing their reports of the switch to Daylight Savings Time. As I wrote Mr. Phillips letter, I feel I was deceived by untrue information and got a real slap-in-the-face when John Langen and Mike West (the morning personalities who frequently pull these kinds of stunts) informed their listeners that it wasn't really Daylight Savings Time . . . that doesn't happen until the third week of April (chuckle-chuckle). I got very little enjoyment out of this joke. Nor do I think that their 'News in Your Face' program which mangles news out of proportion or makes it up entirely to slander political figures and entertainment industry persons is anything that belongs getting broadcast over the air-waves so freely and seemingly without any care as to how it might effect the public.

Obviously, I do not have to listen to KISW, there are plenty of other stations who have much more quality and pride and taste in what they broadcast (KZAM FM 92 in Bellevue for example is excellent), but I ask you how pretend news and pretend game shows (where the phone-in contestants are often hung-up on or ridiculed on-air) and weather reports for any city other than the Seattle area can be beneficial and of real value to the listening public?

I hope you will look into this situation or have someone at the local office (who directed me to write you) take a sincere and serious look of the unfortunate and hap-hazard manner in which this station is managed and the trash they think should make up valueable listening material.

I am reminded of a new d-j who came to Seattle almost a year ago to work the afternoon shift on KPLZ, he was really sharp and has a nice sence of music and commercial balance in his show. One day he tossed out an ethnic joke (Italian) at random and caught a flurry of calls and response from his listeners. The next day he apologized on the air, and the management followed suit. Within two weeks he left the station, presumably from pressure, and I hear he wound up in California.

It's hard to believe that bright guy got the squeeze play for such a minor thing, when he attempted to apologize for and then KISW does continuous slandering, deception and lying on the air and never even gets its wrists slapped. I truly believe their programming is often of no value to the public and while it is a matter of personal opinion, I hope it gets investigated.

Thank you for time in reading this letter, a response would be very appreciated.

(s) (Deleted)[86]

The attachment to this letter by this same complainant addressed to Mr. Beau Phillips, programming director at radio station KISW (FM 100) reads as follows:

Well, I can't explain why I have endured the tasteless humour, tacky verbal abuse and senseless on-air slander-attacks of innocent persons (including some of the listing audience), and I choose to do so no longer. On the morning of Monday, March 29th, 1982, I fell victim to the latest of your bits of hazardous programming and reckless misuse of your license to broadcast in the public interest.

At my job, I keep a radio on for a bit of background music while I move about doing my work. I can not sit still and listen intently to the rantings of the 'dee-jays' word-for-word all day. Sometime on Friday the 26th of March I caught a notice over KISW explaining that Daylight Savings Time would commence over the upcoming weekend and I was told to set my clocks ahead one hour on Sunday night/Monday morning at 2AM.

Over the weekend I didn't listen to the radio at all. I had my son to be with, and my fiancee and her son. It actually wasn't until Monday morning, about five miles from home on my way to work, that I realized the cruel joke your station had played on me. Your morning 'personalities' announced that (chuckle-chuckle) it was still Standard Time. I had woken us all up an hour early for no reason. I had sent my son to wait for his school bus one hour early, my fiance and I got to sit at the Park and Ride for a wasted hour, and her son got to visit with the sitter for an extra hour (at extra expense). It was not amused.

Over the past few years, your programming has become tasteless and stagnant, and your news and information less reliable. Your programming seems less in the public interest than in the selfish interest of some reckless individuals employed by KISW. Other than your strong broadcasting signal, I wonder what has kept me listening to your on-air rantings and slanderous comments this long.

I cannot understand why the FCC would allow such careless abuse of the airwaves unless there has been no public outcry.

You may consider it done: A Xerox of this letter will be mailed to Mr. Stephen F. Sewell at the main office of the Federal Communications Commission along with a note explaining why.

I presume he will contact you directly if he concurs with my feelings on the blatant misuse of your license to broadcast quality material of genuine use to the public. I believe it is the responsibility of station personnel and

---

[86]Appendix page 51.

management to see to it that material is factual and news is above suspicion.

For what it is worth; I will no longer listen to radio station KISW and will attempt to dissuade my friends and persons at work from listening also.

(s) (Deleted)[87]

Hoffart has not located any reply to this complainant by the FCC. The file search in Washington, D.C., however, did produce a letter of admonishment sent to Kaye-Smith Enterprises, Radio Station KISW (FM), Bellevue, Washington, 98009. It reads as follows: dated July 15, 1982.

The Commission has received a complaint that station KISW (FM) may have broadcast "untrue" information so as to deceive the public. Specifically, the complainant alleges that on the morning of March 26, 1982, John Langen and Mike West broadcast information that Daylight Savings Time would commence on the upcoming weekend and advised listeners to advance their clocks one hour on Sunday night/Monday morning at 2:AM. Daylight Savings Time actually went into effect at 2:00AM on Sunday, April 18, 1982. The complainant states that "It actually wasn't until Monday morning, about five miles from home on my way to work (sic), that I realized the cruel joke your station had played on me. Your morning 'personalities' announced that (chuckle-chuckle) it was still Standard Time. I (sic) had woken (sic) us all up an hour early for no reason." The Commission has stated a policy in *En Banc Programming*-Inquiry, 44 FCC 2303, 2304 (1960):

Prior to the *en banc* hearing, the Commission had made its position clear that, in fulfilling its obligation to operate in the public interest, a broadcast station is expected to exercise reasonable care and prudence with respect to its broadcast material in order to assure that no matter is broadcast which will deceive or mislead the public.

Also, the Commission has decided a line of cases involving situations which mislead and deceive the public. For instance in *Doubleday Broadcasting Co, Inc.*, 56 FCC 2d 333 (1975) the Commission dealt with a situation in which the announcements involved a hoax kidnapping of one of the station's announcers. Information received in that matter indicated the announcements were intended to be humorous and, in that context it would be reasonably understood as a prank. In another case, *Action Radio, Inc.*, 51 FCC 2d 803 (1970) the Commission concluded that the licensee engaged in deliberate falsification of news by broadcasting ficticious temperatures during weather reports. Although this was not the sole basis for its decision, the Commission granted the licensee a one year probationary renewal of the station's license. It is important to note that in that case the Commission stated:

---

[87]Appendix page 52.

215

This activity, albeit on a lower plane, falls on the perifery of the type of "nonfact" reporting we referred to as "staged" or "pseudo event" in *Democratic National Convention Television Coverage*, 16 FCC 2d 650, 656-657, (1969) (51 FCC 2d at 807)

The staff does not believe, that in your case, the falsification of the commencement of Daylight Savings Time announcements comes within the range of hoax cases covered in Commission decisions, nevertheless this Commission is concerned when the public is mislead and relies thereon. The time change announcements in your case are not substantially different from the type of announcements in the *Action Radio, Inc.*, case in which the Commission expressed great concern.

Consequently, this matter is being called to your attention so that you may exercise appropriate supervision over station operations and take whatever steps are necessary to assure that statements concerning time changes and similar type announcements are accurate and factual.

This matter is being made part of the records of Station KISW (FM).

Sincerely, (s) Jeffrey W. Malickson
Assistant Chief
Complaints and Compliance Division
Broadcast Bureau.

cc: Fly, Shuebruk, Blume, Gaguine, Boros and Schulkind.[88]

This letter, written some three and one half months after the receipt of the complainant's letter, shows that this matter was made part of the station's records. Hoffart found no such letter in the KISW public file, either in Seattle or in Washington, D.C. This letter, however, triggered a letter from Mr. Smith to Mr. Steve West, KISW and to Mr. Rod Krebs, at KJRB/KEZE in Spokane, Washington. This letter, dated July 20th, 1982 reads as follows:

From: Lester M. Smith, RE: FCC Complaint—KISW (FM).

I am widely circulating this letter from the FCC that we received today.

I want each of you to sit down with your various air people and tell them about the responsibility they have when they are on the air. What might seem funny to them could cause a great deal of problems for the station, especially when it receives a complaint from the FCC.

I will talk to each of you about this.

Best personal regards, (s) Les.

CC: Beau Phillips, KISW, w/enc.
John Sherman, KJRB/KEZE, w/enc.
Jerome S. Boros, w/o enc.[89]
file.

---

[88]Appendix pages 53 and 54.
[89]Appendix page 55.

The significance of the dates on these letters becomes clearer when some of the Oral Argument is presented that related to Hoffart's charges in this matter:

TR:1036   *Chairman Marino:* . . . in his petition to enlarge issues points 4, 18 and 21 seem to deal with the news staging allegation of the daylight saving time matter. What is the response to that? That was after the original license period. Am I correct in that?
Mr. Boros: The news staging was a complaint by Mr. Hoffart about some program efforts, as I recall, and misleading the public. I would say that it may have been after but it is a totally diminmus situation where conceivably and we will say for argument purposes, admittedly, there was an error made on the part of the station's staff. That error has not been repeated because procedures were immediately set into effect. I think the record reflects that. Whether it is the record before you or whether it is what we might call the broader record before the Commission as a whole and we respectfully submit . . .
Mr. Marino: There seems to be, or at least a staff ruling on that on that point.
Mr. Boros: Yes, we respectfully submitted official notice. This applicant, Kaye-Smith, did not sit still when an error occurred, but it took responsible action immediately on an on-going nature.

The reader should immediately recognize that the record does not support the testimony by Mr. Boros. First, the complaint was not filed by Hoffart, but by a Seattle area resident. Second, the commission did not find the matter of diminimus nature. They issued a letter of admonshment and made it part of the KISW file. Third, Mr. Boros states that the record reflects that the licensee put procedures into effect immediately so that the error would not be repeated. In actual fact Mr. Smith took no action until after he received the letter of admonishment from the FCC. His letter is dated five days after the date of the FCC letter. It is also significant that the Beau Phillips memo in the public file is dated the same day that Mr. Smith wrote Steve West his "action" letter with a copy to Mr. Phillips. In short, no action was taken until three and one half months after the non-fact programming. The statements by Mr. Boros that immediate action was taken is untrue, as supported by the record.

Furthermore, the commission told Mr. Smith that he needs to exercise appropriate supervision over stations operations. This notice to

Smith came in July of 1982. The record in this case proves that Smith viewed this FCC admonishment and warning as purely lip service. Let's review the record.

After Smith sent this July 20th letter to his employees, the following transpired:

KISW was in receipt of a letter dated February 18, 1983 wherein a complainant objected to an announcer's references to an infant being a "pain in the ass."

On May 24, 1983 the FCC in Washington, D.C was in receipt of a programming complaint relating to obscene and perverse dialog on KISW.

On March 27th, 1984, KISW allegedly allowed talk-show guest Billy Idol to engage in obscene and indecent utterings for an extended period of time. In this matter the complaint alleged that a female complainant was told to "go masterbate" by Mr. Idol when she telephoned in a complaint. Significantly, Mr. Smith did not personally air an apology.

In October/November of 1982 KISW personnel engaged in what may be classed as perhaps the largest number of statutory violations ever coming to the attention of the commission in the filing of their Direct Written Case. The record in that case establishes that Mr. Smith refused to become involved even after counsel told him that there were problems. He said, "If you got problems, call the radio station."

Mr. Bogel admits in his memo letter that he destroyed complaint letters. Destruction of complaint letters is a rules violation.

In early 1986, Mr. Smith's two station in Portland, Oregon allegedly aired non-fact commercials relating to a non-existent auto, willfully and repeatedly, along with a number of other Portland radio stations. Significantly, Mr. Smith was on notice to police the programming on his stations, as the letter of admonishment clearly states.

In summation, it appears that Mr. Smith has delegated his responsibilities to operate the station in the public interest, convenience or necessity to Mr. West and other employees who are irresponsible and disregard orders that may have been given them. The concept of *respondeat superior* holds that Mr. Smith and the Kayes are liable for the acts of their employees.

Smith and his associates are also responsible for statements made by counsel to the review board in regards to the Daylight Saving Time fiasco. The record simply does not support what Mr. Boros told the review board.

The reader may make up his or her mind if the content of the Beau Phillips memo in the KISW file can be supported by the facts. Do you think that a station in a market of 2.3 million can air non-fact events such as the Daylite Saving Time pseudo event for a period of some thirty or more hours and receive only two complaint letters and no phone calls advising them of the error? And what about the twenty-four KISW employees at the station and eight or more in the Bellevue office? Can it be believed that none of these thirty-two employees was aware that misinformation was being aired? You can be the judge. The author calls the content of the memo inherently unbelievable. If there are any Seattle area residents that called KISW about this non-fact reporting, or who wrote letters complaining about the broadcasts, the author would like to hear from you. Please verify your letters.

The commission no longer requires an appearance before a notary in the filing of verified documents. All that is now required is a statement that the information is true and correct to the best of the author's recollection and belief, and so state under penalty of perjury under the laws of the United States of America.[90]

---

[90]Title 28, U.S.C. section 1746 permits self-verification.

33.

REVIEW BOARD DECISION

The author made two filings with the review board. To his exceptions to the Initial Decision, Hoffart takes excerpts from the board's Decision released June 8, 1984. "We affirm the ALJ's resolution of the designated issues for the reasons set out below and conclude that several petitions to reopen the record have not been justified."

The review board addressed the notarial imperfections issue as follows:

A "notarial imperfections" issue was specified against Kaye-Smith by the ALJ on his own motion after receiving material from Kaye-Smith purporting to remedy such imperfections in affidavits supportive of its direct written case. (TR: 140-144). His findings under this issue are set forth in the Initial Decision paragraphs 93 thru 109 and will be highlighted here only to the extent necessary to place Hoffart's exceptions in perspective. The notarial imperfections grew out of Kaye-Smith's efforts to solicit testimonials from Seattle area residents as to Station KISW's performance during its last license period. Lester Smith, executive director of Kaye-Smith, delegated authority to general manager Stephen L. West and program director Eric S. Bogel to work with counsel and to oversee procurement of the testimonials. Counsel informed West that the testimonials required verification by a notary and that each potential affiant was to be advised that his or her sworn letter was intended for use as testimony in a hearing before the Commission. West, in turn, passed this information to the station personnel specifically recruited for the task of obtaining the letters. Neither West nor Bogel, however, fully comprehended the technical requirements of an affidavit.

All letters received were directed to Margaret (sic) Noren, administrative assistant to West, and a notary in the state of Washington, before being forwarded to counsel. Noren, whose notary experience was limited, had become a notary in order to facilitate station billing, and had never received formal training or taken an examination to become a notary. Carrie Matthews (sic) another station employee, sometimes acted as a substitute notary for Noren. Matthews' experience, too, was very limited, and she also had not received training or taken an examination to become a notary. Prior to the mailing of the letters to counsel, West and Noren discovered that five of the letters lacked notarizations. West thereupon instructed Noren to notarize the letters, and she in turn directed Matthews (sic) to notarize them. None of the three was aware that the letters had to be signed in the presence of a notary. The sworn letters were then mailed to counsel and included in Kaye-Smith's direct written case with affidavits from West and Bogel attesting that the letters had been obtained by them or under their direction and that the affiants had been informed that their letter affidavits would be used as testimony before the Commission.

A few days after the exhibit exchange date, counsel spoke with West and learned that some of the testimonials had been signed outside the presence of a notary; he instructed West to secure re-executed affidavits from the persons as well as two others whose affidavits lacked the date of notarization. An effort was then made by station personnel to obtain proper affidavits for those improperly notarized. Nearly all were subsequently obtained; however, one of the individuals, David Watkins, sent his corrective letter to the station, lacking a notarial seal and signature. Noren spoke by telephone to him about the matter and was instructed by him to affix her signature and seal to the letter, an instruction she carried out. Compounding this shortcoming was the fact that Watkins failed to apprise her that his secretary had affixed his signature to the letter. Noren made one more error and placed her seal on another letter in order to correct an erroneous date on the letter. The re-executed affidavits were substituted for the previously exchanged improperly notarized affidavits, and it was at that point that the ALJ added the issue. Five of the individuals whose testimonials had been originally deficiently notarized appeared as witnesses and testified that they voluntarily authored their letters; all but two understood that their letters would be used in a Commission hearing although only two recalled actually being told that their letters were to be used at hearing.

After observing all of the witnesses and considering their testimony, the ALJ concluded that the notarial imperfections were the result of errors by the station employees assigned to the task of obtaining the letters, that none of the station personnel involved believed that he or she was acting improperly, and that there was no intention to mislead the Commission. There was no motive for submitting improperly notarized testimony or for not informing the potential affiants that their letters would be used as evidence because these facts could have been easily ascertained at hearing, and the fact that some potential affiants were not so informed appeared to have been an oversight. Accordingly, this conduct warranted, at most, no more than a slight demerit against Kaye-Smith.

Hoffart's exceptions pertaining to this issue include a hodgepodge of accusations and allegations which he contends the ALJ failed to consider. These contentions are summarized as follows: *First*, Kaye-Smith should be held strictly liable for submitting documents that were in fact erroneous. *Second*, West, Bogel and Noren gave perjured testimony. *Third*, West and Bogel submitted false jurats. *Fourth*, Noren knowingly affixed her notary seal and signature to the improperly notarized affidavits after having been warned that the practice was illegal, and she conspired with West to have Matthews (sic) illegally notarize other documents. *Finally*, station personnel intimidated potential witnesses into not speaking with Hoffart. Kaye-Smith also challenges the ALJ's conclusion under this issue, arguing that no demerit, however slight, should be assessed against it.

The exceptions of both parties will be denied. Turning first to Hoffart's exceptions, we have fully considered the proffered supporting documentation underlying each allegation and find that the allegations are unfounded. *First*, the ALJ's finding that the notarial imperfections resulted from error, and not an intent to mislead Hoffart or the Commission reflects the record evidence; and his conclusion, that Kaye-Smith warrants no more than a slight demerit fully comports with past Commission precedent. (citing *WIOO, Inc.*), 54 RR 2d 1291, 1304–1305 (1983); *Rocket Radio, Inc.*, 65, FCC 2d 589, 595,596. Accordingly, Hoffart's contention that Kaye-Smith must be disqualified because of the mere fact that the material submitted by it contained imperfections is too draconian. *Second*, the charge that West, Bogel and Noren gave perjured testimony is overblown on the part of Hoffart. Perjury generally connotes a knowingly false statement made under oath. Mere mistakes in recollection or isolated incidents of forgetfullness do not rise to this level. Our examination of the specific statements made by the three individuals above (and addendum A of Hoffart's exceptions) reveals nothing more serious than that the statements are either at times equivocal or show at most an incorrect recollection on the part of the witness. No adequate basis has been demonstrated by Hoffart to support a finding of culpability in this regard. It is much ado about nothing, and a traditional adversarial attempt to puff these matters into deliberate attempts to deceive. (citations omitted)

Third, the allegation that West and Bogel submitted false jurats was obviously considered by the ALJ when he observed the two as witnesses and concluded that their failure in a few instances to inform affiants of the fact that their testimonial letters would be used in a Commission proceeding, as sworn to by both men on their affidavits, appears to have been an oversight. While not condoning the actions of West and Bogel in this regard, we are satisfied that there was no intent to mislead and that the slight demerit assessed against Kaye-Smith by the ALJ under this issue overall is a sufficient sanction.

Fourth, the claims that Noren knew her actions were improper when she affixed her seal and signature on the letters outside the presence of the signatories and that she conspired with West to coerce Matthews (sic) to improperly notarize some of the testimonials are based solely on speculation and conjecture. Noren testified that she never checked with counsel to determine whether it was appropriate to affix her seal to the documents outside the presence of the letter writer. In light of the fact that the letter writers testified that they voluntarily prepared their testimonials, which vitiates any discernible motive to improperly notarize the documents, a simple and more plausible explanation for Noren's conduct is that she was unaware of the requirement that the affiant had to be in her presence when she affixed her seal and signature to the document. Hoffart's claims therefore are rejected. Hoffart also claims that two additional letter writers (John Taylor and Bob Curran) should have appeared at hearing for cross-examination. We agree with the ALJ that the record under this issue was fully developed, and additional testimony would have been merely cumulative.

Finally, the accusation that station personnel intimidated potential witnesses into not responding to Hoffart's inquiries is overstated. Intimidation or harrassment of witnesses requires threats of reprisals or some other unnecessary and abusive conduct reasonably calculated to dissuade a witness from continuing his or her involvement in a proceeding. (citations omitted). Here, the record reveals that some of the letter writers contacted station personnel to determine whether they had to respond to Hoffart's letter concerning whether they had personally appeared before Carrie Matthews (sic) to have their testimonials notarized. The callers were simply told by the KISW employees that they did not think it was necessary to respond. The station employees did not call the letter writers nor did they make any affirmative efforts to prevent the responses to Hoffart. Thus, the behavior described does not rise to the level of intimidation or harrassment of witnesses. (citations omitted) Similarly, we disagree with Kaye-Smith's exception that no demerit under this issue is warranted and with its characterization that only lower echelon and inexperienced staffers were involved in the mistakes. It is clear that the station's general manager and program director participated in the errors and that much of the difficulty could have been avoided had those individuals been more attentive. A slight demerit against Kaye-Smith is fully warranted. (again citing *WIOO, Inc.*)[91]

Before the author takes issue with the review board's Decision, the reader should know that the cited *WIOO* case involved a pre-executed affidavit. In that case the applicant was given a slight demerit when it was adduced that he had reviewed the document prior to submission to the commission. In the instant case it is clear that the *WIOO* case is inapposite. To take a single case of a pre-executed affidavit which was reviewed prior to submission and equate it against the myriad of transgressions by Kaye-Smith falls on the distant side of arbitrary, capricious and abuse of discretion. Smith did not review the Kelsey affidavit, as signed, prior to the submission to the commission, nor could Mr. Bogel have reviewed the attachment list to his affidavit which had an affiant listed for the 9th of November when in actual fact the affidavit was not executed until the 10th.

In summation the review board cited *Cowles Broadcasting Incorporation v. the FCC.* In Cowles a single issue was the unauthorized move of their main studio which the commission found was not disqualifying after first being remanded by the U.S. Court of Appeals. Again, to equate Cowles with the instant Hoffart/Kaye-Smith case is a farce.

... the court indicated that in making a comparative choice between applicants in this type of case, relevant factors "are all to be weighed, all at once, all with an eye toward the public interest. Nothing is to be removed from the scales until the final balance is struck." Our review of the ALJ's conclusions in this case indicates that the ALJ has carried out the Court's directive, and that in doing so, he also correctly applied controlling Commission policy. We therefore affirm the ALJ's holdings that the preferences accorded Hoffart coupled with the slight demerit accruing to Kaye-

---

[91]98 FCC 2d at 679, paragraphs 9 through 16.

Smith are not sufficient to overcome the substantial preference awarded to Kaye-Smith for its past broadcast record.[92]

Joseph A. Marino, Chairman, Review Board.
Federal Communications Commission.

The reader can make up his or her own mind as to whether or not relevant factors were removed from the scales, or not put on the scales in the first instance. Some of the misstatements by the review board, albeit quoting from the Initial Decision, are as follows:

1. Mr. and Mrs. Danny Kaye and Mr. Lester M. Smith, owners of Kaye-Smith Enterprises are not responsible for the illegal acts of their employees.

2. That West or Bogel did not fully comprehend the technical requirements of an affidavit is inherently unbelievable.

3. Noren was an experienced notary. Hoffart had filed three documents notarized by Ms. Noren prior to the notarial imperfections fiasco.

4. The Review Board makes no mention of the four years of notarizations of billings by Ms. Noren when she had no direct knowledge, in all cases, that the commercials had been aired as scheduled.

5. The statement that Carrie Matthew sometimes acted as a substitute notary for Ms. Noren is not supported by the record. In actual fact Ms. Matthew stated that the illegal notarization of the McCullough letter purportedly on the 28th of October was her first notarial act.

6. The Review Board states that prior to the mailing of the letters . . . in actual fact Smith, Young and Noren all testified that Federal Express was used for the exchange to counsel.

7. The board says that West instructed Noren to notarized the letters. The record supports the testimony that West told Ms. Noren to have Ms. Matthew illegally notarize five of the testimonial letters.

8. The board says "a few days after the exhibit exchange counsel spoke to West." The record shows that the exchange was on the 11th and 12th of November and that Counsel Stuart Young called on the 12th—not a few days later, (assuming he was truthful).

9. In regards to the David Watkins' repetition of an illegal notarization, the record supports the fact that KISW asked Mr. Watkins to send his unnotarized letter to them and they would notarize it there. This was after the difficulties had already come to the attention of Ms. Noren. She so stated under oath. The Review Board's findings and conclusions are not based upon the official record.

10. The Review Board makes light of the fact that Ms. Noren also notarized the C. Clark Griffin corrected letter outside the presence of Mr. Griffin, allegedly after she called him on the phone and got his

---

[92]98 FCC 2d at page 687, paragraph 26.

224

permission to do so. This, again, is an act performed after Ms. Noren stated all of the difficulties had already come to her attention.

11. The Review Board agrees with the ALJ that there was no intent to mislead anyone and that there was no motive for submitting improperly executed notarized testimonial letters. Hoffart disagrees. Ms. Noren specifically stated, under oath, that she notarized, or instructed Ms. Matthew to notarize, the unverified letters in order to make them legal before the court. As to intent to deceive, Hoffart was on the receiving end of this deception, and he contends that deception was evident and contemplated, not only in the filing of an initial five (or more) illegally notarized letters, but also the two letters that were similarly affixed with phony notarial verifications and then filed as corrections.

12. The Review Board agrees with the ALJ that the repeated failure of Mr. West and Mr. Bogel to inform the potential affiants that their letters would be used as testimony in a proceeding before the Federal Communications Commission is an oversight. Hoffart disagrees. The filing of false information with a Federal Agency is a statutory violation of Title 18, U.S.C. section 1001.

13. The Review Board says that Hoffart's charges of perjury is overblown. Again Hoffart disagrees. When Mr. West testified that Mr. David Watkins had appeared before him and Ms. Noren, purportedly on the 17th of November, he lied. Hoffart finds no equivocation in his statement. In response to the authors question as to whether or not Mr. Watkins had appeared, he stated, without equivocation, "Yes." Similarly, when Ms. Noren stated "sworn and subscribed to before me this 17th day of November, 1982" on the bottom of the David Watkins corrected letter; she lied.

14. The Board upheld the ALJ in his refusal to order Mr. John Taylor and Mr. Bob Curran to appear as witnesses, holding that their testimony would be cumulative. Hoffart disagrees. Ms. Noren was the only witness to testify that both of these letter authors had appeared before her. Such one-sided adjudication is unlawful. Hoffart had a right to question both of these individuals to ascertain if Ms. Noren stated untruths, particularly in the light of her perjured statement on the David Watkins' corrected letter.

15. Hoffart submits that witness tampering was evident, even though the Review Board holds otherwise. Three of the six witnesses testified that they were told it was not necessary to respond to Hoffart. John Taylor and Mr. Curran have yet to be heard from. Perhaps they were also told not to respond to Hoffart. It would appear, as stated earlier, that a response would be in favor of Kaye-Smith if Ms. Noren's testimony is true.

16. Citing *WIOO* and *Cowles* as dispositive stretches credibility. Neither of these cases comes even close to being on parallel tracks with

the instant Kaye-Smith case. The Review Board, then, just as the ALJ, should be charged with making a decision that is arbitrary, capricious and an abuse of discretion.[93]

Following this decision, Hoffart filed a Petition for Reconsideration citing the newly discovered poronography complaints, and the newly obtained non-entertainment statistics from the FCC that showed KISW as having programmed 25 percent fewer non-entertainment programs than five similarly situated FM stations in the Seattle area. Hoffart also filed the KISW 1984 form 395, their equal employment report, wherein it was shown that KISW had zero ethnic groups employed on its staff of twenty-six people. This qualified as new material, as did the Billy Idol complaint letter.

The review board rejected Hoffart's Petition for Reconsideration on August 7, 1984, releasing the following:

Hoffart's petitions will be denied. Turning first to the petition for reconsideration. Hoffart initially contends that Station KISW has a history of broadcasting obscene, indecent, or objectionable programming. Appended to his brief in support are six letters received by the Commission over a thirty-eight month period, the most recent letter received April 4, 1984, complaining of offensive language allegedly aired over Station KISW. We conclude, however, that the complaint letters are not sufficient to cause us to reconsider our Decision.

The Commission has previously stated that its primary concern at renewal time is not with individual programs, but rather with the more limited issue of whether the licensee's programming on an overall basis has been in the public interest. (see *Pacifica Foundation*, 36 FCC, 147, (1964) Here, we conducted such an evaluation and concluded that Station KISW's overall past broadcast performance has been in the public interest. Thus, we affirm the ALJ's award of a strong comparative preference to Kaye-Smith for Station KISW's past performance during its license term, adopting his findings concerning the licensee's on-going ascertainment of community problems, needs and interests; its contact with numerous community leaders; its handling of issues of interest to the area through regularly scheduled news, public affairs, and other non-entertainment programs, and public service announcements; its local production of programs addressed to community problems; and its noteworthy reputation in the community. Additionally, we noted that KISW's non-entertainment programming as shown by its composite week performance, exceeded the amount promised in its earlier filed renewal application. The complaint letters (assuming, arguendo, their accuracy ... and Kaye-Smith does not dispute them) relate soley to a few isolated instances presented over a thirty-eight month period and are not sufficient to undermine our determination that KISW's overall past broadcast performance was substantial and merited a strong renewal expectancy preference. The letters

---

[93] 5. U.S.C. 706 (2) (A), reproduced in the Appendix as page 63.

do not reflect a clear-cut pattern of operation inconsistent with the public interest standard. As pointed out in our Decision, with respect to the most recent letter, the station acted responsibly in taking corrective measures after offensive material had been aired; that is, the offensive language occurred during a live interview, the interview was discontinued when the interviewee would not modify his language, and a taped apology by the interviewee was subsequently repeatedly broadcast over the station. In the light of the above, we are persuaded that further inquiry concerning this matter is not warranted. (citing *Pacifica Foundation*, 95 FCC 2d, 750, 760-761 (1983).

Hoffart's next contention is that Station KISW violated the Commission's Equal Employment Opportunity (EEO) rules and guidelines. In support he attaches the station's Annual Employment Report for 1984 which he claims shows the station's percentage of ethnic employees to be below the area's workforce. This allegation, too, is insufficient to support reconsideration of our Decision.

The author skips the remainder of the EEO findings by the review board. Suffice to state that the board holds that it is the effectiveness of a station's policy statement and not employment statistics that is germane. Hoffart had previously documented to the commission that KISW had similar short-comings in 1979 and 1982. Hoffart was not allowed to bring in EEO matters relating to other Kaye-Smith stations. At KJR, where Hoffart had charged EEO shortcomings, the commission ordered periodic reporting of their hiring practices. KJR, to the uninitiated, was the AM sister station in Seattle to KISW. Kaye-Smith was the former owner of two stations in Cincinnati, Ohio, WUBE and WCXL. Both of these stations were required to make periodic EEO reporting in two successive renewals. In Kansas City, Kansas, Kaye-Smith was subjected to a sex discrimination charge in 1976. Hoffart lost track of that case in 1980 when it was still pending before the EEO Commission. The charge was filed by an employee of KCKN-FM-AM, a Kaye-Smith station at that time. The overall record of Kaye-Smith in EEO matters is dismal, due, to a large extent, to the failure of the commission to put some teeth into its EEO rules and regulations when influential broadcasters are involved.

Hoffart's third contention will also be rejected. Hoffart submits copies of the 1980 renewal applications of commercial FM stations in the Seattle area which he claims, show, on average, a greater percentage of non-entertainment programming (9%) than that aired by Station KISW (6.61%). This submission is too late. The requiste showing for reopening the record is that the request must be supported by newly discovered evidence, the facts relied on must show that the petitioner could not with due diligence have known or discovered such facts at the time of the hearing, and the evidence, if true, must effect a basic part of the decision. (citation omitted). Here, there has been no showing that any of these requisites have been met. The information was accessible at the time of the hearing, and in view of the positive findings favoring KISW's renewal we do not perceive that it would have affected the Decision. Hoffart's final argument in support of reconsideration is that he was prejudiced because he did not attend the oral argument. This argument is totally unfounded. As noted in our Decision, Hoffart voluntarily chose not to participate in oral argument before the Board, and he cannot now be heard to claim that his non-attendance negatively influenced our Decision.[94]

The Petition for Reconsideration was denied. As with the review board's Decision, it was signed by Joseph A. Marino.

An analysis of the review board's findings and conclusions as they relate to Hoffart's reconsideration petition is in order.

First, as it relates to Hoffart's filing of the obscenity complaints, some of these were in the commission's files at the time of the hearing, and should have been brought to the attention of the ALJ by mass media. However, as the reader already has been informed, mass media did not participate at the hearing. Regardless, the Billy Idol complaint was a new fact, and it definitely had a bearing on the meritorious programming finding. The board, however, swept this under the rug. A precedent now exists wherein complainants who protest obscene and indecent language can be told to "go masterbate" with the blessings of the FCC Review Board members Joseph Marino, Jerold Jacobs and Norman Blumenthal. Since the commission upheld the review board, the full five panel of the commission also appears to sanction this type of rebuff by talk show guests upon concerned citizens.

It is significant that the review board cites the *Pacifica Foundation* cases of 1964 and 1983 but neglects to cite the *Pacifica Foundation* case of 1975.[95]

This is the famous seven dirty words case wherein a complainant advised the commission that *Pacifica Foundation* Station WBAI (FM) in New York aired the George Carlin Album FOOLE at approximately 2 PM on October 30, 1973. This album contains the seven dirty words described by the commission, in their Declaratory Order 75-200, released February 21, 1975, as being shit, fuck, cocksucker, mother-fucker, piss, cunt and tit. The author prints these obscenities with apologies to the reader, but it is necessary to show that a parallel exists between these words and those allegedly aired by KISW, which were pussey, masterbation, fuck, (from the Billy Idol complaint) and mother-fucker, ass, shit and bullshit from the complaint letter in the appendix.[96]

---

[94]98 FCC 20. At page 671 through 673.
[95]56 FCC 2d ct 94. FCC 75-200, released 2-21-1975.
[96]Appendix page 43.

With respect to the airing of the Carlin album, the commission found that the airings were indecent when programmed at times when children can be expected to be in the audience. The Billy Idol airing was around 3:10PM and as such KISW can be reasonably be expected to have a teenage audience. By the *Pacifica* precedent, affirmed by the U.S. Supreme Court, the KISW airings should have merited an indecent rating. The review board, however, appears to find this type of programming in the public interest, convenience or necessity since that is the criteria under which the commission must, by statute, issue licenses. The review board also appears to hold that such programming is meritorious.

One more aspect of the *Pacifica* case of 1975 needs to be reviewed. Of the seven commissioners serving in 1975, only one, Mr. Quello, is still holding office. Mr. Quello filed a concurring statement to the *Pacifica Declaratory* ruling in which he stated:

> ... I agree wholeheartedly with the conclusion that the words listed in paragraph 14 ... are words which depict sexual and excretory activities and organs in a manner patently offensive by contemporary community standards for the broadcast medium and are accordingly indecent when broadcast on radio and television. However, I depart from the majority in its view that such words are less offensive when children are at a minimum in the audience. Garbage is garbage. And by no stretch of the imagination can I conceive of such words being broadcast in the context of serious literary, artistic, political, or scientific value. Under contemporary community standards anywhere in this country, I believe such words are reprehensive no matter what the broadcast hour ... [97]

This is what Commissioner Quello stated in 1975. In 1985 he concurrs with the review board that KISW's broadcasts of similar language when children are expected to be in the audience warrants a meritorious programming rating and is in the public interest, convenience or necessity, or so it seems. Quello should be interrogated by a congressional committee and asked to explain his change in course. Can it be that Mr. Quello took into consideration that KISW was primarily owned by Mr. and Mrs. Danvy Kaye?

The review board found, as mitigating factors, that the Carlin broadcast is inapposite since that airing was a "shock-wave" of repetitions of obscene and indecent utterings. They also considered mitigating the fact that KISW allegedly aired an apology some three days later. Hoffart submits that a responsible broadcaster would have fired all connected with the airing and barred any further airings by Mr. Idol. They should have personally aired an apology, not only to the person who was allegedly told to go masterbate, but to the public in general.

---

[97] *Pacifica Foundation/WBAI*, 56 FCC 2d at page 103.

As to whether or not the airings were protected by the First Amendment, as Ms. Wise from the Enforcement Division at the FCC ruled, The Supreme Court in *Miller v. California*,[98] ruled that utterings without redeemable literary, artistic, political or scientific value can be classed as being obscene and/or indecent. In the case of Mr. Idol, allegedly he was in Seattle for a concert, and it should be clearly evident that his airings were of a commercial nature and were aired to attract customers to his commercial venture. In addition, Title 18, U.S.C. section 1464 prohibits such airings by statute.

The commission requires that each broadcast licensee file an annual report with them showing the station's employment profile. The report is made on the FCC form 395.

The KISW reports for 1979, 1982 and 1984 allegedly show shortcomings in equal employment when compared with the minimum standards acceptable to the commission. The standards are on file with the U.S. Court of Appeals as a result of the court asking the commission for some guidelines that could be the basis for decisions.[99]

The guidelines show that the FCC expects licensees to meet a 50 percent of parity figure in ethnic groups employment with parity being based upon the laborforce available in the station's Standard Metropolitan Statistical Area. (SMSA)

When the station's employment falls below the guidelines the commission states it will conduct an indepth review of the employer's equal opportunity policy in co-operation with the Equal Employment Opportunity Commission.

In the case of the KISW annual reports, which the author has tabulated for the years 1977 through 1984,[100] there appears to be a serious pattern of shortcomings in the employment of ethnic group workers. The tabulations taken from the KISW form 395 reports show zero ethnic employment in four of the eight years. Significantly, there are no employees other than caucasians listed in 1984.

Kaye-Smith's response to Hoffart's charges of EEO shortcomings is that there are not enough qualified ethnic group individuals applying for positions. It is somewhat ironic that all of the KISW employees involved in this case are white but Kaye-Smith found them qualified. The question arises as to what KISW expects from its employees, in the way of qualifications. It appears that honesty is not one of the virtues required.

---

[98]*Miller v. California*, 413 U.S. 15 (1973).
[99]Letter to Mr. George Fisher, Clerk, U.S. Court of Appeals, authored by Vincent Mullins, secretary, FCC. This letter is dated September 16, 1977.
[100]Appendix page 64. KISW annual employment profile statistics.

Hoffart's proof to the commission that KISW was below the zone of reasonableness in ethnic group employment was swept under the rug by the commission.

Next the board refused to accept Hoffart's offer of proof that KISW was below the average of five other similarly situated commercial FM stations in the Seattle area in terms of non-entertainment programming. They ruled that the figures were available to Hoffart at the time of the hearing and therefore cannot now be brought into the case. Even if acceptable, the fact that KISW is 25 percent below the other stations in terms of service to the public would not have made any difference anyway.

Hoffart disagrees. The Policy Statement on Comparative Renewals of 1965 clearly states that average non-entertainment programming does not deserve any credit toward any meritorious programming findings since the commission expects at least an average performance. In this case Hoffart proved that KISW was 25 percent below average, more or less, and the door to that filing was opened by the review board at oral argument. The board makes a large ado about the fact that KISW aired more non-entertainment than promised in their 1977 renewal application. They promised 6 percent and aired 6.61 percent. This is the figure that mysteriously turned into meritorious programming.

As to the board's finding that Hoffart had an opportunity to present those figures at the hearing, he would have obtained them from the FCC files if Kaye-Smith had asked for, and obtained, a meritorious programming issue. They did not, and for obvious reasons. Their record could not support such a finding. All in all, it appears that no matter what Hoffart proves, KISW is deserving renewal on a meritorious programming finding which the author submits was non-existent.

The board also rejected Hoffart's argument that giving fifty-seven minutes of oral argument time to Kaye-Smith when Hoffart and the mass media declined to appear prejudiced his case. The author was given no warning that his twenty minutes of allotted time would revert to Kaye-Smith if he failed to appear.

34.

THE COMMISSION'S EN BANC ORDER

Hoffart filed for review of the review board's decisions with the commission. The five commissioners upheld the review board.[101] Significantly this order was adopted, purportedly on April 15, 1985 by the commission sitting *en banc*. April 15, 1985 was a Monday, and the first day of the National Association of Broadcasters Annual Convention at Las Vegas, Nevada. The media reported that Ms. Dawson and Henry Rivera were in attendance on this opening day. The other commissioners were also at this convention but the author does not know on which days.

It appears, therefore, that the commission was not sitting *en banc* on the 15th of April, 1985, when the Order affirming the review board's Decisions was purportedly arrived at. Perhaps a review of the commission's agenda for April, 1985 is warranted.

The commission's Order reads as follows, in part:

The central issue in this comparative renewal proceeding involves the weighting of the various merits and demerits assessed on the basis of the record. The Review Board determined that Kaye-Smith should be preferred. We agree with that ultimate conclusion, and we will therefore deny review. However, certain matters raised by Hoffart require further discussion.

As Hoffart asserts, Kaye-Smith's record has not been without blemish. Exhibits submitted in the hearing were notarized outside the presence of the signatories. Such action warrants a slight comparative demerit. (citing Rocket Radio, 65 FCC 2d). It further appears that, in 1980, Kaye-Smith violated Section 74.551 (a)(1) of the Commission's rules by substituting a 12 watt microwave transmitter for a 7 watt transmitter without prior Commission approval. However, the violation was the result of an oversight on the part of the licensee's engineer, and the new transmitter had superior adjacent channel interference characteristics. It also appears that the licensee violated Section 74.1251 (b)(2) of the Commission's rules when it constructed an FM translator station using the wrong transmitting antenna. Such a change required prior Commission approval, but the licensee fully described the actual antenna in its application for a license, and the Commission granted that application. The record further reflects that Kaye-Smith violated Section 73.961 of the Rules by failing to conduct approximately half of the required weekly tests of the Emergency Broadcast system. However, that violation is substantially less than other instances in which a minor sanction was imposed. Compare *Oil Shale Broadcasting Co.*, 42 RR 2d 828 (1978) ($200 forfeiture for failure to

---

[101]Order No. 85-192, adopted April 15, 1985 and released April 19, 1985.

conduct any tests for thirteen months). Finally, it appears that Kaye-Smith prematurely executed an affidavit verifying the KISW (FM) renewal application, in that the affidavit was dated before the completion of required equipment performance tests. However, this matter warrants only slight comparative weight, *WIOO, Inc.*, 54 RR 2d 1291, 1304-5 (1983).

In our view, these alleged transgressions amount to nothing more than innocent errors on the part of the licensee, apparently unfamilar (sic) with these particular intricacies of the Commission's rules. As such, even taken together, they do not warrant more than a slight comparative demerit. On balance, we believe that Kaye-Smith's preference based on its meritorious past service is sufficient to outweigh the slight demerits assessed against it and the comparative plus awarded Hoffart. This is so because the preference given for a past broadcast record such as the one provided by Kaye-Smith normally outweighs structural (sic) factors like diversity and predictive factors like integration of ownership and management. *Cowles Broadcasting, Inc.*, (WESH-TV) 86 FCC 2d 993 (1981) affirmed sub nom, *Central Florida Enterprises v FCC*, 683, F 2d 503 (D.C. Circuit, 1982). By affording stations that provide such meritorious service a plus of major significance, we are assured that licensees are encouraged to invest in the provision of a quality service. In this case, Kaye-Smith's past record of substantial public service in the public interest has been sufficiently strong to overcome the licensee's minor transgressions and the challenger's comparative merits.

Accordingly, it is ordered, that, pursuant to Section 1.115(g) of the Commission's Rules, the Petition for Review filed November 19, 1984 by Vincent L. Hoffart is denied . . .

Federal Communications Commission
William J. Tricarico, Secretary.

(footnote to the commission's Order) We fully agree with the review board's assessment of the record evidence and Hoffart's exceptions to the matter of the imperfectly notarized exhibits.

The author now reviews the commission's *en banc* order and will prove, beyond any doubt, that the commissioners themselves have engaged in impermissible misrepresentations and untruths in this denial of Hoffart's review petition.

The commission admits that Kaye-Smith filed a series of documents that were represented as being legally notarized when in actual fact the verifications on seven such documents were phonies affixed by Kaye-Smith notary/employees. This, the five commissioners concluded, warrants only a slight demerit, citing *Rocket Radio*, 65 FCC 2d. Hoffart, however, quotes from *Rocket Radio*, 70 FCC 2d, page 420:

The deliberate and knowing submission of false or improperly certified documents to the Commission is a serious matter which has resulted in disqualifications of applicants in the past. (Citing *Radio Carrollton,*

WIOO, Inc., and *3 J's Broadcasting*) ... the (Blackstock) statement cannot be deemed a valid affidavit since it was not sworn to or signed in the presence of a notary, and the signatory was not even informed that the statement would be notarized. While we believe that (Apostolic) engaged in serious misconduct in submitting the statement as a purported affidavit, we disagree with the Judge's conclusion to disqualify (Apostolic) on this issue. ... While we by no means condone ... we believe the evidence indicates innocent error rather than a deliberate and concious attempt to deceive the Commission ...

We have also concluded that the application of *Rocket* must be denied because it deliberately submitted an affidavit containing misrepresentations to the Commission ... thus denial of both applications would serve the public interest, convenience and necessity.

Leonidas P.B Emerson, Member, Review Board.

Apostolic was disqualified on other matters in the above case. The reader will recognize, the author submits, that there are no parallels between the cited case and the Kaye-Smith case that warrant a finding of no intent to deceive the commission. Kaye-Smith engaged in an initial five (or more) phony verifications and followed those up with two additional phony verifications after the author detected the illegal acts and reported them to the judge. The two repeated acts came after Station Manager Stephen West was warned by counsel that "you can't do that." The commission did not elaborate on the fact that *Rocket Radio* was disqualified for submitting a false affidavit. Just as the review board skirted the *Pacifica Foundation* seven dirty words case, the commission here skirts the fact that both applicants were disqualified.

The commission admits that Kaye-Smith violated the rules when they installed a higher-powered microwave transmitter without prior authority from the commission. They find this excusable on the basis that it was an oversight on the part of the station's engineer. The record evidence, however, shows that the engineer discussed the matter of interference problems with Mr. Stephen West, the KISW manager, and between themselves they decided to order and install a higher-powered transmitter from a different manufacturer without advising the commission. This is no oversight, but a deliberate act that violated the statutory provisions of the Communications Act of 1934, as amended, which prohibits the installation and use of radio apparatus without prior authority from the commission.[102] Compounding this felonious act was the fact that Mr. Smith signed an application to relicense the seven watt transmitter at a time when the twelve watt unit had been in use for about six months. For the commission to hold that Hoffart's revelations are insignificant defies analysis. Their Order establishes a precedent

---

[102]Title 47, U.S.C. Section 301.

wherein broadcasters may install higher-powered equipment without authority and then simply state that the engineer involved engaged in oversights. In actual fact this appears to give pirate station operators a clear case to operate radio apparatus without a license or permit thereto. Like cases require like treatment. The author charges the commission with an appearance of preferential treatment to Kaye-Smith Enterprises in this matter.

What is really egregious in the commission's Order is their findings and conclusions relating to Hoffart's charges that KISW installed and used an unauthorized antenna on their translator located on Queen Anne Hill. The commission states, as a mitigating factor, that Kaye-Smith fully described the actual antenna in their license application, and that the commission granted that application. This is a blatant falsehood and a misrepresentation by the commissioners. While Kaye-Smith did describe the characteristics of the antenna installed, they never had a permit from the FCC for such an installation, and the installation was never authorized. The commission's statement that the application was granted is untrue, and they know it, or should have known it because Hoffart filed proof, beyond any doubt, that the commission never granted authority for the use of a TACO Y-51 5 element antenna for their translator K283AA.

Hoffart files a copy of a response he received from Mr. Laurence E. Harris, Chief, Broadcast Bureau, to an FOIA request that specifically requested a copy of the authorization given Kaye-Smith for the use of a TACO Y-51 5 element directional antenna. It reads as follows:

21 October, 1982
RE: FOIA request No 82-163

Dear Mr. Hoffart:
This refers to your request dated October 5, 1982, pursuant to the Freedom of Informations Act. Specifically, you are requesting a copy of the specific authority given FM Station KISW, Seattle, Washington, to operate FM Translator Station K283AA with an antenna other than the Gibson 3 Colinear vertical dipole antenna specified in its license issued May 22, 1979, File No. BLFT 780822IA.

After careful search of the Commission's file, the Bureau is unable to locate any such authority or record of receiving such a request.

Your letter also claims that this translator station is now operating with a TACO Y-51 5 element Yagi antenna in contravention of Section 74.1251 (2) of the Commission's rules. In this regard, I have forwarded a copy of your letter to the Complaints and Compliance Division for appropriate action.

Sincerely, (s) Laurence E. Harris

Chief, Broadcast Bureau.[103]

The author introduced the letter into the record and the judge granted leave, at the hearing, to file this document as Hoffart's Direct Written Case exhibit 21.

This, then, establishes that the commission made impermissible misrepresentations in their Order and filed this untrue information—that the commission granted the license application for the use of a TACO 5 element transmitting antenna—upon Hoffart and the public.

TR:747   *Mr. Hoffart:* I would like to submit into evidence a letter from the Federal Communications Commission in regards to this. Would you like a copy?

Judge Fitzpatrick: Two copies for the record. What exhibit number do we want to attribute to this? The next one? Mr. Hoffart, you have exchanged Exhibits 1 through 20, so you want to have this marked as Hoffart Exhibit, Hearing Exhibit 21?

Mr. Hoffart: 21.

Judge Fitzpatrick: All right, Hoffart's Exhibit 21, which is a letter from Laurence E. Harris, Chief, Broadcast Bureau, date October 21, 1982, is marked for identification.

Mr. Young: Would that be a direct exhibit or a rebuttal exhibit? In this case a direct, I assume.

Judge Fitzpatrick: I guess my answer would be tweedle dum, tweedle dee.

The judge's response pretty well sums up this misrepresentation by the commission in their Order. In other words, who gives a damn? Hoffart is not going to prevail, no matter what the record establishes.

The FOIA response from Mr. Harris states that the FCC has no record of receiving a request from KISW for use of a TACO antenna, yet counsel for Kaye-Smith filed, after the hearing, a copy of such a request in the form of a license application. This late-filed exhibit was assigned Kaye-Smith Exhibit 19. It was purportedly filed on August 21, 1978, signed by Smith Aug 10, 1978.

TR:726   *Judge Fitzpatrick:* What, if anything, was done when you got a license that authorized an antenna you weren't using, even though you had reported to the Commission that you were using another antenna? What, if anything, did you do then?

Mr. Siegenthaler: Well, we again tried, I believe . . . in the licensing period again . . . stated that we were using this

---

[103]Appendix page 56. FOIA response letter.

antenna. We resubmitted this information once again in hopes that it would get itself cleared up. And again, it cames back specifying the antenna that was originally documented on the construction permit.

Judge Fitzpatrick: Nobody just picked up a phone and got in touch with the FCC and talked to somebody over there?

Mr. Siegenthaler: Well, I can show you the documents of our filings. We have that.

The preponderance of evidence is that KISW never had a construction permit nor a license to install or use a TACO directional antenna on their translator K 283AA. The Complaints and Compliance Division, prodded into action by Mr. Harris, sent a letter to Kaye-Smith Enterprises dated November 5, 1982 in which they requested KISW to describe the antenna installed, *inter alia.* Kaye-Smith responded by acknowledging that they installed a TACO Y-51 antenna and that a license application had been filed to cover this installation. Mr. Smith blamed the commission for not issuing a license for the TACO antenna. Since the construction permit did not allow this directional antenna installation, there was no error or oversight by the Broadcast Bureau. Hoffart submits what was involved is the willfull and repeated use of unauthorized radio apparatus by Kaye-Smith and the illegal installation was probably not known to other Seattle area broadcasters. There can be no question that this unauthorized installation contributed to the KISW ratings since they, at that time, were the only FM station broadcasting from Cougar Mountain to cover Alki Point in West Seattle.

The commission swept this statutory violation under the rug by calling the installation an oversight. It is a well-known precept that there is no need for a showing of willfullness when actions are repeated, and repeated means more than once. Here we have KISW using unauthorized and unlicensed radio apparatus for a period of over four years. The record shows that KISW made two applications for the use of a directional antenna and both were rejected by the bureau.

The author pursued this matter further by filing another FOIA request for a copy of a license issued to KISW that specifically authorized the use of a TACO Y-51 antenna. A response was received and it reads as follows:

Dear Mr. Hoffart:
This is in reference to the Freedom of Informations Act, 5 U.S.C. 552, (FOIA Control No. 86-44), which you filed regarding FM translator Stations K283AA and K259AA, Seattle, Washington.
Pursuant to the Freedom of Informations Act, 5, U.S.C. section 552, you request a copy of the license certificate, and any and all documents relat-

ing thereto, which specifically authorizes K283AA to operate with a directional antenna, namely a TACO Y-51. You further seek copies of any notice of apparent liability that may have been issued to the licensee for the willful and repeated operation of K 283AA with an antenna not authorized by the license granted the station on May 22, 1979. Finally, copies of all documents, including applications, regarding K 259 AA are requested.

Author's note: KISW apparently filed a new application for a translator to cover Alki Point to operate on channel 259. This came after Hoffart blew the whistle on their illegal installation at the hearing via Hoffart's Direct exhibit 21. FCC granted a permit on November 21, 1985. The file number is BPFT-831026MB, with indicates that the application was received on the 26th day of October, 1983. To continue with the FOIA response:

To place the instant request in the proper perspective, it should initially be noted that K283AA was constructed in 1978 using a different transmitting antenna than the one specified in the construction permit issued by the Commission. However, as was developed in the comparative renewal proceeding (BC Docket Nos. 82-265 and 82-266). in which you were involved with Dena Pictures, Incorporated, the licensee of Station KISW (FM), Seattle, Washington, the substituted antenna was identified and its performance characteristics were tabulated and submitted as part of the license application for that station. While that application was granted by the Commission, the license certificate issued May 22, 1979 did not reflect the use of the substituted TACO Y 51 antenna. In reviewing the grant of KISW (FM)'s renewal application and the denial of your competing application, the Commission considered and specifically addressed the above matter. While it found that the licensee had violated Section 74.1251 (b)(2) of the Commission's rules in contructing K283AA with a substituted antenna for which prior approval had not been obtained, that transgression was regarded as minor, amounting under the circumstances to nothing more than an innocent error on the part of the licensee apparently unfamilar (sic) with this particular intricacy of the Commission's rules. See *Kaye-Smith Enterprises*, FCC 85-192, released April 19, 1985.

Turning to the specifics of your document request, please be advised that a thorough review of the records systems maintained by the Mass Media Bureau and the Field Operations Bureau has been conducted. However, no documents of the nature requested with respect to K283AA have been ascertained as a result of this records search . . . [104]

The reader may wish to review this letter as it is printed in the appendix in order to establish the accuracy of the above FOIA response.

---

[104]Appendix pages 57 and 58.

The author now puts this matter into its proper perspective. With reference to the license issued,[105] note that the December 1, 1981 date under item 2, is the expiration date of this license.

Kaye-Smith filed for a renewal on September 18, 1981. A copy of the transmittal letter is in the appendix.[106] This transmittal letter, and the application for the renewal, was filed by Kaye-Smith as Kaye-Smith exhibit 19 on December 8, 1982, after the hearing, as rebuttal and offer of proof that they had advised the commission that their installation did not correspond to the license issued.

This, then, is the application that Mr. Siegenthaler had reference to when he stated, preceded by a question on this matter by the judge, on December 2nd, 1982:

TR:726   *Judge Fitzpatrick:* What, if anything, was done when you got a license that authorized an antenna you weren't using, even though you had reported to the Commission that you were using another antenna? What, if anything, did you do then?

Mr. Siegenthaler: Well, we again tried, I believe, in the licensing period again . . . stated that we were using this antenna. We resubmitted this information once again in hopes that it would get itself cleared up. And again, it came back specifying the antenna that was originally documented on the construction permit.

This is proof that KISW did nothing between the time the invalid license was issued on May 22, 1979 until September 19, 1981, in the way of advising the commission that they were still using an unauthorized antenna. There is more, however.

The invalid license had expired on December 1, 1981 and the FOIA response from Mr. William H. Johnson, acting chief of the Mass Media Bureau, implies that no renewal was issued. Siegenthaler states that one was received, again for the Gibson antenna. The author followed through on this matter and again asked his copy company agent to review the K283AA files. They responded that there was nothing in this file dated after 1981.

The question arises, was another license issued to replace the expired invalid license? If so, why is there no copy in the FCC files? If none was issued, did KISW operate their translator without any authorization, albeit even an invalid license, after December 1, 1981? If no renewal was issued, did the commission make misrepresentations to the public and Hoffart in this matter when they stated, in their Order 85-192,

---

[105]Appendix page No. 40. This is a copy of the invalid license issued by the FCC.
[106]Appendix page 59.

without equivocation, " . . . the licensee fully described the antenna in its application for a license and the commission granted that application"?

One further note on this matter. The review board, at oral argument on February 24, 1984, asked Mr. Boros about this unauthorized installation.

TR:1028 *Chairman Marino*: I will combine the next two because they seem to be possibly related. They are points number N and points number O which appear also at 25 and 26 of the brief.

They deal with some alleged violations by KISW of your translator authorization and your microwave oven (sic) authorization.

Mr. Boros: Yes, I think that is referenced to special authorizations, if I am on the right track which were obtained authorizations for auxilliary equipment, and Mr. Hoffart, as I recall, proceeded on two levels.

He wrote a letter to the Complaints and Compliance Bureau and he also, at trial, made allegations.

All of our authorizations are in good shape. All have been granted by the operating bureaus involved and the Complaints and Compliance Bureau as well as the judge before whom charges were raised, made no findings adverse to it.

Chairman Marino: Well, the judge did find, didn't he, that you had applied for one type of equipment and used another. Then subsequently applied for the right equipment in one of these charges, if I recall.

Mr. Boros: Yes. That is the charge I think I am adverting to. But what I am saying is upon evaluating the situation, the judge which had the benefit of observing the demeanor and, of course, inquiring himself, and Judge Fitzpatrick is not reluctant to do so, found nothing adverse to it.

Mr. Jacobs: Mr. Boros . . .

Mr. Boros: I am not saying that we are infallible. I will say that any errors on our part are errors which do not constitute a pattern, those are errors which top management is not responsible because top management responsibly delegated to other people on the staff and if people on the staff made the error, it is not a case of being on notice.

Certainly, once you are on notice that a member of your staff is sufficient, then you have the two bite doctrine of taught law which is applicable.

But where you hit the right people and they make errors that's no worse that the unfortunate problem we lawyers occasionally have that some lawyer is less experienced . . . the case the way we would like it.

Well, it appears that Mr. Boros is blaming their experienced engineer for "errors" in this matter. The record does not support "errors" but a repetitious filing by Mr. Lester M. Smith for a license to use unauthorized radio apparatus. Smith made and signed applications in 1978 and again in 1981 for the use of a directional antenna on their K283AA translator. He was on notice that the license issued in May of 1979 did not authorize the TACO Y-51 antenna. Thus we do have the two bite doctrine of taught law. Both Smith and the Broadcast Bureau were aware of this illegal installation. The question arises why FCC did not issue a cease and desist order.

The commission's Order 85-192 states that all transgressions were errors and due to unfamiliarity of the rules. This implies that Mr. Siegenthaler was incompetent to perform his assigned tasks. This stigmatization by the commission reflects upon the character of Mr. Siegenthaler and is unwarranted. There is nothing in the record to support the fact that Siegenthaler was unfamiliar with the rules. The preponderance of evidence is that he acted under orders from Mr. Smith and his manager in the matter of the installation and operation of unauthorized radio apparatus.

The commission's Order is a matter of public record. They are required, by law, to widely circulate their decisions. At least one library in each state is a repository for the FCC 2d Reports, as distributed by the U.S. Government Printing Office. In addition, there is wide circulation in Pike and Fisher and other law book printers of the FCC's actions. It follows, then, that Mr. Siegenthaler has been maligned by a federal agency as to his ability to perform assigned tasks and his knowledge of the FCC rules and regulations. This stigmatization was also carried forward by counsel for Kaye-Smith as a mitigating factor. The author does not feel Mr. Siegenthaler is an incompetent engineer, but that he was acting under orders to install and operate illegal apparatus under penalty of being discharged if he did not do so.

Siegenthaler is now branded as being an incompetent engineer, courtesy of Kaye-Smith and the Federal Communications Commission. Perhaps he will take steps to clear his name.

The author now turns to the Emergency Broadcast rules violations by Kaye-Smith. The commission admits that the rules were violated. They cite *Oil Shale Broadcasting* as being dispositive.[107] This station in Rifle, Colorado was fined two hundred dollars for EBS rules violations. It appears logical that the KISW transgressions were more serious than those at Rifle, Colorado, because KISW programs in an area of approximately 2.3 million people and EBS failures could have more serious consequences. The commission, however, is not known for using logic in making decisions. They look at who is involved and not what is involved.

To go further in this matter, Hoffart prints a notice of a monetary forfeiture assessed against *Capitol Media, Inc.,* of Cheyenne, Wyoming.[108] This FCC Memorandum and Order assesses a forfeiture in the amount of four thousand dollars for, *inter alia:* "Failure to make appropriate entries in the station log indicating reasons why weekly test EBS transmissions were not received," citing section 73.932 (d) of the rules, one of the rules that Hoffart had charged that KISW personnel repeatedly violated.

It is significant that this forfeiture was assessed by the commission *en banc* on December 9, 1985, about six months after their Las Vegas decision wherein KISW was held blameless for similar violations. Here again we have preferential treatment given an influential broadcaster. It is well-known that the commission takes into consideration the financial condition of licensees when it assesses forfeitures. Here we have Mr. and Mrs. Danny Kaye and Lester M. Smith being given a clean bill of health and no fine while a small station in Cheyenne, Wyoming deserves being hit in the pocketbook. This shows the two faces of the commission. Influential broadcasters are given preferential treatment. The author trusts that a congressional committee will ask Mr. Fowler, *et al,* why this *Capitol Media* forfeiture was warranted and the Kaye's and Smith go scot free.

Finally, the commission acknowledges that Mr. Smith pre-executed his certification of the 1980 license renewal and represented to the commission that the performance measurements had been made when this was not the case. They cite *WIOO* again in this mitigation, holding that misrepresentations warrant only a slight demerit. The case is clearly inapposite. Smith engaged in active indifference by failing to check the accuracy of his application.

The author has charged the commission with engaging in preferential treatment in this case. The commission's KISW renewal supports such a charge. Preferential treatment, or the appearance of preferential treatment, is prohibited by statute. Part nineteen of the FCC Rules and

---

[107]*Oil Shale Broadcasting v. FCC.,* 42 RR 2d at 828 (1978).
[108]Appendix pages 60 and 61. Underscoring by the author, Hoffart.

Regulations, Volume No. 1, is entitled Employee Responsibility and Conduct. It reads, in part: (19.735-201a,) Proscribed actions:

An employee shall avoid any action, whether or not specifically prohibited by this subpart, which, might result in, or create the appearance of:
(b) Giving preferential treatment to any person;
(c) Impeding Government efficiency or economy;
(d) Losing complete independence or impartiality;
(f) Affecting adversely the confidence of the public in the integrity of the Government.[109]

Note particularly that the author does not have to prove preferential treatment, he only needs to show that there is an appearance of such conduct. The reader may decide for him or herself if the authors charges are warranted.

Under another section of this ethical conduct regulation, it is stated that the word "Employees" means an officer or employee of the commission, including the commissioners. It is further stated that the Office of Personnel Management has the responsibility to enforce the regulation, which was codified by Executive Order Number 11222, May 8, 1965.

The question now arises whether or not the Office of Personnel Management will conduct an impartial investigation of the charges made by Hoffart. It will be up to the public to demand a special prosecutor and a grand jury investigation into the allegations by Hoffart. The commission has not been subjected to a scrutiny since the late 1950s when a Commissioner was charged with selling his vote.

Commission chairman Fowler should be the first to call for an unbiased investigation in order to prove to the public that preferential treatment was not accorded Kaye-Smith in this case.

Post-editing update: Hoffart filed another FOIA for the KISW translator documents on December 20, 1986. On February 20, 1987, Hoffart was advised by phone, that the documents had been located. Mr. Jim Brown, the FCC employee who called Hoffart, said, "you wouldn't believe it." To date, April 1, 1987, the "you wouldn't believe it" documents have not been released to Hoffart. It is now over ninety days since the FOIA request was received by the FCC managing director.

It appears that the FCC is in violation of 5, U.S.C. 552, by refusing to release public documents to Hoffart.

---

[109]Federal Register, 32 FR. 13457, (9-26-1967).

243

35.

THE U.S. COURT OF APPEALS JUDGMENT

The author filed an appeal of the FCC Order 85-192 with the U.S. Court of Appeals, District of Columbia Circuit. This court has jurisdiction over federal agency actions. The filing was dated July 15, 1985 and case number 85-1266 was assigned. Hoffart followed the federal rules of appellate procedures and the local rules of the court to the best of his ability.

The court was made aware of the commission's actions on all major transgressions by Kaye-Smith as outlined in this book. Kaye-Smith filed a motion to intervene on behalf of the FCC who was the appellee to Hoffart's appeal.

As part of the Kaye-Smith filings, they filed their Brief on October 23, 1985. In that Brief, as Hoffart outlined to the court, Kaye-Smith made three misrepresentations. First, they filed upon the court:

> The various adjudicatory authorities charged with resolving the contest between Kaye-Smith and Hoffart, on an agency level, consistently have held that KISW's past performance to be meritorious. That conclusion derived not only from station operation but also from local evaluation thereof. Thus station KISW has received numerous letters from community leaders, throughout the license period, commending the station for its public service programming. As the Mayor of Seattle stated during hearing, Kaye-Smith has demonstrated a " . . . strong, effective commitment to broadcasting in the public interest . . . "[110]

The author has already revealed to the reader that the mayor's participation in the hearing was limited to the filing of a solicited letter of commendation. A fair reading of the above representation to the court by Counsel Boros indicates that Mr. Boros stated to the court that Mr. Charles Royer, Seattle Mayor, made his statements praising KISW programming at the hearing. Since Mayor Royer did not personally appear at the hearing, the statement, "As the Mayor of Seattle stated during hearing," is untrue.

Second, counsel for Kaye-Smith, in their Brief filed with the court, made the following misrepresentation:

> Weighted against this substantial preference were minor preferences accorded Hoffart for diversification and integration . . . (also page 7, Intervenor Brief)

Hoffart can find no references anywhere in the record where the ALJ, the review board or the commission targeted Hoffart's preferences as

---

[110]Kaye-Smith Intervenor's Brief, excerpt from page 7.

minor. The term was willfully added to the case by counsel in order to make their case more palatable to the court. Since it is untrue that any of the adjudicatory parties so termed Hoffart's integration and mass media preferences, counsel has to stand as having filed misrepresentations with the court of appeals.

Third, counsel filed the following with the court:

The Commission carefully considered the "alleged transgressions" of Kaye-Smith which were:
(i) the notarization of exhibits outside the presence of the signatories;
(ii) The substitution of a 12 watt transmitter without prior approval . . . but the licensee fully described the actual antenna in its license application which was granted by the Commission.
(iii) failure to conduct approximately half of the required weekly tests of the emergency broadcast system and
(iv) the premature execution of an affidavit verifying the KISW (FM) renewal application, in that the affidavit was dated before the completion of required equipment performance tests. (page 20, Intervenor Brief)

The author takes exception the (ii), *supra*. Here counsel lump-sums two discrete statutory violations into one by stating that the antenna substitution was connected with the microwave transmitter installation. Hoffart made no such claims. The antenna substitution was connected with the KISW translator installation. The two installations, that of the KISW microwave and the KISW translator, are separately licensed, when licensed. By representing these as one installation, counsel has, in actual fact, made misrepresentations to the U.S. Court of Appeals.

The Court of Appeals, in a judgment handed down April 16, 1986, after suspending oral argument, affirmed the commission's Order 85-192. This single-page document is reproduced in the appendix.[111] The reader may note that the court ordered that the judgment was not to be published.

Hoffart is not surprised by the court's Order not to publish the judgment. The judgment can be classed as an embarrassment to the court because their decision was not based upon the facts supplied by Hoffart.

In any event, Judges Wald, Edwards and Kozinski (9th circuit, sitting by des.) ordered and adjudged:

While the issues presented occasion no need for an opinion, they have been accorded full consideration by the Court."
. . . the order of the Federal Communications Commission on appeal herein is hereby affirmed.

Per Curiam, for the Court
George Fisher, Clerk.

---

[111]Appendix page 62.

Hoffart next filed a Petition for Rehearing and a suggestion for rehearing *en banc*.

No judge in active service voted for a rehearing.

The next judicial step would be to file a Writ of Certiorari with the U.S. Supreme Court. Hoffart leaves that move for a later date. Perhaps some concerned Seattle area citizens will write Hoffart verified letters of facts which they have direct knowledge of that prove Kaye-Smith lacked candor in their presentations. There are many questionable areas, such as whether or not Federal Express picked up a package at KISW studios on November 9th or 10th of 1982, as Ms. Noren stated in sworn testimony, later altered to show that the Direct Case exchange was by mail, by counsel. This contradictory description could lead to a "lack of candor" issue and grounds for reopening the record.

36.

CONCLUSION

The author would also like to hear from the following testimonial letters authors whose testimony was not presented in person at the hearing in order to verify to the author that KISW personnel informed them that their testimonial letters would be used in a proceeding before the Federal Communications Commission. The names are taken from the attachment lists printed in the appendix as pages 4, 6 and 8.

Charles Royer, Mayor of Seattle
Nina L. Evers, Muscular Dystrophy
Patricia Frank, Big Sisters of Puget Sound
Wanda Harrison, Leukemia Society of America
Jeanne Beall, Space Needle Corporation
John Taylor, Seattle Arts Festival
Tom Fortin, Lynnwood Senior High School
Lynne A Freeman, Boys and Girls Clubs of King County
Lou Lavinthal, Variety Club
Lynne A Freeman, Gerber/Meyers Wolfe and Kilgore
Michael Campbell, Campbell Sports, Inc.
Robert L. Steil, President, Squire.
Todd M. Bitts, President, PSRBA (Broadcasters Ass'n.)
Patricia P. Fearey, Pat Fearey and Associates
Bob L. Curran, Military Coordinator, Seafair.
Scott Hickey, Public Relations, Alpac Corporation
James M. Foster, Rainier Brewing Company
C. Clark Griffin, C.C. Griffin and Company
Douglas Weisfield, Weisfield's Inc.,

Station Manager Stephen West and Program Director Eric Bogel stated, under oath, that each of the above were told that their letters of commendation would be used as sworn testimony in a proceeding before the Federal Communications Commission. True or False?[112]

There are many others listed in this book that may take exceptions to what is printed in this book. The witnesses that appeared may, for the first time, become aware of what was involved in this case and what the KISW employees testified to that, in some cases, appears to establish that those witnesses were untruthful.

These witnesses may wish to clear the records where disparate testimony has been elicited.

---

[112]Appendix pages 3 through 8.

247

Similarly, Seattle area residents who sent letters of complaint to KISW during 1977 through 1985, which have not been mentioned in this book, may wish to provide the author with details. If proof exists that KISW personnel kept complaint letters from him is his inspection of their public files, there is a good chance that the record may be reopened for further hearings.

Individuals who think that the decisions and orders reached in this case by the Federal Communications Commission are arbitrary, capricious, an abuse of discretion, and contrary to congressional intent when they enacted the Communications Act of 1934 may wish to write their congressional representatives and ask for an investigation of this case. It would be interesting to see which ones vote for a special prosecutor to investigate the commission and which ones vote for a whitewash. Senators have a zip code of 20510 and representatives can be reached by using zip code 20515. It would also be interesting to find out which broadcast licensees would support such a project, and which will support the commission, the agency that holds their license in their hands.

The author's zip code is 99207, Spokane, Washington. Mail sent to the Hays Park Station, 99207 should reach him.

This is by no means an isolated case where the FCC has engaged in an appearance of preferential treatment and it is high time that somebody does something about it. The public, and not the broadcasters, own the airwaves, and it is time that the commission be reminded of that fact.

The Communications Act of 1934, as amended, reads, in part:

It is the purpose of this Act, among other things, to maintain the control of the United States over all channels of radio transmission; and to provide for the use of such channels, but not the ownership thereof . . . [113]

The "Fifth Estate" does not like the fact that the act specifically states that they do not own their licenses but are only temporary public trustees subject to the operations of their stations in the public interest, convenience or necessity in order to warrant renewal. The public should be wary of the repeated introduction of bills in congress which would give broadcasters their licenses in perpetuity. This would be one of the biggest give-aways of a scarce and valuable public resource in the history of the United States.

The public should demand greater diversification of allocation of broadcast channels. There are only about 12,000 channels licensed and the present rules allow any one entity to be licensed up to thirty-six stations, under certain conditions. Minority licensees amount to about 2 percent. The instant Kaye-Smith and Hoffart case proves that challenges at renewals times are an exercise in futility. Mr. Fowler has been

---

[113]Communications Act of 1934, as amended, Section 301.

248

quoted as saying that it is unamerican to revoke or not renew a broadcasters license. Mr. Quello has been quoted as urging broadcasters to lobby for elimination of comparative challenges. Ms. Dawson favors removing all caps to ownership. With such biased individuals sitting in judgment it should be clear to the public that renewals based upon incumbency *per se* is already an actual fact and the hearings are held only because they are a statutory requirement. They are a mockery, to say the least.

There is support for wider distribution of licenses in a landmark decision by the U.S. Supreme Court:

> The First Amendment . . . rests on the assumption that the widest possible dissemination of information from diverse and antagonistic sources is essential to the welfare of the public, that a free press is a condition of a free society.[114]

The commission's policies of granting licenses to those that are already multiple owners and denying applications by applicants that have no media interests appears to violate the First Amendment of the Constitution. In the instant case Hoffart has zero media interests and Mr. and Mrs. Danny Kaye and Mr. Smith had five channels, down from ten at one time. In short, the commission's grant of the KISW renewal is not based upon the public interest, if the court's Associated Press decision precedent is relied upon.

The commission, however, is not known to make any decisions based upon existing policy statements, laws, statutes, the Constitution or even common sense. The facts are that the commission makes decisions based upon who is involved and not what is involved, and this notarial imperfections case proves this, beyond any doubt.

The commission will be the first to argue that the U.S. Court of Appeals, D.C. Circuit has affirmed their Order 85-182. This is true, but only raises questions as to why the court rubber-stamped this case, without oral argument and without articulating or explaining why they reached such a decision.

Perhaps congress or a special grand jury should ask the judges involved how they could reach such a conclusion when the official record virtually demands prosecution of the individuals who filed false information with a federal agency. The Constitution of the United States supports diversification of mass media.

The author has stopped short of calling the Federal Communications Commission corrupt. Perhaps some of the readers of this book will not be that generous and will demand grand jury action and congressional

---

[114]*Associated Press v. United States*, 326, U.S. (1945).

investigation of this case and many others on record where challengers have lost before the commission.

A broadcaster seeks and is granted the free and exclusive use of a limited and valuable part of the public domain; when he accepts that franchise it is burdened by enforceable public obligations. A newspaper can be operated at the whim or caprice of its owners; a broadcast station cannot. After nearly five decades of operation the broadcast industry does not seem to have grasped the simple fact that a broadcast license is a public trust subject to termination for breach of duty . . .

Judge Warren Burger
Court of Appeals decision on WLBT,
Jackson, Miss (citing from—)

Office of Communications of United Church of Christ v. FCC. (March, 1966)

EXHIBITS
AND
TABLE OF AUTHORITIES
AND CITATIONS

INDEX TO APPENDIX EXHIBITS

1. K/S Exhibit 16, page 14—Judy Balint letter
2. Judy Balint letter to Hoffart, 11/16/82
3. K/S Exhibit 16, page 2—Eric Bogel affidavit
4. K/S Exhibit 16, page 3—attachment to Bogel affidavit
5. K/S Exhibit 16, page 15—Stephen West affidavit
6. K/S Exhibit 16, page 16—attachment to West affidavit
7. K/S Exhibit 17, page 2—Stephen West affidavit
8. K/S Exhibit 17, page 3—attachment to West affidavit
9. K/S Exhibit 16, page 6—Julie McCullough letter
10. Counsel's transmittal letter to notarial corrections 11/23/82
11. Counsel's transmittal letter to notarial corrections 11/24/82
12. K/S Exhibit 16, page 6 (A)—McCullough notarial correction
13. K/S Exhibit 17, page 5—David Watkins original letter
14. K/S Exhibit 17, page 5 (A)—Watkins corrected letter
15. K/S Exhibit 16, page 7—Shawn Taylor original letter
16. K/S Exhibit 16, page 8—Shawn Taylor original letter
17. K/S Exhibit 16, page 7 (A)—Shawn Taylor corrected letter
18. K/S Exhibit 16, page 8 (A)—Shawn Taylor corrected letter
19. K/S Exhibit 16, page 13—John R. Taylor, original letter
20. K/S Exhibit 16, page 13 (A)—Taylor corrected letter
21. K/S Exhibit 16, page 28—Bob L. Curran letter
22. K/S Exhibit 17, page 6—Daniel McConnell original letter
23. K/S Exhibit 17, page 6 (A)—McConnell corrected letter
24. K/S Exhibit 16, page 24—C.E. Blacksmith original letter
25. K/S Exhibit 16, page 24 (A)—Blacksmith corrected letter
26. K/S Exhibit 17, page 8—C.C. Griffin original letter
27. K/S Exhibit 17, page 8 (A)—Griffin corrected letter
28. K/S Exhibit 15, page 22—L.M. Smith preexecuted affidavit
29. K/S Exhibit 15, page 16—Anthony Kelsey affidavit
30. K/S Exhibit 15, page 17—Anthony Kelsey affidavit
31. K/S Exhibit 16, page 5—Nina L. Evers letter
32. K/S Exhibit 16, page 4—Mayor Charles Royer letter

FOCUS —|⊢ ALTERNATIVE WORK PATTERNS

October 29, 1982

TO WHOM IT MAY CONCERN

Focus is a non-profit agency which promotes alternative work patterns in
the Seattle area. We have been in existence since 1974 and have used
both print and broadcast media since that time to publicize our activities.

KISW has been responsive to our requests to air Public Service Announcements
and has expressed interest in our activities. We have found their
staff to be concerned with community needs and genuinely interested in
informing the public .

Judy Balint

Judy Balint
Office Coordinator

Carrie Matthew
Notary Public
King Co.

1

FOCUS ALTERNATIVE WORK PATTERNS

November 16, 1982

Dear Mr. Hoffart,

In response to your letter of Nov. 13, 1982, I did not appear in front of a notary with regard to my letter of support for KISW.

I was also not aware that the purpose of these testimonials was to bolster a legal case.

Sincerely,

Judy Balint

Judy Balint
Office coordinator.

509 TENTH AVENUE EAST · SEATTLE WASHINGTON 98102 · 206 329-7918

State Of Washington   )   ss
County Of King   )

Eric S. Bogel, being duly sworn, deposes and says:

1. Each of the affidavits described on the attachment was obtained by me or those under my direction. It was explained to each affiant that his or her affidavit would be used as testimony in a proceeding before the Federal Communications Commission.

_____
Eric S. Bogel

Subscribed and sworn to before me
this   day of November, 1982.

Notary Public

My commission expires: June 1, 1986

3

Attached is the written testimony from the following

Seattle area community members:

-Charles Royer, Mayor of Seattle
-Nina L. Evers, District Director, Muscular Dystrophy
    Association
-Julie McCullough, Trustee, Greenpeace, Seattle
-Shawn Taylor, Boy Scouts of America
-Patricia Frank, Executive Director, Puget Sound Big
    Sisters
-Wanda Harrison, Program Coordinator, Leukemia Society
    Of America, Inc.
-Jeanne Beall, Space Needle Corporation
-John Taylor, The Seattle Arts Festival
-Judy Balint, Office Coordinator, Focus

State Of Washington) ss
County Of King   )

Stephen L. West, being duly sworn, deposes and says:

1.   Each of the affidavits described on the attachment was obtained by me or those under my direction. It was explained to each affiant that his or her affidavit would be used as testimony in a proceeding before the Federal Communications Commission.

_____
                    Stephen L. West

Subscribed and sworn to before me
this   day of November, 1982.

_____
         Notary Public

My commission expires: June 1, 1986

5

Attached is the written testimony from the following

Seattle area community members:

   -Tom Fortin, Instructor, Lynnwood Senior High School
   -Lynne A. Freeman, Board of Directors, Boys and
      Girls Clubs of King County
   -Lou Lavinthal, International Ambassador, Variety
      Club
   -Lynne A. Freeman, Vice President, Gerber/Meyers
      Wolfe and Kilgore
   -Michael Campbell, Campbell Sports, Inc.
   -Charles E. Blacksmith, Merchandiser, Roundup
      Music Distributors
   -Robert L. Steil, President, Squire
   -Todd M. Bitts, President, PSRBA (Puget Sound
      Radio Broadcasters Association)
   -Patricia P. Fearey, President, Pat Fearey &
      Associates
   -Bob L. Curran, Military Coordinator, Seafair

6

State Of Washington   )   ss
County Of King   )

    Stephen L. West, being duly sworn, deposes and says:

    1. Each of the affidavits described on the attachment
was obtained by me or those under my direction. It was
explained to each affiant that his or her affidavit would
be used as testimony in a proceeding before the Federal
Communications Commission.

                                            Stephen L. West

Subscribed and sworn to before me
this _____ day of November, 1982.

Carrie Matthew
     Notary Public

My commission expires: June 1, 1986

7

Attached is the written testimony from the following

Seattle area community members:

-Scott Hickey, Director of Advertising and
Public Relations, Alpac Corporation
-David Watkins, Assistant General Manager/
Director of Marketing, Seattle
Supersonics
-J. Daniel McConnell, President, The McConnell
Company
-James M. Foster, Advertising Manager, Rainier
Brewing Company
-C. Clark Griffin, President, C.C. Griffin &
Company, Inc.
-Douglas Weisfield, Advertising Director,
Weisfield's, Inc.

Paul Sullivan
KISW
712 Aurora North
Seattle, WA 98109

22 October 82

Dear Paul,

Many thanks to you and all the good folks of KISW.
Greenpeace began its environmental work here in the Northwest five years ago. We are pleased with the consistant
support KISW has given Greenpeace over these years through
public service announcements and news coverage. We feel
that the station helps us reach an important segment in
the community that would otherwise not hear about our
efforts.

And thank <u>you</u> Paul. Your guidance on promotional and
administrative matters has been of tremendous help to
our organization. It is especially nice of the station to
allow you to work with us during regular business hours.

We look forward to working more with you and KISW in
the future.

Sincerely,

Julie McCullough
Promotions Director / Trustee
Greenpeace, Seattle

DATE 10/28/82

CARRIE MATTHEW/NOTARY PUBLIC

9

FLY, SHUEBRUK, GAGUINE, BOROS, SCHULKIND and BRAUN

JAMES LAWRENCE FLY (1966)
PETER SHUEBRUK
BENITO GAGUINE
JEROME S. BOROS
HERBERT M. SCHULKIND
HOWARD J. BRAUN *
IRVING GASTFREUND *

RUSSELL C. BALCH *
ZAVE M. UNGER * *
HEIDI P. SANCHEZ *

JACK P. BLUME
ASHER H. ENDE
STEVEN D. BURTON * *
COUNSEL

* D. C. BAR ONLY
* * N. Y. BAR ONLY

New York, New York
November 23, 1982

45 ROCKEFELLER PLAZA
NEW YORK, NEW YORK 10111-0151
(212) 247-3040
TELECOPIER (212) 247-3628
D. C. - N. Y. TIE LINE (202) 293-1397

1211 CONNECTICUT AVENUE, N. W.
WASHINGTON, D. C. 20036-2768
(202) 293-1260
TELECOPIER (202) 293-1311

Re: Kaye-Smith Enterprises
BC Docket No. 82-265

BY HAND

Dear Judge Fitzpatrick

I am enclosing herewith corrections to Kaye-Smith Direct Exhibits 5-10, 13 and 16-17. These will remedy notorial imperfections in the foregoing Exhibits.

The pages enclosed under Attachment I are to be added as the final pages of each of the foregoing Exhibits, as their respective markings and pagination indicate. The pages enclosed under Attachment II are to be substituted for the existing Exhibit pages indentically marked and paginated.

By copies of this letter and enclosures, I am supplying Mr. Hoffart and Mr. Sarno of the Broadcast Bureau with these corrected pages.

Very truly yours

FLY, SHUEBRUK, GAGUINE, BOROS,
SCHULKIND AND BRAUN

Stuart J. Young

Honorable Thomas B. Fizpatrick
Assistant Chief Administrative Law Judge
Federal Communications Commission
Washington, D.C. 20554

Enclosures (2)

cc: Vincent L. Hoffart - w/encl. (Federal Express)
    Daniel Sarno, Esq. - w/encl. (By Hand)

10

FLY, SHUEBRUK, GAGUINE, BOROS, SCHULKIND AND BRAUN

JAMES LAWRENCE FLY (1966)
PETER SHUEBRUK
BENITO GAGUINE
JEROME S. BOROS
HERBERT M. SCHULKIND
HOWARD J. BRAUN *
IRVING GASTFREUND *

RUSSELL C. BALCH *
ZAVE M. UNGER * *
HEIDI P. SANCHEZ *

JACK P. BLUME
ASHER H. ENDE
STEVEN D. BURTON * *
COUNSEL

* D. C. BAR ONLY
* * N. Y. BAR ONLY

New York, New York
November 24, 1982

45 ROCKEFELLER PLAZA
NEW YORK, NEW YORK 10111-0151
(212) 247-3040
TELECOPIER (212) 247-3628
D. C.-N. Y. TIE LINE (202) 293-1397

1211 CONNECTICUT AVENUE, N. W.
WASHINGTON, D. C. 20036-2768
(202) 293-1280
TELECOPIER (202) 293-1311

Re: Kaye-Smith Enterprises
BC Docket No. 82-265

VIA FEDERAL EXPRESS

Dear Judge Fitzpatrick

I am enclosing herewith three pages, marked and paginated, to be substituted for the identically marked and paginated pages in Kaye-Smith Direct Exhibits 16 and 17. These will serve to correct notorial imperfections.

By copies of this letter and enclosures, I am supplying Mr. Hoffart and Mr. Sarno of the Broadcast Bureau with these pages.

Very truly yours

FLY, SHUEBRUK, GAGUINE, BOROS,
SCHULKIND AND BRAUN

Stuart J. Young

Honorable Thomas B. Fitzpatrick
Assistant Chief Administrative Law Judge
Federal Communications Commission
c/o Seattle District Office
3256 Federal Building
915 Second Avenue
Seattle, Washington 98174

Enclosures (3)

cc: Vincent L. Hoffart - w/encl. (Federal Express)
    Daniel Sarno, Esq. - w/encl. (By Hand)

11

Kaye-Smith Exhibit 16
(page 6A)

Paul Sullivan
KISW
712 Aurora North
Seattle, WA 98109

16 November 82

Dear Paul

GREENPEACE,
SEATTLE

GOOD SHEPHERD
CENTER
4649 SUNNYSIDE
AVENUE NORTH
SEATTLE, WA
98103

TELEPHONE
206/632-4326

Many thanks to you and all the good folks of KISW.
Greenpeace began its environmental work here in the Northwest
five years ago. We are pleased with the consistant support
KISW has given Greenpeace over these years through public service
announcements and news coverage. We feel that the station
helps us reach an important segment in the community that
would otherwise not hear about our efforts.

And thank you Paul. Your guidance on promotional and administrative
matters has been of tremendous help to our organization. It is
especially nice of the station to allow you to work with us
during regular business hours.

We look forward to working more with you and KISW in the future.

Sincerely,

Julie McCullough
Promotions Director / Trustee
Greenpeace, Seattle

cc Vincent L. Hoffart

11-16-82
Date

Diana Blane / Notary Public

King Co. / Seattle

12

SEATTLE
SUPERSONICS
C Box 14102 — Seattle, WA 98114

October 22, 1982

Steve West
KISW RADIO
712 Aurora Avenue N.
Seattle, WA 98109

Dear Steve:

Every once in a while, we have the habit of remember-
ing how well someone has been treating us, and we've
neglected to say thanks.

Thanks.

Our relationship with KISW has been a bright spot
over the past few years. You've been able to help
us out in both the normal and even the unusual times,
and always with efficiency, a smile, and a pleasant
tone.

The Sonics have benefitted greatly for the services
you have rendered, and I might add that I hear nothing
but good things on the "street" about KISW, from old
and young alike.

Keep up the good work, and tell your staff we think
you're wonderful!

Sincerely,

David Watkins
Assistant G.M./Dir. of Marketing

DW:mbn

13

**SEATTLE
SUPERSONICS**

C Box 14102 — Seattle. WA 98114

November 17, 1982

Steve West
KISW RADIO
712 Aurora Avenue North
Seattle, WA 98109

Dear Steve:

Every once in a while, we have the habit of remember-
ing how well someone has been treating us, and we've
neglected to say thanks.

Thanks.

Our relationship with KISW has been a bright spot
over the past few years. You've been able to help
us out in both the normal and even the unusual times,
and always with efficiency, a smile, and a pleasant
tone.

The Sonics have benefitted greatly for the services
you have rendered, and I might add that I hear nothing
but good things on the "street" about KISW, from old
and young alike.

Keep up the good work, and tell your staff we think
you're wonderful!

Sincerely,

David Watkins
Vice President
Marketing/Advertising

DW:mbn

Subscribed and sworn before me
this 17ᵗʰ day of November 1982.

Notary Public
My commission expires: 6-15-83

Business Office: 206/628-8400   Ticket Information: 628-8448   Season & Group Sales: 628-8444

119 Occidental Avenue South

14

BOY SCOUTS OF AMERICA
CHIEF SEATTLE COUNCIL
3120 Rainier Avenue South
Seattle, Washington 98144
725 5200

November 5, 1982

Beau Phillips
Program Director
712 Aurora N
Seattle WA 98109

Mr. Phillips:

A major aspect of my position in the Exploring Division of the Boy Scouts of America, is that of locating corporate and community groups willing to commit time, energy, and other resources to showing a group of young adults about their interests or business. We work across a very wide spectrum of kinds of people and many unique fields.

In the Seattle area, it has been my experience that in the communications/broadcast area, it is singularly hard to get adults and their businesses to work in our program. It is for that reason I'm writing this letter.

I know of the involvement of KISW and its personnel in several Exploring related projects over the past five years. In most cases, those were individual engagements as opposed to a regularly scheduled, on-going commitment. We've certainly appreciated those occasions and I feel the young people of our community have benefited from them.

Your current commitment to charter an Exploring post is however, a different level of contribution to Exploring and to Seattle area high schoolers. You are meeting with a group of kids regularly in a program designed by KISW staff people and the kids. This involves people from many different departments volunteering their time to share their expertise. It means opening your studios, facilities, and offices to members of the general public. It represents a willingness on the part of KISW to participate voluntarily in your community.

Council President
BRUCE F. BAKER

Council Vice President
CHRISTOPHER L. BRITTON

Council Commissioner
PAUL E. GILBERT

Scout Executive
CHAEL HOOVER, JR.

A United Way Agency

15

Kaye-Smith Exhibit 16
(page 8)

On behalf of the students who will be the recipents of your
efforts, thanks for using your considerable influence and
reputation in such a positive direction.

Sincerely,

Shawn Taylor
Exploring Post Program

ST:mg

CARRIE MATTHEW/NOTARY PUBLIC

DATE: 11/5/82

16

BOY SCOUTS OF AMERICA
CHIEF SEATTLE COUNCIL
3120 Rainier Avenue South
Seattle, Washington 98144
725 5200

November 23, 1982

Beau Phillips
Program Director
712 Aurora N
Seattle WA 98109

Mr. Phillips:

A major aspect of my position in the Exploring Division of the Boy Scouts of America, is that of locating corporate and community groups willing to commit time, energy, and other resources to showing a group of young adults about their interests or business. We work across a very wide spectrum of kinds of people and many unique fields.

In the Seattle area, it has been my experience that in the communications/broadcast area, it is singlularly hard to get adults and their businesses to work in our program. It is for that reason I'm writing this letter.

I know of the involvement of KISW and its personnel in several Exploring related projects over the past five years. In most cases, those were individual engagements as opposed to a regularly scheduled, on-going commitment. We've certainly appreciated those occasions and I feel the young people of our community have benefited from them.

Your current commitment to charter an Exploring post is however, a different level of contribution to Exploring and to Seattle area high schoolers. You are meeting with a group of kids regularly in a program designed by KISW staff people and the kids. This involves people from many different departments volunteering their time to share their expertise. It means opening your studios, facilities, and offices to members of the general public. It represents a willingness on the part of KISW to participate voluntarily in your community.

Council President
BRUCE F. BAKER

Council Vice President
CHRISTOPHER L. BRITTON

Council Commissioner
PAUL E. GILBERT

Scout Executive
'ICHAEL HOOVER, JR

A United Way Agency

17

Kaye-Smith Exhibit 16
(page 8A)

Mr. Phillips
November 23, 1982
Page 2

On behalf of the students who will be the recipients of your
efforts, thanks for using your considerable influence and
reputation in such a positive direction.

Sincerely,

Shawn Taylor
Exploring Post Program

ST:mg

18

Seattle Center • 305 Harrison Street

BUMBERSHOOT
The Seattle Arts Festival 1982

Seattle • WA • 98109 • 206-625-4275

October 25, 1982

To whom it may concern:

We have had the pleasure of working with KISW for the
past several years, first on the promotion of the artful
coaster derby called The Bumbernationals, and later on
the promotion of Rock Day at Bumbershoot, the large
Coliseum rock show at the festival. For these events,
KISW has provided $40,000 worth of air time at no cost
to the festival, resulting in large, well-rounded audiences.

We have found the management and staff at KISW to be very
cooperative, enthusiastic, responsible and efficient in
our dealings with them, and look forward to continuing
our success in bringing the arts to the people of Seattle
for many years to come.

Sincerely yours,

John Taylor
Promotion Director
BUMBERSHOOT

JT:mab

NOTARY PUBLIC FOR THE STATE OF WASH.
RESIDING IN THE COUNTY OF KING.

comm. expires: 6-15-83

Kaye-Smith Exhibit 16
(page 13A)

The Seattle Arts Festival 1982

November 22, 1982

To whom it may concern:

We have had the pleasure of working with KISW for the past several years, first on the promotion of the artful coaster derby called The Bumbernationals, and later on the promotion of Rock Day at Bumbershoot, the large Coliseum rock show at the annual Seattle arts festival. For these events, KISW has provided $40,000 worth of air time at no cost to the festival, resulting in large, well rounded audiences.

We have found the management and staff at KISW to be very cooperative, enthusiastic, responsible and efficient in our dealings with them. We look forward to continuing our relationship, and joining KISW in bringing the arts to the people of Seattle for many years to come.

Sincerely yours,

John Taylor
Promotion Director
BUMBERSHOOT

JT:an

Subscribed and sworn before me this 23ʳᵈ day of November 1982.

Notary Public

My commission expires: 6-15-83

**32 YEARS OF
COMMUNITY
SERVICE
1950-1982**

901 OCCIDENTAL SOUTH
SEATTLE, WASHINGTON 98134
(206) 623-7100

PRESIDENT
Gerald J. Alfers

**FIRST
VICE PRESIDENT**
Ward Sax

VICE PRESIDENTS
Daniel Doyle
Oris Dunham, Jr.
S. Josef Selak
James F. Vatn
Geoff Vernon
Steve West

SECRETARY
Jack Link

TREASURER
William W. Jeude

EXECUTIVE COMMITTEE
Carl Behnke
Todd M. Bitts
Fred Burrow
Paul Dennis
Pat Fearey
Frank H. Hattori
Boyd Holding
Lou Lavinthal
Gene Merlino
Leone O'Neill
Gary Palmer
John Reiche
Robert Steil
Margot Wigley
R/Adm. J.D. Williams

**EXECUTIVE
VICE PRESIDENT
AND MANAGING
DIRECTOR**
Donald C. Jones

**PUBLIC RELATIONS
DIRECTOR**
Sharon Hasson

DIRECTOR OF EVENTS
Price L. Winemiller

TO WHOM IT MAY CONCERN

I WISH TO THANK RADIO STATION KISW FOR THEIR PUBLIC
SERVICE SUPPORT IN ANNOUNCEMENT ON ARMED FORCES DAY
AND OTHER MILITARY PROGRAMS FOR THE INTEREST OF THE
PUBLIC EACH YEAR.

THEY ARE VERY COOPERATIVE DURING SEAFAIR IN GIVING
THE VOLUNTEERS OF THE MILITARY CREDIT FOR SUPPORTING
NON-PROFIT ORGANIZATIONS.

EACH YEAR THEIR ASSISTANCE OF SEAFAIR, THE MILITARY
AND OTHER CHARITABLE ORGANIZATIONS IS GREATLY
APPRECIATED.

IT IS THROUGH THEIR EFFORT AND SUPPORT THAT THESE
PROGRAMS ARE MORE SUCCESSFUL EACH YEAR.

BOB L. CURRAN
Major, Retd (Army)
Military Coordinator

DATED THIS 24 CF OCTOBER, 1982,

NOTARY PUBLIC FOR THE STATE OF WASHINGTON
RESIDING IN KING CO. 6-15-83

21

PUBLIC RELATIONS COUNSEL
MANAGEMENT ASSISTANCE
IN THE BUSINESS, FINANCIAL,
GOVERNMENTAL AND
COMMUNITY SECTORS.

October 29, 1982

To Whom It May Concern:

As a active public relations counselor in the Northwest region and publisher of the Puget Sound News Media Directory, I work-regularly with the broadcast media. During the past few years, I have dealt directly with the management of KISW radio through a number of my clients.

The station is exceedingly well run and respected in the Seattle Market and is held in high regard by radio people around the country. From my personal observation on a number of promotional and community affairs, their management practices have been ethical, fiscally responsible and effective.

KISW has held a high ranking in this market for some time now and should continue to excel under current management.

Regards,

J. Daniel McConnell
President
THE McCONNELL COMPANY

DM:si

Notary Public
King Co.

QUEEN ANNE SQUARE
SUITE 505
220 WEST MERCER STREET
SEATTLE, WASHINGTON 98119
(206) 285-0140

22

MANAGEMENT ASSISTANCE
IN THE BUSINESS, FINANCIAL,
GOVERNMENTAL AND
COMMUNITY SECTORS.

November 16, 1982

To Whom It May Concern:

As a active public relations counselor in the Northwest region
and publisher of the Puget Sound News Media Directory, I work
regularly with the broadcast media. During the past few years,
I have dealt directly with the management of KISW radio through
a number of my clients.

The station is exceedingly well run and respected in the Seattle
Market and is held in high regard by radio people around the
country. From my personal observation on a number of promotional
and community affairs, their management practices have been
ethical, fiscally responsible and effective.

KISW has held a high ranking in this market for some time now
and should continue to excel under current management.

Regards,

S. Daniel McConnell

S. Daniel McConnell
President
THE McCONNELL COMPANY

DM:si

Subscribed and sworn before me
this 16th day of November 1982.

Margret E Moren

Notary Public

My Comm. expires 6/15/83 GLEN ANNE SQUARE
SUITE 505
220 WEST MERCER STREET
SEATTLE, WASHINGTON 98119
(206) 285-0140

23

roundup
music distributors

A DIVISION OF
18300 MIDVALE A
Mailing Address: P.O. BOX 77003 SEATTLE, WA 98177

(206) 542-7551

October 27, 1982

Mr. Steve West
KISW Radio
P.O. Box 21449
Seattle, Washington   98111

Dear Steve:

Let this letter serve as formal acknowledgement that
Roundup Music recognizes KISW to be a Company with
substantially good business practices.

Our relationship over the past several years has con-
sistantly been nothing less than upfront and in every
way a model of customer-client integrity.

I am also personally aware of the results of your
community services and you and the staff should be
commended for same.

Sincerely,

Charles E. Blacksmith
Merchandiser

CEB/sjc

NOTARY PUBLIC
Comm. Expires: 6/1/86

24

roundup
music distributors

A DIVISION OF FR
18300 MIDVALE AVE.
Mailing Address: P.O. BOX 7.

(206) 542-7551

November 17, 1982

Mr. Steve West
KISW Radio
P.O. Box 21449
Seattle, Washington   98111

Dear Steve:

Let this letter serve as formal acknowledgement that
Roundup Music recognizes KISW to be a Company with
substantially good business practices.

Our relationship over the past several years has consistently been nothing less than upfront and in every
way a model of customer-client integrity.

I am also personally aware of the results of your
community services and you and the staff should be
commended for same.

Sincerely,

C.E. Blacksmith
Merchandiser

CEB/sjc

Signed before me this 17th day of November, 1982

Notary Public

25

CC GRIFFIN & COMPANY INC

October 21, 1982

Paul Sullivan
KISW

Dear Paul,

Desperado has used KISW for the last three years helping to promote the
Desperado brand name awareness to the younger male demographic.

It is our experience that advertising on KISW has helped at retail and it
is our intent to continue to use KISW in our media planning for the future.

Sincerely,

C. Clark Griffin
President

RS/vas

Christine Woolson
10/29/82   King Co., Wa

Suite 4227
Seattle Trade Center
2601 F1tn Avenue
Seattle, Washington 95121
(206) 624 3298

CC GRIFFIN & COMPANY INC

November 23, 1982

Paul Sullivan
KISW

Dear Paul,

Desperado has used KISW for the last three years helping to promote the Desperado brand name awareness to the younger male demographic.

It is our experience that advertising on KISW has helped at retail and it is our intent to continue to use KISW in our media planning for the future.

Sincerely,

C. Clark Griffin
President

RS/vas

State of Washington) ss
County of King)

Notary Public in and for the State
of Washington.

Date: November 23, 1982

27

Kaye-Smith Exhibit 15
(page 22)

State Of Washington   )
County Of King   )

AFFIDAVIT OF LESTER M. SMITH

    1.   I am Lester M. Smith, Executive Director of Kaye-Smith Enterprises, licensee of Station KISW(FM).

    2.   I have read the foregoing Kaye-Smith Exhibit 15 concerning the Seattle-Everett-Tacoma Arbitron Radio Audience Estimates ("audience estimate books") and it is true and correct to the best of my knowledge. As a broadcast professional, I regularly subscribe to and rely upon the data in these audience estimate books in the course of my business to guage the size of radio station listenership among various demographic segments of the greater Seattle area.

Lester M. Smith

Subscribed and sworn before me
this 9th day of November, 1982.

Notary Public

My commission expires: July 15, 1985

28

State of New York)
County of New York)

AFFIDAVIT OF A. ANTHONY KELSEY

1. I am A. ANTHONY KELSEY, General Counsel and Assistant
Secretary of the Arbitron Company.

2. I have read the foregoing Kaye-Smith Exhibit and state
that it is true and correct to the best of my knowledge.

3. Tables I - IV attached thereto are true and correct
copies of pages 6 - 9 of the Seattle-Everett-Tacoma Arbitron
Radio Audience Estimates Book ("audience estimates book") for
the Fall of 1980. Tables V - X are true and correct copies of
page 72 of each of the Spring and Fall audience estimates books
for the years 1978, 1979 and 1980 covering the Seattle-Everett-
Tacoma market.

4. The Arbitron audience estimates referred to in the
foregoing exhibit are regularly published compilations of market
data widely and regularly relied upon in the course of business
by broadcasting professionals, including radio station management
and programming personnel, advertisers and advertising agencies.

5. The methodology of the Arbitron surveys referred to in
the foregoing exhibit is described on the pages immediately following this affidavit. These explanatory pages are true and
correct copies of pages 1, 2, i and ii which appeared in the

Kaye-Smith Exhibit 15
(page 17)

Seattle-Everett-Tacoma Arbitron audience estimates book

for the Fall 1980.

A. Anthony Kelsey

Subscribed and sworn to before
me this /o7l day of November,
1982.

Notary Public

My Commission expires:

MUSCULAR DYSTROPHY ASSOCIATION
Fighting 40 Neuromuscular Diseases
Active Member, National Health Council

Please Reply To: 215 SIXTH AVENUE NORTH, SEATTLE, WASHINGTON 98109, (206) 624-5220

November 8, 1982

To Whom It May Concern,

The Northwest Washington Chapter of the Muscular Dystrophy Association is a non-profit organization dedicated in the fight against neuromuscular diseases.

KISW has participated and supported our bed racing program in both 1980 and 1981. This included their co-sponsorship of a bed race entry as well as on-air promotion of our bed race.

KISW has continuously helped us by promoting our special events and fund raising efforts. We greatly appreciate their support and look forward to working wih them in the future.

Sincerely,

Nina L. Evers
District Director

NLE:ts

SUBSCRIBED AND SWORN TO
BEFORE ME THIS 10th DAY
OF Nov, 1982

Office Of The Mayor
City of Seattle

Charles Royer, Mayor

October 25, 1982

KISW
712 Aurora Avenue North
Seattle, Washington 98109

Attention: Beau Phillips, Program Director

After working with KISW staff on two public service
campaigns, I am very impressed with the station's civic
consciousness and high professional standards.

In the winter of 1980 and again in July of this year,
KISW staff came to my office to tape public service
announcements for special station-sponsored activities
benefiting our Seattle area food banks. I understand
the 1980 campaign brought proceeds from 84,000 sticker
sales to Northwest Second Harvest, and this summer's
charity softball game sent 5,000 pounds of food to the
same very deserving organization.

It was a pleasure to participate in both projects, which
clearly show a strong, effective commitment to broadcasting
in the public interest.

Charles Royer, Mayor

Signed and sworn before me this _25ᵀᴴ_ day of _October_ ,
1982, in witness whereof I have hereunto set my hand and
official seal.

Notary Public in and for the
State of Washington, residing at
Seattle.

An equal employment opportunity · affirmative action employer.
1200 Municipal Building, Seattle, Washington 98104, (206) 625-4000

32

SEATTLE'S BEST

KISW•FM 100

7/20/82

TO: Public File
FROM: Beau Phillips
RE: Daylight Savings

    This memo is intended to clear up any confusion regarding the announcement of Daylight Savings Time on KISW earlier this year. While the first actual day of Daylight Savings was April 25th, we learned of current legislation that would've turned the clocks forward March 27th. The House of Representatives has already passed a bill that would allow one extra month of daylight in an energy conservation effort. This bill is now before the Senate.

    KISW's broadcast of Daylight Savings Time beginning on March 27th arose out of uncertainty surrounding this bill. Our news department was doing a story on energy conservation and the Daylight Savings Bill issue came up. We received word from what we considered at the time to be a credible source that the early D.S.T. date would be implemented this year starting in March. As it happens, Daylight Savings Time is set to start one month ahead of schedule in 1983.

    We first broadcast the incorrect clock setting information on Friday, March 26th of this year. It was not until 4pm the following day that the error was caught and immediately corrected. We ran live disclaimers throughout the remainder of the weekend explaining the mistake and restating the correct start date. Inevitably there were some people who never heard those disclaimers. I received 2 complaint letters (which I regrettably did not save) and explained to them what I've said above.

    KISW does not make a habit of broadcasting mis-information. We apologized to those who called and wrote and to our listening audiences as well. It was an honest mistake that arose while investigating a news item we felt would be of interest. This was simply an instance of sketchy communication and human error on my part. There was no intent to deceive listeners or knowingly broadcast false information.

Sincerely

Beau Phillips
Program Director

omm. expires; 6-15-'83
Burck

33

	6A-10	M-F	60 SEC	4 BROADCASTS @	31.00 -	124.00
9:	0640AM					
0:	0910AM					
1:	0725AM					
5:	0755AM					**611**

	10A-2P					
2:		HOFFART Q.	Do you check those bills against the logs first			31.00
	10		to see that the spots were run?			
9:	11					306.00
0:		NOREN A.	No. That's done by Carrie Matthew.			
1:	12					
2:		Q.	You don't personally do it?			
5:	13					
		A.	No.			
9:	14		Q.	But you notarize the bills that that's what's		62.00
5:	15					
0:	16	happened?				93.00
1:		A.	Yes.			
2:	17					

BOROS Q. What was the routine?   _537_

	11	BOROS Q.	What was the routine?	62.00
3:	12	NOREN A.	That we have a rubber stamp that says that	
4:			according to the best of my knowledge in accordance with	
4:	13		our laws, that on this date and this month, and then I	102.00
	14		sign it, that according to our logs this is what ran to	780.00
	15		the best of my knowledge, and I date it and sign it and	117.00
	16		then affix my seal over it. And that had been the same	663.00
	17		routine prior to when I came.	
	18			

	19	Q.	For how long have you been performing that	
	20	routine?		
AFFIDAVIT	21	A.	Four years.	IN LOG

NEWS

News media information 202 / 254-7674
Recorded listing of releases and texts
202 / 632-0002

FEDERAL COMMUNICATIONS COMMISSION
1919 M STREET, N.W.
WASHINGTON, D.C. 20554

2068

This is an unofficial announcement of Commission action. Release of the full text of a Commission order constitutes official action. See MCI v FCC 515 F 2d 385 (D C Circ 1975)

Report No. 18221   ACTION IN DOCKET CASE   January 22, 1985

SIX OUTDATED BROADCAST BUSINESS PRACTICES POLICIES DELETED; DELETION OR MODIFICATION OF THREE MORE PROPOSED
(MM DOCKET NO. 83-842)

In the latest action in the on-going broadcast "underbrush" proceeding in which the Commission is attempting to eliminate or modify various policies, doctrines, declaratory rulings, rules, informal rulings and interpretive statements ("underbrush") that have grown up around major regulations over the years and which are no longer warranted, the Commission has deleted the following policy areas which broadly deal with broadcast business practices:

— Licensee distortion of audience ratings (Section 73.4040);

— Conflict of interest (Section 73.4085) and sports announcer selection (Section 73.4245);

— Promotion of non-broadcast business of a station (Section 73.4225) and use of a station for personal advantage in other business activities;

— Concert promotion announcements;

— Failure to perform sales contracts (Section 73.4230); and

— False, misleading and deceptive commercials (Section 73.4070).

The Commission, in a separate but related rulemaking notice, proposed deleting or substantially modifying three additional policy areas:

— Fraudulent billing practices (Sections 73.4115, 73.1205);

— Network clipping (Sections 73.4155. 73.1205); and

— Combination advertising rates; joint sales practices (Section 73.4065).

The policies involved either business practices permitted by federal antitrust laws or practices that are unlawful under other legal structures at either the federal or state level.

(over)

35

The FCC noted that parties involved in these broadcast business practices generally are very knowledgeable and well-represented and it was appropriate to leave them to private remedial mechanisms. The FCC should not directly enforce private rights and obligations of its licensees without a clear and convincing showing that without such enforcement a substantial and immediate danger to viewers or listeners would ensue, the agency concluded.

With respect to policies which circumscribe economic arrangements more tightly than the antitrust laws, the Commission observed that the FCC should not attempt to outlaw practices sanctioned by the antitrust laws, at least where the viewers or listeners receive no offsetting benefits. It also noted the compliance with such policies imposed certain unwarranted managerial costs upon licensees, particularly smaller broadcasters, and their elimination will free the licensees to concentrate their managerial effort on more important matters such as programing and sales.

Insofar as these actions prohibited by these policies and rules may be considered as reflecting on the "character" of a licensee, the Commission noted that it is considering this question in a separate proceeding (Gen. Docket 81-500).

Action by the Commission January 18, 1985, by Policy Statement and Order (FCC 85-25) and by Notice of Proposed Rulemaking (FCC 85-26). Commissioners Fowler (Chairman), Quello, Dawson and Patrick, with Commissioner Rivera concurring in part and issuing a statement.

-FCC-

For more information contact James A. Hudgens at (202) 653-5940.

STATE OF WASHINGTON }
ss
County of ___KING___

On this ___18th___ day of ___May___, 19 82, before me the undersigned,
a Notary Public in and for the State of Washington, personally appeared ___CARRIE MATTHEW___
Principal
personally known to me to be the person described in and who executed this bond as Principal, and acknowledged to me
that he/she signed the same freely and voluntarily for the uses and purposes therein expressed.
IN WITNESS WHEREOF, I have hereunto set my hand and affixed my official seal the day and year last written above.

Margt E Piper
Notary Public in and for the State of Washington,

(Seal)

Residing at ___King Co___

OATH OF OFFICE

STATE OF WASHINGTON }
ss
County of ___KING___

I, ___CARRIE MATTHEW___, do solemnly swear
(Notary Applicant)
that I will support the Constitution of the United States and the Constitution and Laws of the State of Washington, and
that I will faithfully and impartially discharge the duties of Notary Public to the best of my ability.

x _Carrie Matthew_
Notary Applicant

Subscribed and sworn to before me this ___18th___

day of ___May___, 19 82

Margt E Piper
Notary Public in and for the State of Washington,

residing at ___King Co.___

Kenneth S. Helm Clerk of the Superior Court
For King County, Wash.

MAY 19 1982

Bond approved _____, 19___

By _____ Deputy
County Clerk

(County Clerk's seal here)

King County, Washington

<table>
<tr><td>No</td><td>Notice mailed to County Clerk</td><td>Term Expires</td><td>Commissioned</td><td>Seal Approved</td><td></td><td>Place two clear impressions of Seal here</td><td>(County) KING</td><td>(City) SEATTLE</td><td>(Address) 800 Queen Anne Av</td><td>(Name) CARRIE MATTHEW</td><td>OATH OF OFFICE AND SEAL IMPRESSIO OF</td><td>Notary Bond</td><td>303.775</td></tr>
</table>

37

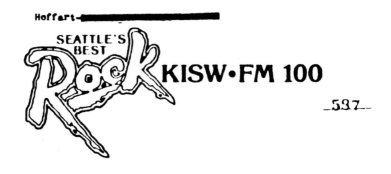

SEATTLE'S BEST

KISW•FM 100

_537_

KISW RENEWAL

HEARING NOTICE - BROADCAST DATES

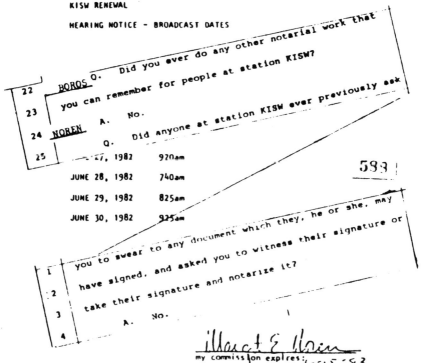

	BOROS		
22			
23			
24	NOREN		
25		___ 27, 1982	920am
	JUNE 28, 1982	740am
	JUNE 29, 1982	825am
	JUNE 30, 1982	925am

Q. Did you ever do any other notarial work that you can remember for people at station KISW?

A. No.

Q. Did anyone at station KISW ever previously ask

_533_

you to swear to any document which they, he or she, may have signed, and asked you to witness their signature or take their signature and notarize it?

A. No.

my commission expires: 6-15-83

38

APPLICATION FOR:

NOTARY PUBLIC COMMIS?I

11-1 (D)

FEE $10.00

DEPARTMENT OF LICENSING
DIVISION OF PROFESSIONAL LICENSING
P.O. BOX 9649
Olympia, WA 98504

MONEY CTL (6,7,8)

Make remittance payable to
STATE TREASURER

FOR OFFICE USE ONLY

	TRANS(3)	PROF CODE (4)	PC/C(C(5)			EXPIRATION DATE(9)	EXP(10)	STAT(11)	TYPE(1)
LA	11	25601							I
KEY DATE (13)	CLASS (14)	ASSN (16)	BILLED AMOUNT (16)	SIGN	SPLIT	QHTD			
			10.00						

PLEASE TYPE OR PRINT

NAME __Matthew, Carrie___
LAST   FIRST   MIDDLE

DATE OF BIRTH 2 /17/61
MO DAY YEAR

RESIDENCE ADDRESS __800 Queen Ave. N__

CITY __Seattle__ STATE __WA__ ZIP CODE __98109__ COUNTY (27) __King__

TELEPHONE NUMBER __285-7625__
Enter number to be used during normal business hours

SOCIAL SECURITY NUMBER __(deleted by the author__
Requested for identification purposes only. Entering SSN is
voluntary and is not mandatory for commission approval.

– THIS FORM MAY BE USED FOR REINSTATEMENT – BUT NOT FOR REAPPOINTMENT –

PREVIOUS COMMISSION DATE AND NUMBER IF APPLICABLE: Expiration Date: _____ Commission Number: _____

CERTIFICATION
I HEREBY CERTIFY THAT I HAVE NOT BEEN CONVICTED OF A FELONY OR MALFEASANCE IN
OFFICE. I UNDERSTAND THAT ANY CONVICTION OF A FELONY OR ANY MALFEASANCE IN THE
OFFICE OF NOTARY WILL IMMEDIATELY FORFEIT MY COMMISSION AS A NOTARY (RCW 9.92.120).

SIGNATURE __Carrie Matthew__
(EXACTLY AS NAME ON SEAL OR STAMP)

OFFICE USE ONLY
CERT DATE (44)
CERT. NO. (45)

CERTIFICATION BY FREEHOLDERS
I, AN UNDERSIGNED FREEHOLDER RESIDING IN THE COUNTY WHEREIN THE APPLICANT RESIDES, DO HEREBY CERTIFY THAT THE
APPLICANT NAMED HEREIN IS PERSONALLY KNOWN BY ME AND IS A CITIZEN OF GOOD MORAL CHARACTER AND REPUTE. I DO
THEREFORE PETITION THE GOVERNOR OF THE STATE OF WASHINGTON TO COMMISSION SAID APPLICANT AS A NOTARY PUBLIC.

NOTE: FREEHOLDER SIGNATURES REQUIRED ONLY ON ORIGINAL APPLICATION

FREEHOLDER SIGNATURE   CITY   COUNTY OF RESIDENCE

39

FCC Form 365
Jan 1974

UNITED STATES OF AMERICA
FEDERAL COMMUNICATIONS COMMISSION

File No.: **BLFT-780822IA**

LICENSE FOR A
BROADCAST TRANSLATOR STATION

Call Sign: **K283AA**

Subject to the provisions of the Communications Act of 1934, subsequent acts, and treaties, and all regulations heretofore or hereafter made by this Commission, and further subject to conditions set forth in this license, the licensee is hereby authorized to use and operate the radio transmitting apparatus hereinafter described.

1. Name of LICENSEE . . . . DENA Pictures, Inc. & Alexander Broadcasting Co., a joint venture dba Kaye-Smith Enterprises

2. License term ending 3 a.m. Local Time . . . . December 1, 1981

3. Principal community to be served . . . . Seattle, Washington

4. Primary station . . . . KISW (FM) Ch-260, 99.6 MHz, Seattle, Washington

5. Via . . . . : --------

6. Operating assignment . . . . : Channel 283, 104.5 MHz

7. Hours of operation . . . . : Unlimited.

8. Transmitter . . . . ROBERT A. JONES, J-317

9. Transmitter power output . . . . 10 watts

10. Transmitting antenna location . . . . 111 Tower Place, Seattle, Washington

11. North Latitude 47 37 52
    West Longitude 122 21 17

12. Transmitting Antenna . . . . GIBSON, 3 Colinear vertical dipoles mounted on a
13. Antenna supporting structure . . . . 32-foot building

14. Overall height above ground . . . . 53 feet
15. Main radiation lobe oriented . . . . Omnidirectional
16. Obstruction marking specifications . . . . In accordance with the following paragraphs of FCC Form 715
    (attached). None Required

17. Conditions . . . .
THE AUTHOR DIRECTS THE READER'S ATTENTION TO THE LAST PARAGRAPH.
. . .THIS LICENSE SHALL NOT VEST IN THE LICENSE ANY RIGHT TO
OPERATE THE STATION. . .IN ANY OTHER MANNER THAN AUTHORIZED HEREIN.

The Commission reserves the right during said license period of terminating this license or making effective any changes or modification of this license which may be necessary to comply with any decision of the Commission rendered as a result of any hearing held under the rules of the Commission prior to the commencement of this license period or any decision rendered as a result of any such hearing which has been designated but not held, prior to the Commencement of this license period.

This license is issued on the licensee's representation that the statements contained in licensee's application are true and that the undertakings therein contained, so far as they are consistent herewith, will be carried out in good faith. The licensee shall, during the terms of this license, render such service as will serve public interest, convenience, or necessity to the full extent of the privileges herein conferred.

This license shall not vest in the license any right to operate the station nor any right in the use of the frequencies designated in the license beyond the term hereof, nor in any other manner than authorized herein. Neither the license nor the rights herein granted shall be transferred, assigned, or in any manner either voluntarily or involuntarily disposed of, or indirectly by transfer of control of the licensee, if a corporation, to any person without the written consent of the Commission. This license is subject to the right of use or control by the Government of the United States conferred by Section 606 of the Communications Act of 1934.

Issued at: **May 22, 1979**
1b

FEDERAL
COMMUNICATIONS
COMMISSION

(address deleted)

February 7,
1981.

Federal Communication Commission,   (2 - 13t
Washington, D.C.

                    Sir;
        I have a complaint to give to your off-
ice and perhaps your Commission can give me the
help I need;-- I have lived here for some 20
years;I am also a professional within the state
of Washington.

        My request is this;Is it possible your
Commission may stop/prohibit the filthy/hog
slop,obsene,programs which are being given to
us over the television/radio reports these days.
Do not inform me that all I need do to stop
such programs is to turn the dial to "OFF" and
I shall no longer view the obsene programs.
        I am aware of the above fact,but the
so called "JHOWS" continue whether I watch
such or whether I do not;Children still see and
"eat" the filthy shows and if such is wrong for
me to see,the same is true for any child.

        Also is it feasible that the radio stat-
ion in Seattle (Washingto)which is KISW. may
be prohibited from cursing and "enjoying" the
obsene language which is done each day;I am
certain of this because I hear it each day
until I can bear up under such curses as
is provided via radio;usually in the A.M.on
Sunday from 6--9 a.m.Cannot such cursing be
STOPPED in some manner;are we forced to hear
such filthy words over the air.
        Some years ago,I had a part in stopp-
ing a "show" via radio due to the fact the
people were using obsene/swearing language
day after day;that program soon was taken
off the air;I am sure there are yet folk
who are decent and I am pos ive I am one
of such people.
        Hoping your Commission may give me the

41

help I need;We love good clean "shows" given via the media
but I shall fight HOG SLOP,/OBSENE/CURSING being aired via
any manner whatsoever;May we have this STOPPED NOW/AT ONCE.
Thanking you kindly,

                              Respectfully,

(signature deleted)

(address deleted)

FCC COMM Jan 9, 198:
DISTRICT COMMISSION 3
Seattle, Wa
JAN 12 1981 9817
JAN 15 1981
COMPL
SEATTLE, WASHINGTON

To Whom It May Concern
This is to protest the obscene language used on the radio station K T S W.

My radio was tuned to this station by someone else in my home so I left it on to this talk show.

The d. j. had a pimp com on + talk + his language was filthy including mother fucker, ass, shit + bull shit.

Has the FCC become so lax that they now allow this thing? It was my experience up to now that they either bleeped it out or cut them off the air. I know there is a seven second second delay.

Please look into this

43

matter:
The time was between
7:30 am + 8:00 am. Sat Ja
9, 1982.

Sincerely,

(signature deleted)

P.S. I called the station an
am sending them a
letter also. Talk show
are very good, but not
this kind of talk!

FEB 4 1982

'$ 3'10 -'{{}}
C1-302

Dear (name deleted)

(This part of this
letter deleted by
the FCC)

- 2

Your January 9 letter to the Commission's Seattle office has been forwarded
to this office.

Please see Sections 1(b), 4(d), 5(a), 10 and 18 in "The FCC and Broadcasting,"
and our second enclosure entitled "Obscenity, Indecency and Profanity in Broadcasting." The information in your letter is not sufficient to indicate whether
the KISW talk show you have objected to would be considered violative of the
criminal statute discussed in our enclosures. If you wish to send this office
additional detailed information concerning the program--for example, accurate
quotations of statements broadcast--it will be given full consideration. But
there is no law prohibiting broadcast discussion of any given subject, and
the FCC cannot direct stations in the selection of talk show participants.
Comments in writing to stations about specific programs can be effective in
influencing broadcasters' programming practices.

Patrick, W/cc. B

45

18 February 1983

Mr. Steven West, General Manager
KISW-FM
712 Aurora Avenue North
Seattle, Wa. 98109

Dear Mr. West;

I am writing to complain about something I heard on KISW-FM Thursday,
17 February that I feel was offensive and in very poor taste.
At approximately 2:24 p.m. that day, a record ended and the sound
of a crying infant was heard. The announcer said something to the effect
'What the hell is this? Hey, close the door, will 'ya'
The crying ended with the slam of a door followed by the announcer saying
'That's our rock baby we picked up a month or two ago. He was alright then,
now he's a pain in the ass.' I believe this sort of 'bush league'
radio would be more expected from a small, far away radio station
where professionalism's sorely lacking and not from a highly rated
station in this country's 15th largest radio market, which professes
to play Seattle's best new Rock.

It's common knowledge that deregulation has freed radio to be more 'blue'
which is usually tolerable since it reflects what's spoken in society.
But I believe that reference to an infant as a 'pain in the ass'
is inherently harmful and mean and intolerable on any media under
any circumstances. As a result, I will no longer listen to KISW-FM
and I'll advise others I meet and know to do the same. A copy of this letter
has been sent to Complaints and Compliance, FCC Broadcast Bureau
and the Regional Director of the FCC office in Seattle.

Regretfully,

(signature deleted)

(address deleted)

46

May 24 1983

FCC.
Mass Media Bureau
Washington, BC 20554

Sir:

Enclosed find a letter which I sent to radio station KISW, Seattle, Wa. I would appreciate any help that you can offer in eliminating obscene and perverse dialog from radio station KISW which primarily services adolescents and teenage audiences.

Thank you

(signature deleted)
(address deleted)

112 [illegible] W.   May 21, 1983

Seattle, Wa

Sir:

At approximately 7:00 a.m. Thursday
May 19 1983, while listening to your
radio station, KISW, I heard what
I considered to be obscene and
perverse dialog. The dialog was of
a man who was sad because she
wouldn't do it with him but would
do it with him and with him
and with them, etc. The man also
went onto talk about a various
woman.

I would appreciate in the future
if your disc jockeys would monitor
what they consider to be appropriate
material for their teenage and adult
audiences.

Thank you for your cooperation.

Sincerely,

(signature deleted)

copy: FCC
Mass Media Bureau
Washington, D.C. 20554

48

Dear F.C.C. On March 27, 1984 at 3:10 P.M.
a local rock station in the Seattle area
had a rock star who goes by the name
of Billy Idol on the air. Wave live.
The station was K I S W. Billy Idol started
telling about how he liked to eat Pussy,
then he went on to tell about Masterbation.
He went on to make sound effects. The whole
time the radio announcers laughed their
butts off. Then he got some phone calls on
the air and told one girl to go masterbate.
He also said Fuck several times. Also
the radio announcer told him that this
is America and he could say anything the wanted to over the radio. What
I want to know is is that true? If its
not true who the hell is going to do
something about it.

Sincerly (signature deleted)

(address deleted)

49

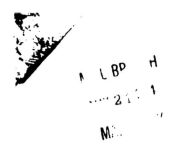

8310-TD
C4-531

Dear Mr.

This is in response to your most recent letter to the Commission concerning remarks alleged to have been made by a "rock" musician who was interviewed on Radio Station KISW(FM), Seattle, WA, on March 27, 1934. Your previous letter (which the Commission has already answered) described the objectionable language you state was used in the interview, and your recent letter asks for Commission action on the matter.

As we stated in our previous response to you on this matter, Court decisions distinguishing between material protected by the First Amendment and that which is obscene or indecent (the use of which can be subjected to government regulation) are clearly stated, and the Commission is necessarily guided by decisions of the Supreme Court in making determinations regarding specific material. In regard to sexually-oriented programming, unless it can be demonstrated that a connection exists between a specific presentation and the Court's standards for identifying obscenity or indecency (the threshhold requirement of evidence in establishing a _prima facie_ case) that material would be protected under the First Amendment to the Constitution. Based on the information you have provided, we are unable to make the required connection and, thus, Commission action on your unsupported allegations would be unwarranted.

Sincerely,

Edythe Wise, Chief
Complaints and Investigations Branch
Enforcement Division
Mass Media Bureau

MR. STEPHEN F. SEWELL

I wrote this letter to Mr. Beau Phillips of radio station KISW (FM 100) in Seattle, WA after being care-
*   enough to allow myself decieved into believing their reports of the switch to Daylight Savings Time.*
ᴧs I wrote Mr. Phillips letter, I feel I was deceived by untrue information and got a real slap-in-the-face
when John Langen & Mike West (the morning personalities who frequently pull these kinds of stunts)
informed their listeners that it wasn't really Daylight Savings Time...that doesn't happen until the third
week of April (chuckle-chuckle). I got very little enjoyment out of this joke. Nor do I think that their
'News In YOur Face' program which mangles news out of proportion or makes it up entirely to sladner
political figures and entertainment-industry persons is anything that belongs getting broadcast over the
air-waves so freely and seemingly without any care as to how it might affect the public.

*   Obviously, I do not have to listen to KISW, there are plenty of other stations who have much more*
quality and pride and taste in what they broadcast (KZAM FM-92 in Bellevue for example is excellent)
but I ask you how pretend news and pretend game shows (where the phone-in contestents are often
hung-up on or ridiculed on-air) and weather reports for any city other than the Seattle area can be
beneficial and of real value to the listening public.

*   I hope you will look into this situation or have someone in the local office (who directed me to write*
you) take a sincere and serious look ot the unfortunate and haphazard manner in which this station is
managed and the trash they think should make up valueable listening material.

*   I am reminded of a new 'd-j' who came to Seattle almost a year ago to work the afternoon shift on*
KPLZ, he was really sharp and has a nice sence of music and commercial balance in his show. One
day he tossed out an ethnic joke (Itilian) at random and caught a flurry of calls and responce from
his listeners. The next day he apologized on the air, and the management followed suit. Within two
weeks he left the station, presumably from pressure, and I hear he wound up in California.

*   It's hard to believe that bright guy got the squeeze play for such a minor thing, which he attempted*
to apologize for and then KISW does continuous slandering, deception and lying on the air and never
even gets its wrists slapped. I truly believe their programming is often of no value to the public and
while it is a matter of personal ponion, I hope it gets investigated.

*   ınk you for your time in reading this letter, a response would be very appreciated.*

(signature and
address deleted)

51

Mr. Beau Phillips; Programming Director at radio station KISW (FM 100).

Well, I can't explain why I have endured the tasteless humour, tacky verbal abuse and senseless on-air slander-attacks of innocent persons (including some of the listening audience), and I choose to do so no longer. On the morning of Monday, March 29th, 1982, I fell victim to the latest of your bits of hazardous programming and reckless misuse of your license to broadcast in the public interest.

At my job, I keep a radio on for a bit of background music while I move about doing my work. I can not sit still and listen intently to the rantings of the 'dee-jays' word-for-word all day. Sometime on Friday the 26th of March I caught a notice over KISW explaining that Daylight Savings Time would commence over the upcoming weekend and I was told to set my clocks ahead one hour on Sunday night/ Monday morning at 2 am.

Over the weekend I didn't listen to the radio at all. I had my son to be with, and my fiancee and her son.

It actually wasn't until Monday morning, about five miles from home on my way to wkrk, that I realized the cruel joke your station had played on me. Your morning 'personslities' announced that (chuckle-chuckle) it was still Standard Time. I had woken us all up an hour early for no reason. I had sent my son to wait for his schbol bus one hour early, my fiancee and I got to sit at the Park & Ride for a wasted hour, and her son got to visit with the sitter for an extra hour (at an extra expense). I was not amused.

Over the past few years, your programming has become tasteless and stagnant, and your news & information less reliable. Your programming seems less in the public interest than in the selfish interest of some reckless individuals employed at KISW. Other than your strong broadcasting signal, I wonder what has kept me listening to your on-air rantings & slanderous comments this long.

I cannot understand why the F.C.C. would allow such careless abuse of the airwaves unless there has been no public outcry.

You may consider it donwe: A Xerox of this letter will be mailed to Mr. Stephen F. Sewell at the main office of the Fedemal Communications Commission along with a note explaining why .

I presume he will contact you directly if he concurs with my feelings on the blatant misuse of your license to broadcast quality material of genuine use to the public. I believe it is the responsibility of station personnel & management to see to it that material is factual and news above suspicion.

For what it is worth; I will no longer listen to radio station KISW and will attempt to dissuade my friends and persons at work from listening also.

(signature and
address deleted)

52

JUL 1 5 1982

IN REPLY REFER TO

8310-W
C4-362

Kaye-Smith Enterprises
Radio Station KISW(FM)
P. O. Box 3010
Bellevue, Washington 98009

Gentlemen:

The Commission has received a complaint that station KISW(FM) may have broadcast "untrue" information so as to deceive the public.

Specifically, the complainant alleges that on the morning of March 26, 1982, John Langen and Mike West broadcast information that Daylight Savings Time would commence on the upcoming weekend and advised listeners to advance their clocks one hour on Sunday night/Monday morning at 2:00 a.m. Daylight Saving Time actually went into effect at 2:00 a.m. on Sunday, April 18, 1982. The complainant states that "It actually wasn't until Monday morning, about five miles from home on my way to wkrk (sic), that I realized the cruel joke your station had played on me. Your morning 'personalities' announced that (chuckle-chuckle) it was still Standard Time. I (sic) had woken (sic) us all up an hour early for no reason."

The Commission has stated a policy in En Banc Programming Inquiry, 44 FCC 2303, 2304 (1960):

> Prior to the en banc hearing, the Commission had made its position clear that, in fulfilling its obligation to operate in the public interest, a broadcast station is expected to exercise reasonable care and prudence with respect to its broadcast material in order to assure that no matter is broadcast which will deceive or mislead the public.

Also, the Commission has decided a line of cases involving situations which mislead and deceive the public. For instance in Doubleday Broadcasting Co. Inc., 56 FCC 2d 333 (1975) the Commission dealt with a situation in which the announcements involved a hoax kidnapping of one of the station's announcers. Information received in that matter indicated the announcements were intended to be humorous and, that in that context it would be reasonably understood as a prank. In another case, Action Radio, Inc., 51 FCC 2d 803 (1970), the Commission concluded that the licensee engaged in deliberate falsification of news by broadcasting ficticious temperatures during weather reports. Although this was not the sole basis for its decision, the Commission granted the licensee a one year probationary renewal of the station's license. It is important to note that in that case the Commission stated:

53

This activity, albeit on a lower plane, falls on the perifery of the type of "nonfact" reporting we referred to as "staged," or "pseudo event" in Democratic National Convention Television Coverage, 16 FCC 2d 650, 656-657 (1969). [51 FCC 2d at 807].

The staff does not believe, that in your case, the falsification of the commencement of Daylight Saving Time announcements comes within the range of hoax cases covered in Commission decisions, nevertheless this Commission is concerned when the public is mislead and relies thereon. The time change announcements in your case are not substantially different from the type of announcements in the Action Radio, Inc. case in which the Commission expressed great concern.

Consequently, this matter is being called to your attention so that you may exercise appropriate supervision over station operations and take whatever steps are necessary to assure that statements concerning time changes and similar type announcements are accurate and factual.

This matter is being made part of the records of Station KISW(FM).

                               Sincerely,

                               Jeffrey W. Malickson
                               Jeffrey W. Malickson
                               Assistant Chief
                               Complaints and Compliance Division
                               Broadcast Bureau

cc: Fly, Shuebruk, Blume, Gaguine, Boros & Schulkind

KAYE-SMITH ENTERPRISES
P O Box 3010
Bellevue Washington 98009
Telephone (206) 455-0923

July 20, 1982

MEMO TO: STEVE WEST - KISW
             ROD KREBS   - KJRB/KEZE

FROM: Lester M. Smith

RE: FCC COMPLAINT - KISW(FM)

I am widely circulating this letter from the FCC that we received today.

I want each of you to sit down with your various air people and tell them about the responsibility they have when they are on the air. What might seem funny to them could cause a great deal of problems for the station, especially when it receives a complaint from the FCC.

I will talk to each of you about this.

Best personal regards.

LMS:amc
cc: Beau Phillips, KISW, w/enc.
    John Sherman, KJRB/KEZE, w/enc.
    Jerome S. Boros, w/o enc.
    File

55

FEDERAL COMMUNICATIONS COMMISSION
WASHINGTON. D C. 20554

2 1 OCT 1982

IN REPLY REFER TO:
8900-RH

Mr. Vincent L. Hoffart
N. 1748 Lacey Street
Spokane, Washington 99207

RE: FOIA Request No. 82-163

Dear Mr. Hoffart:

This refers to your request dated October 5, 1982, pursuant to the
Freedom of Information Act. Specifically, you are requesting a copy of
the specific authority given FM Station KISW, Seattle, Washington, to
operate FM Translator Station K283AA with an antenna other than the
Gibson 3 Colinear vertical dipole antenna specified in its license
issued May 22, 1979 (File No. BLFT-780822IA).

After careful search of the·Commission's file, the Bureau is unable to
locate any such authority or record of receiving such a request.

Your letter also claims that this translator station is now operating
with a Taco Y-51 5 element Yagi antenna in contravention of Section 74.1251(2)
of the Commission's Rules. In this regard, I have forwarded a copy of
your letter to the Complaints and Compliance Division for appropriate
action.

Sincerely,

Laurence E. Harris
Chief, Broadcast Bureau

56

2 c ᵕ ℓ ᵧ - 16 · ℓ ℓ

IN REPLY REFER TO

Mr. Vincent L. Hoffart
N. 1748 Lacey Street
Spokane, Washington   99207-5330

Dear Mr. Hoffart:

This is in reference to the Freedom of Information Act request
(FOIA Control No. 86-44), which you filed regarding FM translator
Stations K283AA and K259AA, Seattle, Washington.

Pursuant to the Freedom of Information Act, 5 U.S.C. Section 552,
you request a copy of the license certificate, and any and all
documents relating thereto, which specifically authorizes K283AA
to operate with a directional antenna, namely, a Taco Y 51. You
further seek copies of any notices of apparent liability that may
have been issued to the licensee for the willful and repeated
operation of K283AA with an antenna not authorized by the license
granted the station on May 22, 1979. Finally, copies of all
documents, including applications, regarding K259AA are requested.

To place the instant request in the proper prospective, it should
initially be noted that K283AA was constructed in 1978 using a
different transmitting antenna than the one specified in the
construction permit issued by the Commission. However, as was
developed in the comparative renewal proceeding (BC Docket Nos.
82-265 and 82-266), in which you are involved with Dena Pictures,
Incorporated, the licensee of Station KISW(FM), Seattle,
Washington, the substituted antenna was identified and its
performance characteristics were tabulated and submitted as part
of the license application for that station. While that
application was granted by the Commission, the license certificate
issued on May 22, 1979 did not reflect the use of the substituted
TACO Y 51 antenna. In reviewing the grant of KISW(FM)'s renewal
application and the denial of your competing application, the
Commission considered and specifically addressed the above matter.
While it found that the licensee had violated Section
74.1251(b)(2) of the Commission's rules in constructing K283AA
with a substituted antenna for which prior approval had not been
obtained, that transgression was regarded as minor, amounting
under the circumstances to nothing more than an innocent error on
the part of the licensee apparently unfamiliar with this particular
intricacy of the Commission's rules. See Kaye-Smith Enterprises,
FCC 85-192, released April 19, 1985.

Turning to the specifics of your document request, please be
advised that a thorough review of the records systems maintained
by the Mass Media Bureau and the Field Operations Bureau has been

conducted. However, no documents of the nature requested with respect to K283AA have been ascertained as a result of this records search. With respect to K259AA, the documents requested are contained in a station file maintained by the Auxiliary Services Branch in Room 7310 at the Commission offices located at 2025 M Street, N.W., Washington, D.C. 20554. These materials are routinely available Commission records, and access thereto can be arranged by contacting Mr. Thomas English at Telephone No. (202) 634-6307.

The Commission does not possess the personnel and other resources that would enable it to provide the public with copies of its records. However, arrangements to have any of the documents in the K259AA station file copied and mailed to you can be made by contacting International Transcription Services, Inc., the exclusive contractor for duplication of all Commission records. Enclosed for your information and use is a bulletin regarding this contractor and the prices charged for its services.

I trust the foregoing is responsive to your request.

Sincerely,

William H. Johnson
Acting Chief
Mass Media Bureau

Enclosure

JAMES LAWRENCE FLY
  (1966)
PETER SHUEBRUK
BENITO GAGUINE
JEROME S. BOROS
HERBERT M. SCHULKIND
HOWARD J. BRAUN*

IRVING GASTFREUND*
RUSSELL C. BALCH*
ZAVE H. UNGER**
JOEL E. STILLMAN***

JACK P. BLUME
ASHER H. ENDE
COUNSEL

*D. C. BAR ONLY
**N. Y. BAR ONLY
***MASS. & FLA. BARS ONLY

45 ROCKEFELLER PLAZA
NEW YORK, NEW YORK 10111
(212) C17-3040

1211 CONNECTICUT AVENUE N W
WASHINGTON D C 20036
(202) 293-1280

New York, New York
September 18, 1981

Re: Station K283AA
     Seattle, Washington

Dear Mr. Tricarico

Enclosed for filing, on behalf of Dena Pictures, Incorporated
and Alexander Broadcasting Company, a joint venture, d/b/a
Kaye-Smith Enterprises, are an original and two copies of an
application for renewal of FM Translator Station K283AA for
operation with Primary Station KISW(FM), Seattle, Washington.

Please direct any communications with respect to the above
matter to the undersigned at:

          Suite 1759
          45 Rockefeller Plaza
          New York, New York 10111
          (202) 293-1397 (Tie Line)

                              Very truly yours

                              Jerome S. Boros

Mr. William J. Tricarico
Secretary
Federal Communications Commission
1919 M Street, N.W.
Washington, D.C. 20554

Enclosures (3)

---

bcc: Melvin M. Bailey - w/encl.
      Lester M. Smith - w/encl.
      Steve West - w/encl. (2 - 1 for LPF)

In the Matter of)
)
Liability of Capitol Media, Inc.)
)
Former Licensee of Station KFBC,)
Cheyenne, WY)
)
for a Forfeiture)

SUPPLEMENTAL BRIEF
EXHIBIT PAGE NO. -10-

CERTIFIED MAIL/

No.9 71 2 7

RETURN RECEIPT REQUESTED
FEE PAID

MEMORANDUM OPINION AND ORDER

Adopted: **DEC 9 1985** Released: **DEC 9 1985**

1. The Commission, by the Chief of the Mass Media Bureau acting pursuant
to authority delegated by Section 0.283 of the Commission's Rules, has under
consideration (1) a Notice of Apparent Liability for a forfeiture issued
September 5, 1985, and (2) the response of the former licensee thereto, dated
September 20, 1985, requesting a $300 reduction of the forfeiture.

2. The Notice of Apparent Liability for $4,300 was issued for the
following apparent violations:

SECTION 73.44(a)(3): The main transmitter was emitting, on 2480 kHz (the
second harmonic), a spurious signal suppressed 32 dB below the level of
the carrier. This must be reduced to at least 73 dB.

SECTION 73.44(a)(3): The main transmitter was emitting, on 3720 kHz (the
third harmonic), a spurious signal suppressed 70.7 dB below the level of
the carrier. This must be reduced to at least 73 dB.

SECTION 73.49(a)(8): Failure to enclose the antenna tower with radio
frequency potential at the base within an effective locked fence.

SECTION 73.932(a): Failure to have installed an operating Emergency
Broadcast System (EBS) receiver at the time of the inspection.

SECTION 73.932(d): Failure to make appropriate entries in the station log
indicating reasons why weekly test EBS transmissions were not received.

SECTION 73.1590(a)(6): Failure to make equipment performance measurements
during calendar years 1983 and 1984.

60

SECTION 73.3526(a): Failure to make available the complete public inspection file during routine business hours; the quarterly issues-programs list was missing from the file.

3. In its request for a rescission of $300 of the forfeiture amount, counsel for Capitol Media advises that his client is no longer the licensee of KFBC. However, in the financial accountings attendant to transferring the station, $4,000 not $4,300 was set aside for payment of the forfeiture. Counsel requests that, under the circumstances, $4,000 be accepted in payment of the forfeiture and that the matter be closed.

4. The Commission believes that Capitol Media, Inc. has acted in good faith regarding the forfeiture assessment. In view of the fact that KFBC has been sold, the Commission is persuaded to relieve the former licensee of the remaining forfeiture amount.

5. Accordingly, pursuant to Section 504(b) of the Communications Act of 1934, as amended, IT IS ORDERED, That the remaining $300 forfeiture assessment to Capitol Media, Inc., IS SET ASIDE.

FEDERAL COMMUNICATIONS COMMISSION

James C. McKinney
Chief, Mass Media Bureau

United States Court of Appeals
FOR THE DISTRICT OF COLUMBIA CIRCUIT

No. 85-1266   September Term, 19 85

Vincent L. Hoffart, d/b/a
Hoffart Broadcasting,
       Appellant

v.

Federal Communications Commission,
       Appellee

Dena Pictures, Incorporated,
Dena Pictures, Incorporated and Alexander
Broadcasting Company, d/b/a Kay-Smith
Enterprises,
Alexander Broadcasting Company,
       Intervenors

United States Court of Appeals
for the District of Columbia Circuit

FILED   APR 1 6 1986

GEORGE A. FISHER
CLERK

APPEAL FROM AN ORDER OF THE FEDERAL COMMUNICATIONS COMMISSION

Before: WALD, EDWARDS and *KOZINSKI, Circuit Judges.

J U D G M E N T

     This cause came on for consideration on an appeal from an order of the Federal Communications Commission, and briefs were filed herein by the parties. While the issues presented occasion no need for an opinion, they have been accorded full consideration by the Court. See Local Rule 13(c). On consideration thereof, it is

     ORDERED and ADJUDGED, by this Court, that the order of the Federal Communications Commission on appeal herein is hereby affirmed. It is

     FURTHER ORDERED, by this Court, sua sponte, that the Clerk shall withhold issuance of the mandate herein until seven days after disposition of any timely petition for rehearing. See Local Rule 14, as amended on November 30, 1981 and June 15, 1982. This instruction to the Clerk is without prejudice to the right of any party at any time to move for expedited issuance of the mandate for good cause shown.

Bills of cost must be filed within 14 days after entry of judgment. The Court looks with disfavor upon motions to file bills of costs out of time.

Per Curiam
For The Court

George C. Fisher

George A. Fisher
Clerk

*Of the United States Court of Appeals for the
Ninth Circuit, sitting by designation pursuant to

IS KENNETH STARR "DIRTY" ?

United States Court of Appeals
FOR THE DISTRICT OF COLUMBIA CIRCUIT

No. 85-1266

September Term, 19 85

Vincent L. Hoffart, d/b/a
Hoffart Broadcasting

v.

Federal Communications Commission

BEFORE: Robinson, Chief Judge; Wright, Wald, Mikva, Edwards, Ginsburg, Bork, Scalia, Starr, Silberman and Buckley, Circuit Judges; Kozinski*, Circuit Judge, U.S. Court of Appeals for the Ninth Circuit

O R D E R

The suggestion for rehearing en banc of appellant Vincent L. Hoffart, d/b/a Hoffart Broadcasting, has been circulated to the full Court and no member has requested the taking of a vote thereon. Upon consideration of the foregoing, it is

ORDERED, by the Court en banc, that the suggestion is denied.

Per Curiam

FOR THE COURT
GEORGE A. FISHER, CLERK

BY: _Robert A. Bonner_
Robert A. Bonner
Chief Deputy Clerk

*Sitting by designation pursuant to 28 U.S.C. 291 (a).

§ 706. Scope of review

To the extent necessary to decision and when presented, the reviewing court shall decide all relevant questions of law, interpret constitutional and statutory provisions, and determine the meaning or applicability of the terms of an agency action. The reviewing court shall—

(1) compel agency action unlawfully withheld or unreasonably delayed; and

(2) hold unlawful and set aside agency action, findings, and conclusions found to be—

(A) arbitrary, capricious, an abuse of discretion, or otherwise not in accordance with law;

(B) contrary to constitutional right, power, privilege, or immunity;

(C) in excess of statutory jurisdiction, authority, or limitations, or short of statutory right;

(D) without observance of procedure required by law;

(E) unsupported by substantial evidence in a case subject to sections 556 and 557 of this title or otherwise reviewed on the record of an agency hearing provided by statute; or

(F) unwarranted by the facts to the extent that the facts are subject to trial de novo by the reviewing court.

In making the foregoing determinations, the court shall review the whole record or those parts of it cited by a party, and due account shall be taken of the rule of prejudicial error.

TABULATION--KISW (FM), SEATTLE
EQUAL EMPLOYMENT OPPORTUNITY RECORD.

Year	Fulltime Emp.	Men	Women	Ethnic	Race
1977	16	13	3	0	
1978	17	13	4	1	Black male
1979	19	13	6	0	
1980	18	15	3	1	Black female
1981	20	15	5	1	" "
1982	24	17	7	0	
1983	24	18	6	1	Hispanic male
1984	26	19	7	0	

SEATTLE/EVERETT SMSA LABORFORCE
(1979 data taken from the KISW (FM) renewal application)

WOMEN	BLACK	AM. IND.	HISP.	OTHER	TOTAL ETHNIC
42.1%	3.0%	0.6%	2.1%	3.4%	9.1%

Hoffart certifies that this is a true and accurate
tabulation taken from the annual KISW (FM) forms
No. 395 filed by Kaye-Smith. In addition, the
forms show zero parttime employees in women or
ethnic groups in all eight years. On the trainee
report sheet, there are no trainees listed in any
of the eight years. This tabulation is printed in
lieu of printing four pages for each of the eight
years listed.

TABLE OF AUTHORITIES AND CITATIONS

Supporting Hoffart's charges of Preferential Treatment by the Federal Communications Commission.

Alabama Educational Technical Institute, 50 FCC 2d, 461, (1975) Non-renewal is the proper remedy for substandard performance in the field of Equal Employment.

Asheboro Broadcasting Co., 20 FCC 2d, 1,3 (1969) advice from counsel cannot excuse a clear breach of duty by a licensee. The client becomes fully responsible at some point, and that point is reached more quickly in practice before the FCC than in courts of law.

Barnett Implement Co, Inc., Mt. Vernon, Washington, 89 FCC 2d, 616. . . . it must be concluded that . . . violations were willful since they were neither inadvertent nor accidental . . . it is concluded that Business Radio Stations licensed to Barnett Implement Co., Inc., have as set forth in their licenses . . . Barnett Implement and/or Jerald Rindal, its owner/president, do not have the requisite qualifications to hold Commission licenses. It is ordered that the licenses be revoked. (10-5-81) Lenore G. Ehrig, Chief Administrative Law Judge. (retired, 1983). (Decision upheld by the Review Board).

Berryville Broadcasting Co., 70 FCC 2d, 11. (Thomas) has not demonstrated a reasonable likelyhood of spending 30 hours per week (at the station) since he owns two other stations. (12-15-78)

Broadcast Communications, Evanston, Ill., 97 FCC, 64. (1984) . . . just as we compared similarly situated TV stations in Cowles WESH (86 FCC 2d), we find it more meaningful in measuring broadcast communications performance to compare similarly situated FM stations than to compare all radio stations in the Chicago (Evanston) market.

Brownsfield Broadcasting Co., 93 FCC 2d, 1203. The Policy Statement on Comparative Renewals specifies that full-time integration into management by an owner is of substantial importance. (4-28-1983)

Central Pennsylvania Broadcasting Co., 22 FCC 2d 632, 18 RR 2d 1128 (1970). The Commission's issuance of a radio operators license does not relieve a licensee employing the holder thereof from its obligation to supervise the operation of the station and to assure compliance with applicable technical standards.

Chronicle Broadcasting, 91 FCC 2d, 890. Evidence to a designated issue . . . will not be excluded because it is not specifically mentioned. (cited from G.E. Cameron, Jr.)

Columbia Broadcasting System, Inc., FCC 434, F 2d, 1018, 1026, D.C. Circuit, (1971), . . . when the Commission changes course, it has a legal duty to provide an opinion or analysis indicating that the standard is being changed and assuring that it is faithfully not indifferent to the rules of law.

Continental Broadcasting, Inc., 15 FCC 2d, 120 (1968) (certiorari denied, 403, U.S. 905, (1971). . . . the fact that (WFAB's) local managerial personnel were neither officers or principals has long been considered irrelevant in determining licensee's responsibility for its conduct.

Davis v. United Fruit, 402 F 2d 328 (2nd Circuit, 1968) A client is responsible for the acts of counsel. (certiorari denied, 393 U.S. 1085, 1969)

Eleven-Ten Broadcasting Corp., 32 FCC 2d 706, 22 RR 699 (1962) . . . the fact that these violations were not discovered and corrected on the permittee's own initiative is itself a serious matter . . . a corollary to the axiom of licensee responsibility is that effective licensee supervision of employees is required to discharge that responsibility. Retention of effective control by a licensee of a station's management and operation is a fundamental oblgation of the licensee, and a licensee's lack of familiarity with stations operation and management may reflect an indifference tantamount to lack of control.

Executive Broadcasting Corp., 3 FCC 2d, 699 (1966). Licensee's are not relieved of their liability because of corrective actions.

EZ Communications, Inc., 86 FCC 2d, 120—citing 56 FCC 2d, 371 (1975)— Licensee's Responsibility to Verify Accuracy of Stations Invoices, etc., "Licensees are reminded of their responsibility to verify completeness and accuracy of stations bills, invoices, affidavits, etc., by checking relevant program logs or equivalent stations records. (1981)

Fox River Broadcasting, 88 FCC 2d, 1132, 1135, 50 RR 2d 1321, 1324 (Review Board, 1982). 'an intent to deceive the FCC . . . is the heart of a misrepresentation case. Misrepresentation connotes a false statement of an objective fact intentionally made to deceive.

Gainsville Media, Inc., 70 FCC 2d, 58, 42 RR 2d 489 (reconsideration denied). 'the proposition that applicants for broadcast licenses be examined for predictive compliance with FCC rules is hardly novel. It is, and always been, an important element in the Commission's licensing process. (2-16-78)

Golden Broadcasting System, 68 FCC 2d, 1099. License renewal denied. Applicant made repeated misrepresentations and also concealed false statements, thus undercutting the regulatory system.

Grenco, Inc., 39 FCC 2d, 732, 26 RR 2d 1046 (1973). An applicant that deliberately lies in its testimony before the Commission will be disqualified.

Gulf Coast Communications, Inc., 81 FCC 2d 499, 513-515. (Review Board, 1980) . . . a party found to have abused the Commission's processes in the described manner should not hope to escape with a mere demerit. (11-21-1980)

Happy Broadcasting, Co., 67 FCC 2d, 272. Short Term renewal ordered for misrepresentations in renewal application regarding equipment performance measurements. (1-4-78)

Leflore Broadcasting Co., 636 F 2d, 454, 462 (D.C. Circuit 1980) . . . (the) fact of misrepresentations coupled with proof that the party making it had knowledge of its falsity would be ⸱⸱⸱ ᵹh to justify a conclusion that there was fraudulent intent. (quoting from U.S. Appeals, D.C. Circuit case No. 82-1235 and 83-2105.)

Lewel Broadcasting, Inc., 86 FCC 2d, 912 (citing from California Broadcasting, 98 FCC 2d, 1045) . . . the Commission rejected an applicant's contention that "there had been no deliberate scheme to conceal a wrongful act and that any misstatements were inadvertent" on the grounds that the self-serving testimony was "inherently unbelievable."

Lowndes County Broadcasting Co., 10 FCC 2d, 91, RR 2d 45 (1970) . . . licensees are expected to know and comply with the terms of their authorizations and our rules, and will not be excused for violations of them absent clear mitigating circumstances.

McIllguham v. Barber, 53 N.W. 902, 905. 83 Wis 500 (1892) (cited by the Commission in KCLE, Inc., 66 FCC 2d, 1059.) Incompetence of employees is not a mitigating factor. Competence was defined as sufficient skill or intelligence to understand the act one is performing.

Milton Broadcasting, 34 FCC 2d, 1086, 1047, (1973). We have repeatedly stated that it is the licensees obligation to take affirmative steps to ascertain the true facts and supply accurate information to the Commission.

McLendon Corp., 18 FCC 2d, 244, 288, 16 RR 2d 657 (1969) . . . the Commission has consistently held that licensees are responsible for the acts of their employees performed within the scope of their employment, especially those charged with the management and supervision of the day-to-day operation of the station.

New Continental Broadcasting Co., 88 FCC 2d, 837. A determination of lack of candor or misrepresentations requires evidence of an intention and a motive to deceive, mislead or conceal. (12-30-1981)

New Mexico Broadcasting Co, 87 FCC 2d, 279. Ineptness does not excuse a broadcast licensee's failure to meet its obligations. (7-6-1981)

Oil Shale Broadcasting., 70 FCC 2d, 992, 1003. No credit for non-entertainment public service certificates. "These are run-of-the-mill certificates of thanks, sent to all radio stations who have run PSA's on their behalf."

Old Time Religion Hour, 95 FCC 2d, 719. (Review Board, 10-7, 1983). Disqualified for lack of candor. "It is now clear that an applicant may be disqualified on the basis of its principal's candorless testimony when lack of candor occurs 'before the judge's own eyes'." (citing RKO General, Inc., 670, F 2d, 215, 234, D.C. Circuit, 1981) (citing Taylor v. Hayes, 418 U.S. 488, 499, (1974). Moreover, the Commission has long held that false statements in the course of a hearing process are, in and of themselves, of substantial significance. (citing Nick J. Chaconas, 28 FCC 2d, 231, 233, 21 RR 2d 576, 579, 1971), that specific notice to an applicant that he must testify truthfully is superfluous, and that such false testimony may lead to disqualification. (citing Grenco, Inc., 39 FCC 2d, 732, 736, 26 RR 2d 1046, 1051, 1973). Lack of candor need not specifically be designated as a hearing issue because, 'truth and candor' are always at issue. (citing William M. Rogers, 92 FCC 2d, 187, 199-201, 52 RR 2d 831, 842, 843,

1982) See also Peoples Broadcasting Corp., 52 RR 2d, 1617, 1625, reconsideration denied, 53 RR 2d, 1210 (Review Board, 1983)

Pan American Broadcasting, 89 FCC 2d, 167. Applicants are required to strict adherence to hearing orders, absent unusual or very special circumstances. (2-24-1982)

Password, Inc., 76, FCC 2d 516. Where there has been a pattern of deliberate deception, past meritorious performance and public service by the station generally are insufficient to mitigate any adverse inferences raised. (3-12-1980)

Payne of Virginia, 83 FCC 2d, 49. Virginia Seashore has demonstrated that it cannot be trusted to supply the accurate information expected of licensees. Denial of its application is therefore required. (and at 43) the fundamental importance of truthfullness and complete candor on the part of applicants, as well as licensees, in their dealings with the Commission is well established. (citing 3 J's, 41 FCC 2d, 664,667 (Review Board, 1973.) Milton Broadcasting, 34 FCC 2d 1036, 1047.

Lenore G. Ehrig, Chief Administrative Law Judge.

Paul A. Stewart Enterprises, 45 FCC 2d 773, 25 RR 375 (1963) . . . since we found the violations to be repeated, no additional findings of willfullness was required for the imposition of a forfeiture. We believe that repeated violations warrant imposition of maximum forfeiture. Were we to determine that the violations were willful, still stronger sanctions would be called for . . . Broadcast licensee's are responsible for the proper operations of their stations. While they may hire others to perform certain duties . . . they cannot delegate *responsibility* for stations operations. (citing from J.B. Broadcasting of Baltimore, Ltd., 55 FCC 2d at 596.)

Peoples Broadcasting Corp., 92 FCC 2d, 137. We find (Kiley) seriously lacked candor in certain testimony in the instant proceeding and the initial decision was in error in failing to penalize this misconduct. (Review Board, January, 1983). (Application denied. Case involved false affidavits.)

Radio Carrollton, 69 FCC 2d, 1151. Where a petition contains outright misrepresentations, they will of course be relevant not only to an abuse of processes evaluation, but will also raise independent questions regarding the licensee's basic character qualifications. (5-31-1978)

Red Lion Broadcasting Co., 395 U.S. 367, (1969). It is the right of the viewers and listeners, not the right of the broadcasters, that is paramount . . . it is the purpose of the First Amendment to preserve an uninhibited marketplace of ideas in which truth will ultimately prevail, rather then to countenance monopolization of that market, whether it be by the government itself or a private licensee . . . it is the right of the public to receive suitable access to social, political, esthetic, moral and other ideas and experiences which is crutial here.

Rust Communications, 75 FCC 2d, 445. Short term renewals for stations WHAM and WHFM (FM) for Equal Employment Opportunity shortcomings. January 2, 1980 by the Commission, Memorandum Opinion and Order No. 79-871.

Smith Broadcasting Co., 87 FCC 2d, 1136. Forfeiture assessed for statutory violation—airing lottery information. When the Commission approved a reduction of forfeiture from $500. to $200., Commissioner Fogarty, in a Dissenting Statement stated: "I assumed it was Hornbook law that a statute enacted by Congress does not bow to this agency's contrary policy predelictions, expressed in a legislative proposal or otherwise . . . "Administrative discretion" is one thing: lawlessness another. I hope the Commission will continue to recognize the distinction."

Southern Broadcasting Co, 68 FCC 2d, 854. Accordingly, we hereby put on notice this licensee . . . and all licensees . . . that we anticipate that their non-entertainment programming will be broadcast when it "reasonably could be expected to be effective." (7-6-1978)

Stereo Broadcasting Inc., 87 FCC 2d, 187. False statements in response to Commission inquiries and in the course of the hearing process are, in and of themselves, of substantial significance. (License renewal denied, June, 1981.)

United Broadcasting of Florida, 55 FCC 2d. Commission denied renewal of license where the licensee claimed lack of knowledge of improprieties engaged in by the station. The Commission held that lack of supervision and failure to respond adequately to prevent wrongdoing was tantamount to an intentional disregard to Commission rules . . . United's conduct constitutes an abandonment of its responsibility of control and supervision and it must be held accountable for having willfully put in motion the very forces that resulted in the wrongful conduct. (This was a double-billing case.)

United Broadcasting of Florida, 94 FCC 2d, 950. We agree with the ALJ that the overall performance evaluation that constitutes the renewal expectancy analysis must encompass licensee conduct as well as program performance, for both factors have important predictive value and must be weighed simultaneously. (Review Board, August, 1983, citing WESH, Central Florida, 90 FCC 2d, 250, 270.)

Video 44, Harrisburg of Chicago, et al, 102 FCC 2d, 408. Review Board remanded comparative renewal proceeding to determine whether (Video 44) transmitted obscene material in violation of Title 18, U.S.C. section 1464 when operating in a subscription television mode, (STV). Quoting from separate statement of Review Board member Blumenthal: (Testimony of Senator Dennis DeConcini, June 20, 1985—) " . . . the law is clear on at least one facet of the interminable debate over pronography: Obscene utterances are not protected speech under the First Amendment." (Miller v. California, 413, U.S. 15, 34-36, (1973). Quoting from a footnote by Blumenthal: "had our Media Bureau heeded the injuction of the court in *Berlin Communications, Inc.*, v FCC, 628 F 2d 869, 873 (D.C. Circuit, 1979), and referred the material adduced by the license challenger to the Department of Justice, this agency might have been spared the task of civil enforcement of the criminal code provisions on obscene broadcasts."

Walton Broadcasting Inc., KIKX, Tucson, Arizona, 83 FCC 2d, 440, 441, 442. . . . here (John Walton) received a call from the manager of KIKX advising him of problems . . . his failure to make a reasonable inquiry and to take prompt corrective action permitted the continued broadcast of hoax announcements. Rather than a mere lack of due diligence, this conduct amounted to 'active indifference' sufficient to sustain a finding of gross negligence . . . the fact that (Walton) could not have forseen the misconduct is not relevant because the misconduct could have been prevented . . . (12-18-1980)

WJPD, Inc., 79 FCC 2d, 125. The insulation of licensee responsibility (from his manager) is precisely what the Commission has announced it will not and cannot tolerate. (7-28-80)

WNST Radio, 70 FCC 2d, 1030. (Review Board, 1978). We have concluded that the judge properly found that (Putnam) was lacking in candor . . . and that it persisted in its misrepresentations during the course of the hearing . . . we conclude . . . that (Putnam) should be disqualified for its failure to be truthful.

FEDERAL COMMUNICATIONS COMMISSION POLICIES

Character qualifications, 87 FCC 2d, 856. quoting Mark Fowler, chairman of the Commission. "In dealing with the Commission, I refer to acts of deceit, abuse of processes and other dishonorable conduct which must be viewed as highly objectionable by an agency of limited enforcement resources." (8-6-1981)

Policy Statement on Comparative Renewals, FCC 2d 1, (1946) Diversification of control of the media of mass communications constitutes a primary objective in the licensing scheme . . . fulltime participation in station operations by owners is a factor of substantial importance. It is inherently desirable that legal responsibility and day-to-day performance be closely associated . . . a past record within the bounds of average performance will be disregarded, since average future performance is expected . . . the Communications Act makes character a relevant consideration in the issuance of a license.(308 (b), 47 U.S.C.)

Policy Statement on Violations of Laws by Applicants, FCC 51-317 (1951). Establishment of a Uniform Policy to be followed in licensing radio broadcast stations in connection with Violations by an Applicant of Laws of the United States other than the Communications Act of 1934, as amended. The Communications Act provides that the Commission may grant applications only if the public interest, convenience or necessity is served thereby. (307 (a), 309 (a) and 310 (b). No intelligent appraisal of applicants in terms of this standard can be made without an examination of the basic character qualifications of the applicants, and Congress in 308 (b) of the Act, specifically gave the Commission authority and imposed upon it the duty to make such examination in evaluating applicants for radio facilities . . . it is appropriate that the Commission examine pertinent aspects of the past history of ·' plicant . . . including any violation of Federal Law, including violations of Internal Revenue Laws, antitrust laws, false advertising and other deceptive practices ... it must be concluded, therefore, that the Commission's authority to consider violations of Federal laws, other than the Communications Act of 1934, in evaluating applicants for radio facilities is well established and that a positive duty is imposed upon (the Commission) to exercise this authority. (Quotes from the policy)

FCC RULES AND REGULATIONS—VOL III, MARCH, 1980.

Emergency Broadcasting System (EBS) rules. Section 73.901-73.962, with specific reference to 73.961—failure to conduct the required weekly tests of the Emergency Broadcast System.

Administrative Procedures—Part 74, *74.13*, Equipment tests: (c) The authorization for tests embodied in this section shall not be construed as constituting a license to operate. *74.14* —Upon completion of a radio station in accordance with the terms of the construction permit, the technical provisions of the application therefor, technical requirements of this chapter, and applicable engineering standards, and when an application for station license has been filed showing the station to be in satisfactory operating condition, the permittee of any class of station listed in this part may, without further authority of the Commission, conduct service or program tests.

FCC Rules and Regulations, Volume III, March, 1980. Section 73.3514 (a). Each application shall include all information called for by the particular form on which the application is required to be filed, unless the information called for is inapplicable, in which case this fact shall be indicated.

FCC Rules and Regulations, Volume III, March, 1980. Section 74.501, Aural Broadcast STL and Intercity Relay Stations. Specifically, 74.551, Equipment changes: (a) Prior Commission approval, upon appropriate application (FCC form 313) therefor, is required for any of the following changes: (1)—A change in the transmitter as a whole (except replacement with an identical transmitter) or a change in power output.

FCC Rules and Regulations. Volume III, March, 1980. Section 74.1201, Subpart L—FM Broadcast Translator Stations and FM Broadcast Booster stations. Specifically, Section 74.1251 (b)(2)—Modification of transmission systems. (b) Formal application is required for any of the following changes to be made on FCC forms 346 in the case of FM translator stations booster stations: (2) A change in the transmission system, including the direction of radiation or directive antenna pattern.

FCC Public Notice B, 87794, April 29, 1960 ... Strict adherence to the rules, standards and technical requirements set forth in the rules governing commercial radio operators and the rules governing radio broadcast services (Part III) is considered a basic requirement to the operation in the public interest.

FCC Rules and Regulations, Part 19—19.735-101, et seq.—Employee Responsibility and Conduct. Specifically, 19.735-201. The regulations issued under this subpart contain provisions covering the standards of and governing the ethical and other conduct of FCC employees set forth in Sections 735.201a through 735, 210 of the Civil service regulations (5 CFR, 735.201a-735.210), as well as those set forth in the Executive order and the Federal Conflicts of Interest statutes and the Federal Communications Act of 1934, as amended . . .

Section 19.735-201a—Proscribed actions.

An employee shall avoid any action, whether or not specifically prohibited by this subpart, which might result in, or create the appearance of:

(a)—

(b)—Giving preferential treatment to any person;

(c)—

(d)—Losing complete independence of impartiality;

(e)—

(f)—Affecting adversely the confidence of the public in the integrity of the Government.

FCC Rules and Regulations, Part 19, Subpart A—19.735-101. The effectiveness of the Commission in serving the public interest depends upon the extent to which the Commission holds the confidence and esteem of the Nations citizens. To hold the public confidence, unusually high standards of honesty, integrity, impartiality and conduct must be maintained within the Commission and all officers and employees must not only obey the literal requirements of the Federal laws and orders governing official conduct, but also show by their conduct that they support the ethical principles which underlie these laws and regulations. The avoidance of misconduct and conflicts of interest on the part of the Commission employees through informed judgement is indispensable to the maintenance of these standards. To again call the attention of Federal employees to the importance of maintaining these high moral and ethical standards, the President has issued Executive Order 11222 to codify, clarify, and strengthen the standards of ethical conduct and to set forth a new program assigning central responsibility to the Civil Service Commission for supervising agency action in this regard. In consequence thereof, the Commission has revised its long standing regulations promulgating standards of conduct for all Commission employees and has delegated to the Chairman responsibility for the detection and prevention of acts, short of criminal violations, which could bring discredit upon the Commission and the Federal service. *19.735-102—(a)* "Commission" means the Federal Communications Commission. (b), "Employee" means an officer or employee of the Commission, including the Commissioners.

STATUTES

18, U.S.C. section 1001. Statements or entries generally. Whoever, in any matter within the jurisdiction of any department or agency of the United States

73

knowingly and willfully falsifies, conceals or covers up by any trick, scheme, or device a material fact, or makes any false, fictitious or fraudulent statements or representations, or makes or uses any false writing or document knowing the same to contain any false, fictitious or fraudulent statement or entry, shall be fined not more than $10,000. or imprisoned not more than five years, or both.

18, U.S.C. section 371, Chapter 19, conspiracy to commit offense: If two or more persons conspire either to commit any offense against the United States, or to defraud the United States or any agency thereof in any manner or for any purpose and one or more of such persons do any act to effect the object of the conspiracy, each shall be find not more than $10,000. or imprisoned not more than five years or both.

18, U.S.C. section 1621, Chapter 79, perjury generally: Whoever (1) having taken an oath before a competent tribunal officer, or person, in any case in which a law of the United States authorizes an oath to be administered, that he will testify, declare, depose, or certify truly, or that any written testimony, declaration, deposition or certificate by him subscribed, is true, willfully and contrary to such oath states or subscribes any material matter which he does not believe to be true; or (2) In any declaration, certificate, verification, or statement under penalty of perjury as permitted under section 1746 of title 28, U.S.C., willfully subscribes as true any material matter which he does not believe is true: is guilty of perjury and shall, except as otherwise expressly provided by law, be fined not more than $2,000. or imprisoned not more than five years, or both.

18, U.S.C. section 1512, Tampering with a witness, victim, or an informant. (a) Whoever knowingly uses intimidation or physical force, or threatens another person, or attempts to do so, or engages in misleading conduct toward another person, with intent to—(1)—influence the testimony of any person in an official proceeding . . .

18, U.S.C. section 1464, Broadcasting obscene language. Whoever utters any obscene, indecent or profane language by means of radio communication shall be fined not more than $10,000. or imprisoned not more than two years, or both.

47, U.S.C. Section 301, Communications Act of 1934, as amended. . . . No person shall use or operate any apparatus for the transmission of energy or communications or signals by radio . . . except under and in accordance with this Act and with a license in that behalf granted under the provisions of this Act.

About the Author

Raised in North Dakota, Vincent L. Hoffart, after graduating from high school, worked for several years as a communication technician in that area until his job with the US Signal Corps took him to Spokane, Washington. There he accepted the position of engineer for a new radio station. He later became chief engineer of that station while working in maintenance and installation at several other stations in Washington.

At one station Mr. Hoffart worked for Mr. Lester Smith, owner, along with Mr. and Mrs. Danny Kaye, of station KISW. Mr. Hoffart had been discharged by Mr. Smith in 1976 for what later was explained as job unsuitability, being out of step with other employees and for recommending a woman as manager of his Spokane station. Hoffart, however, believes his dismissal was due to his exposure of payola activities in 1975. Management denied the charges, and Mr. Smith backed management.

Hoffart is a charter member of the Society of Broadcast Engineers with certified senior status. He was recently granted Life Membership. The author married in 1942 and has two sons and three grandchildren. His wife is the former Alvina Krieg from Linton, North Dakota.

ISBN 141207818-0

9 781412 078184